The Conquest of Violence

by the same author

A HISTORY OF POLICE IN ENGLAND AND WALES
900–1966 (1967)
THE CIVIL SERVICE TODAY (GOLLANCZ 1951)

Frontispiece   A Serenade for Tolerance. Aftermath of the
demonstrations in Grosvenor Square, London, 27th October 1968

The Conquest of Violence

Order and Liberty in Britain

by T. A. Critchley

Constable London

First published in 1970
by Constable & Co Ltd
10 Orange Street, London WC2

Copyright © 1970 by T. A. Critchley

SBN 09 456880 4

Set in 11 on 12 pt Monotype Garamond
Printed in Great Britain by The Anchor Press Ltd,
and bound by Wm. Brendon & Son Ltd
both of Tiptree, Essex

Let not England forget her precedence of teaching nations how to live – MILTON

The Reason and End, and for which all Government was at first appointed was to prevent Disorder and Confusion among the People; that is, in few words to prevent Mobs and Rabbles in the world – DANIEL DEFOE

Contents

Illustrations

Introduction

War is the failure of diplomacy, domestic violence the failure of civilisation. Each, in its own way, is a flight from reason. The nature of war has often been examined, but the causes and prevention of violence in society comprise a study which until recently has been neglected, although its importance is now widely recognised.

We do not know the answer to the question, Why are some societies more violent than others? It is, however, possible to approach the problem in one (or both) of two ways: by mounting a comparative survey which would examine the condition of several contemporary societies, or nations; or by a historical study whose object would be to provide the material on which to judge the condition of a single nation at the present time, and perhaps to identify some of the lessons which it might be able to hand on to others. This book attempts the second course. It deals with our experience in Britain of violent events in the past, their failure or occasional success in creating a more just or more stable community, and the ways in which they have influenced our relatively favourable situation in the world today.

Two points about the sub-title, *Order and Liberty in Britain*, require brief explanation. First, although the main purpose of the book is to deal with collective violence (as an extension of protest), its subject cannot be isolated from a consideration of liberty, that other supreme value which must always be weighed against order in the scales of a good civilisation. In tracing the steps by which the British have attained a reasonable degree of order, I have accordingly sought to assess the price that has had to be paid in curtailing individual liberty.

The second point to be made about the sub-title is that the violent events with which the book is concerned are confined, in the main, to England and Wales and rarely touch Scotland. The reason for this is that it seemed to me unwise, in treating of a subject so intimately bound up with a national culture and national customs and laws, to extend the study to the larger ethnic group. The claim to cover Britain, however, rests on the belief that the general conclusions that emerge are valid equally for Scotland as for England and Wales. I do not deal with Northern Ireland, and the typescript had, in any case, gone to press before the recent outbreaks of violence in Belfast and Londonderry; but parts of the book may nevertheless be found to offer an incidental commentary on that situation.

I gratefully acknowledge help from many of the sources set out in the Bibliography and in addition I am indebted to Professor B. C. Roberts, of the London School of Economics, for kindly making available to me an early copy of material provided by scholars of world-wide repute for the American National Commission on the Causes and Prevention of Violence. Some of their ideas I have exploited in Chapter 1 in discussing some theories of collective violence. I am also deeply grateful to Professor A. L. Goodhart, K.B.E., Q.C., of Oxford University for very kindly reading the book in draft. I have greatly benefited from his generous advice and suggestions, but any errors that remain are my responsibility.

T.A.C.
October 1969

The Conquest of Violence

1: Why Violence?

The year 1968 saw appalling violence in the streets of Paris, Berlin, Chicago and Tokyo, and some predicted that London's turn would come on Sunday, 27th October, a day selected for mass demonstrations against a variety of public issues, the most prominent of which was American involvement in the war in Vietnam. In the event, the British gave a striking display of civilised behaviour. Some 30,000 people are estimated to have taken part in the protests, of whom a number had openly professed themselves in favour of violence. But there was virtually none, and the Home Secretary, Mr. Callaghan, after referring to the self-control shown by the mass of the demonstrators and the discipline and restraint of the police, commented: 'I doubt if this kind of demonstration could have taken place so peacefully in any other part of the world.' Two days later the chief London correspondent of the *Washington Post*, writing in *The Times*, praised Britain's moral example as her most potent appeal to the world. 'What did not happen, quite simply, was something that has occurred in every other major western country this year, a truly violent confrontation between angry students and sadistic police. . . . British experience in building a non-violent relatively gentle society seems of paramount importance to a world beset by police brutality and student nihilism.'

Yet for centuries the British were themselves amongst the most turbulent of peoples.* It is only during the last half century that

* This, a commonly accepted view, is open to argument. A nation which commemorates 10th May, 1768, when about half a dozen rioters were killed, as the 'massacre' of St. George's Fields; 15th August, 1819, when eleven

they have settled down to be one of the most tranquil. Moreover, the transformation has been effected without any significant erosion of free speech. This is a remarkable achievement by any standards. The object of this book is to attempt to explain how it came about.

The achievement is the more remarkable when it is remembered that democratic government, by its very nature, is obliged to work within the confines of a dilemma from which there is no escape. Free speech, raised in protest, is the life-blood of democracy, yet the freer the speech the more likely it is to inflame its audience to violence. But violence can kill democracy, for if given rein it will destroy the democracy that licensed it; while to curb it freedom itself may have to be restricted, and democracy thus impaled on the other horn of the dilemma. Any nation which so orders its affairs as to achieve a maximum of freedom of speech with a maximum of freedom from public disorder may fairly claim a prize among the highest achievements of the human race. In terms of individual happiness it surely ranks higher than a successful landing on the moon. How has the prize been won? Can it be held?

To answer these questions it is necessary to examine the causes of violence at selected periods, and note how authority (local and central) responded to its threat. The choice of events is bound to be an arbitrary one, but selection of some sort is unavoidable if the subject is to be kept within manageable limits. Moreover it is the responses to violence (which tend to be unique to Britain) rather than its causes (which tend to be common to mankind everywhere) which repay study. For much the same reason, moral judgments enter very little into the matter. It is not particularly relevant (although it is not possible entirely to disregard the point) to enquire whether politically motivated violence was inspired by good or bad reasons, or those which seemed good or bad at the time. On the other hand it is pertinent to ask whether, with the advantage of hindsight, violence has ever achieved a worth-while object in our society, and whether the means taken to counteract it have themselves always been wise and good or –

people were killed, as the 'massacre' of Peterloo; and 13th November, 1887, when no-one was killed, as 'Bloody Sunday', measures its public violence by high standards.

as will appear – sometimes provocative of more violence. The crux of our enquiry is to ask repeatedly why violence erupted, how it was quelled, and what lessons were brought to bear when it erupted next time. Above all, by what responses and slow accumulation of experience did a maturing nation curb, and then – at all events for a time – conquer collective violence?

As we shall see, authority's responses took many forms, of which the application of counter-violence, by soldiers or professional policemen, has been only one. Some of these responses are rooted in antiquity. The joint principles of self-discipline and voluntary service in a community, for example, go back to Saxon times: the continuous thread they give to the story remains unbroken today. The principle of preventive justice stretches back for 600 years. The principle (if it can be so described) of no more force than necessary, perhaps the most important of all, can be seen to have emerged at latest during the eighteenth century and it was probably active much earlier. It is the same if we study the history of the laws by which successive governments have sought to discourage violence. The common and statute laws about the right of public assembly and free speech can be traced back to very early times. So, too, can the growth of institutions and their attitudes to the job they were set up to do. The courts (with dishonourable exceptions) seem to have tended, in administering justice to rioters, towards a characteristically British principle of no more severity than seemed necessary to match the particular time and situation, although less charitable remarks might be made of the British secret service of Tudor times – which the Special Branch of police of today might no doubt, if they wished, claim as their ancestors.

An important conclusion emerges from this preliminary glance at some of the legal and administrative means available to counter violence in Britain. Varied and plentiful as they are, they provide only the framework, or scaffolding, within which our society has settled down; equally important are the human attitudes that have influenced their employment. A crucial factor in any contest that disrupts public order is the mood and temper of both sides of the affray. It is necessary to evaluate, however tentatively, whatever characteristics distinguish the British, in their public behaviour, from those of other nations; and, most

B

important, to recognise the contribution to public tranquillity that has been made by the relatively gentle character of our police, and their forbearance under provocation. Finally it is proper to ask to what extent the British, in their growth towards political maturity, have shown wisdom or folly in making, or refusing, concessions to rioters.

These are large issues, to some of which only the most tentative answers are possible. They are discussed in subsequent chapters, but before returning to them it is necessary to start with what is perhaps the most fundamental question of all. What are the causes, and nature, of violence in public life?

The term needs first to be defined, and this is no easy matter. According to the *Oxford English Dictionary*, violence is related to the use of 'great physical force' and 'the unlawful exercise of physical force'. Its appeal is largely, but not exclusively, to the young. It thrives on muddle. It has moral overtones: in war it is good, in murder bad; in cops good, in robbers bad. Used in furtherance of political action it might be either: good against Hitler, bad against the Kennedys and Luther King. When Brutus stabbed Caesar his violence (aided by Shakespeare's genius) earned him as enviable a reputation with posterity as Caesar had already secured by acts of violence more barbarous and prolonged, and wrought on a much more massive scale, in Gaul. As the epigram puts it –

> Treason doth never prosper; what's the reason?
> For if it prosper, none dare call it treason.

The concept of public violence is elusive, complex, multi-dimensional. We may draw nearer to it along several distinct planes of thought.

Viewed along the simplest of these, violence is seen as the end-product of a chain reaction: discontent, protest, frustration, violence (illegal), counter-violence (legal). The next step might be continuing protest, violent or non-violent, or possibly concession by either side. But the ultimate end, if authority is not strong enough to assert itself, must be civil war, when questions of legality will be set aside until the victor chooses to re-open them to his own advantage. Invariably the starting-point is a group (or groups) who seek to obtain, or to defend, liberty, justice or privilege – in a sophisticated state, political power. Notable instances of such violent groupings, impotent against an immovable or oppressive Government, occurred in England in 1381, 1642, 1831 and 1912. (More dramatic, but different only in scale and achievement, were the revolutions in America in 1775, France in 1789 and Russia in 1917.) At such times the oppressed have rebelled in the name of freedom and justice, the privileged have struck back in the name of order and legitimacy; and for a while the voices of sanity on either side have been drowned in violence.

This classic progression is familiar enough. A second dimension of collective violence appears when we approach it by examining its particular causes, rather than its more general cause. They can be broken down in several ways. A convenient one is to look at the causes of violence due to the economic pressure of want; that which results from social and political aspirations; and that provoked by religious quarrels.

There is, in addition, yet a third dimension along which we may explore the nature of public violence, and this imports a sub-dimension of time. We look now not at the causes of violence but at its objects; and these may be defined as primitive, or un-differentiated; reactionary; and forward-looking and modern. Each tends to follow the stages of a nation's growth to maturity, though it may sometimes (and primitive violence always does) interrupt growth. This three-fold classification of the objects of violence is a useful one, and it runs through much of this book. Before going on we must examine it in a little more detail.

The first, primitive, object of violence generally works itself out on a small scale, and is localised. It is elemental, brutish, and largely un-political. Historically it is seen in the convulsions of a nation-state being hammered out of its separate parts, as was England in the reign of King Stephen, or during the Wars of the Roses. It lies behind all rowdyism, foreigner-baiting, race-rioting, hooliganism, and, in the contemporary scene, the behaviour of some people at football matches. Today's dangerous drivers share a common stock with Caligula and Warwick the Kingmaker. There is no reason to suppose that primitive violence will ever be eliminated from human society, though there is evidence that its level varies between nations: Manhattan Island, for example, with a population of 1·7 millions has more murders in a year than England and Wales, with a population of 49 millions. Our concern with it here is incidental, and is confined, in the main, to the early part of Chapter 2.

The second object of violence, the reactionary, implies a resort to illegality to recover rights and privileges that were once enjoyed by a group and are now no longer enjoyed because they have been 'stolen'. It is more advanced than primitive violence, and tends to manifest itself later in time. Its typical forms in England are the Peasants' Rising of 1381, when Tyler's men set out to recover the ancient liberties of Saxon England, filched by the Normans; food riots to extract from eighteenth-century landlords the justice and fair prices their Tudor predecessors had granted in half-forgotten times; and the grim Luddite attacks on machinery that seemed to be threatening good ways of work and a high standard of life.

The third object of violence, forward-looking and modern, stands out in contrast to the first two by its thrusting optimism and large-scale, sophisticated organisation. It aspires to gain for a minority group rights and privileges which it has never before enjoyed. The Reform Bill rioters of 1831, demanding 'One man one vote', the Chartists, some of the insurrectionary strikers of 1911–12, and all the 'Votes for Women' suffragettes had in common this forward-looking motivation. It can be seen in many forms throughout the world today in civil rights movements, in the demands of students for greater participation in the control of their universities, and in protests against authoritarianism and a materialistic way of life. Sometimes it assumes a missionary fervour, as with the suffragettes, or it may set about its business with cool determination, as when strikers parade a sullen show of force that spills over into violence by accident.

We shall return to this convenient three-fold classification of the objects of violence in looking more closely, later in this chapter, at the principal causes of disorder in Britain. Before doing so, however, it is necessary, to complete our preliminary exploration of the concept of violence in the abstract, to glance at it briefly through the eyes not only of the sociologist and historian, but also those of the psychologist and ethologist.

Aggressiveness, like crime, is part of the human condition, and

6

violence lies at varying depths below its surface. In young males it is near the top: it is as natural to growing boys to fight as to eat, sleep or breathe. A child must assert his identity. Naturally aggressive, he will strive with others, master them by proofs of superiority, and often pitch his ambitions absurdly beyond the reach of his talent. The livelier, more vigorous he is, the greater will be his rebellion, usually a struggle to break out of the protective cocoon of ordered family life. Total success in such a struggle is rare, and on any conventional view undesirable. Sooner or later most men come to terms with the imagined opponent – parents, family, or other 'normal' institution – since with adulthood and independence the need for opposition to it vanishes. In early adult life a man has recognised his own separate identity and is then ready to merge part of it, as in marriage, with that of another. Reluctantly, or perhaps with secret relief, he clips the wings of ambition and settles for compromise in the business of everyday life, playing out a series of assertive or meek roles: the alternations of which, however, depend not only on his situation and temperament, but also on the tactical advantages he sees from time to time. For man remains an aggressor, accepting challenges and mastering so much of the world outside himself as he can, until he dies. The combative component in his make-up may be compromised. It can never be eliminated.

To be an aggressor, however, a man need not be violent, and most people find it preferable to assert themselves by exploiting qualities of personality, intelligence and perhaps cunning, and probing the weaknesses of others, rather than by attempts at physical intimidation or conquest. The natural leader will emerge because of the vigour of his aggressive drive. Having reached his goal he can then propagate ideas, run enterprises, control companies, attract women, govern men, or in many other ways exercise that superiority over others which is the outward and visible sign of the socially acceptable – indeed, the socially desirable – aggressor. The ambitious man who has 'arrived' feels no need for violence because he can get most of what he wants without it; moreover the restraints of law and custom discourage its use. He illustrates Bacon's principle: 'As in nature things move violently to their place and calmly in their place, so virtue in ambition is violent, in authority settled and calm.'

The point need not be laboured. Aggression serves an essential social purpose. It is a necessary condition of orderly society in which authority is recognised and respected because it is self-proven. Anthony Storr, in a recent book, *Human Aggression*, argues that it is to the consequences of the aggressive drive in moulding a disciplined society that a nation owes its survival in war or against natural calamities, and he aptly quotes the anthropologist, Professor Washburn: 'Throughout most of human history society has depended on young adult males to hunt, to fight, and to maintain the social order with violence.' This is certainly not, however, true of all human history, as will appear in the next chapter, for when in England feudalism collapsed, with its in-built discipline, the English (unlike the French) deliberately refrained for centuries from replacing it by a professional army or police force. They preferred to pay the price of disorder for an accretion of liberty. As we shall see this choice was of crucial importance, since it delayed the creation of an army, and later of a police force, until the nation was sufficiently advanced to be able to live with these new hazards to liberty on acceptable terms, and hence could mould the character of its police in the matrix of a mellowing, and not an untamed, national character. It is obvious that if a police force had been set up in England during, say, the Tudor period, when all adult males were required to keep arms, the police themselves would have been armed; and it is unlikely that any later government would ever have felt it safe to disarm them.

The general line of thought so far is reassuring, and if our main point could be left there a reasonably optimistic conclusion would be possible. Somehow or other man's aggressiveness, potentially a destructive force, nevertheless promotes the best interests of peaceful community life. It would be comforting to think that this was the end of the matter, but it is not: so restricted a view of the consequences of the aggressive drive takes no account of war, the most spectacular of all outbreaks of mass violence; and one is obliged to ask whether not only aggressiveness, but also violence itself, is part of the human condition, which can never be subdued. On this at least two views are possible, each equally pessimistic.

The first has recently been set out in this country by two

ethologists, Mr. and Mrs. Russell, in their book, *Violence, Monkeys and Man*. They argue that violence in man, like violence in animals, is not endemic, but is merely a response to social stress. In common with other writers they observe that violence is not implicit in animals, but is stimulated by external circumstances over which the animal has no control, such as sudden over-population, shortage of food, or the stress of confinement in a zoo. Any of these causes is liable to provoke an animal to destructive hostilities which, under normal conditions, will tend to restore the animal population once more into harmony with its environment. A potent cause of violence, on this view, is lack of living space (one is reminded of Hitler's demand for *lebensraum*); and, pursuing the analogy with man, the Russells contend that if the social environment in which people (or some people) live were bettered, the urge to violence would diminish: 'We can confidently expect that those conditions in which space abounds and all needs are satisfied, which produce peaceful societies of monkeys, can also produce peaceful societies of men.' The logic of this argument, superficially comforting, is nevertheless terrifying. The very conditions which the Russells propose are rapidly being withdrawn from much of the world. The crowded, urban indignities which more and more people are obliged to suffer are the very conditions most conducive to violence; and the conclusion seems inescapable that the world population explosion will be a likely cause of nuclear war.

The other view, that violence is implicit in the human condition and not merely a response to an unfavourable environment, offers an equally bleak prospect for the future of mankind. Its argument is that man shares with animals an instinctive violence, but lacks the restraints on its use that protect an animal species from self-extermination. For reasons which can be traced back to infancy we all grow up harbouring resentments, and these feed the potential of violence within us. It may break out at any time, and each of us is liable to cry with Lear, on the brink of madness –

> I will do such things –
> What they are yet I know not – but they shall be
> The terror of the earth.

The paranoid, seeing enemies everywhere as projections of his own hostility, is merely a degree or two more mad than most of us. A Hitler or Stalin will therefore never lack popular support, at all events in the early stages of violent revolution. War, on this argument, is a safety valve, which mankind screws down at its peril, for if the rulers of the great powers are sane enough and sufficiently in accord with one another to avoid embroiling the world in nuclear war, a traditional outlet for violence will be blocked. The latent violence in man's nature will then have to find fresh primitive outlets. We must be prepared for an upsurge of civil disorder at home, with increased hooliganism, and more aggressive driving on our over-crowded highways. This may be what is happening in many countries, including Britain, today.

These alternative conclusions would be less depressing if the element of truth which each may well contain were widely recognised, for then it might be possible to avert their consequences. Aware and enlightened protest marchers would demand immediate action by all governments to control the growth of world population, and set up study groups on birth control rather than nihilism. Anarchists would cease to exhort each other with brave slogans – 'Pacifism is the contraceptive of revolutionary action' – and, instead, would go out to the under-developed countries as doctors or medical auxiliaries, skilled in socially valuable contraceptive techniques. Perhaps some are already: taking heart from a generation of young idealists who care enough to march for Oxfam, we may resume discussion of the objects of past violence in Britain with cautious optimism for the future.

For much of our history violence in public life has been of the primitive order – violence for its own sake, small in scale, local, and reasonably good-humoured. It is no exaggeration to say that to generations of British people brawling and general disorder, far from being a last resort, were pastimes. They offered a way of life, a natural element of a turbulent society. For a characteristic view of England by a foreigner it is perhaps unnecessary to go back earlier than Tudor times. 'Now,' wrote the urbane Italian, Andreas Franciscius, who visited London in 1497, 'I shall say something about the inhabitants, their culture, and methods of government, thinking that readers will find no less entertainment in these. Londoners have such fierce tempers and wicked dispositions that they not only despise the way in which Italians live, but

actually pursue them with uncontrollable hatred . . . they sometimes drive us off with kicks and blows of the truncheon.'¹ Some
three hundred years later, in 1765, a Frenchman, Pierre Grosley,
wrote in the same vein. Londoners were 'as insolent a rabble as
can be met with', showering foreigners – and particularly the
French – with 'shocking abuse and ill-language' in the hope of
starting a brawl.

But it was not only against foreigners that the British directed
this primitive violence. Public disorder and violent crime were
such normal features of everyday life that an outbreak of rioting
which occurred in London on 24th and 25th March 1668, for
example, on a scale which today would have shocked the nation,
is only lightly touched on in Pepys's Diary (his entry is quoted
on pages 60 and 61). Disorder and brawling might be sparked off
by any temporary and local grievance, or by minor events such as
witch-hunts, fairs and public executions. Elections, in un-policed
Britain, were a constant source of danger, as Mr. Pickwick
discovered at Eatanswill –

'Don't ask any questions,' he warned Mr. Snodgrass. 'It's
always best on these occasions to do what the mob do.'

'But suppose there are two mobs?' suggested Mr. Snodgrass.

'Shout with the largest,' replied Mr. Pickwick.

Mr. Pickwick's advice accorded with long tradition. Edward
Chamberlayne, in the 1702 edition of his work, *Angliae Notitia*,
after referring to the 'rude and even barbarous' nature of the
'common sort', and the 'great courage and virtue' required of
magistrates who opposed the mob, went on:

> I would give the Reader one wholesome Caution, to wit that if
> ever he happens to fall under the displeasure of the Mobile* in a
> Tumult, that he doth not *vim vi repellere* oppose 'em by Force, but
> by kind Words, pitiable Harangues, Condescensions or some such
> resigning Method get free from 'em and leave them to themselves;
> for he who treats them so divides them, and hereupon they
> generally fall out one among another.²

There is a certain contemporary interest in the fact that for
generations our universities and schools played their full part in
this national pastime of violence. In 1355, after a pitched battle

* Later contracted to 'mob', to the displeasure of Swift, who insisted that
the correct word to describe a disorderly crowd was 'rabble'.

in Oxford High Street between factions armed with daggers, swords and bows and arrows, the University was closed until the King intervened to protect the scholars. 'At Winchester in the late eighteenth century,' writes Philippe Ariès, 'the boys occupied the school for two days and hoisted the red flag. In 1818 two companies of troops with fixed bayonets had to be called in to suppress a rising of the pupils. At Rugby, the pupils set fire to their books and desks and withdrew to an island which had to be taken by assault by the army.' [3]

It was this national propensity for primitive violence that generations of local leaders, and a sprinkling of national ones, diverted into purposeful channels of their own, expressing it in the characteristic forms of reactionary violence. This may be broken down into the violence due to economic motives and the violence, generally much more dangerous, due to religious or political motives.

Reactionary-economic violence was common in this country during Tudor and Stuart times, but it reached its peak from about 1740–1830 (in France as well as England) a period of first importance to the present enquiry since it spans the transition from the simple, reactionary riots of pre-industrial England, when the object of most rioters was simply to preserve their standards of living and to take vengeance against an identifiable, individual oppressor, to the post-industrial period, when men gave themselves to causes that spilled over into violence by accident rather than design. Moreover the period presents a classic case-study for the popular theory that collective violence is essentially a by-product of industrialisation, following a standard cycle which in England would run as follows: a society disintegrates under the first impact of industrialisation, say between 1790 and 1820; its early reactions are unco-ordinated and violent, rising to a peak with the Luddite attacks in 1811–12; the rage of the masses drives them to coalesce into a movement – the Hampden Clubs that preceded Peterloo (1819) and Chartism (1838–48); then, with the passage of time, comes re-integration, and disorder diminishes as civil rights are conceded – in the form of local self-government, social legislation, and parliamentary reform. (This tidy theory is not one to which all modern scholars would subscribe. It fails, for example, to explain some of the more impressive risings in

British history, such as the Peasants' Revolt, Aske's rebellion, 'Bloody Sunday' in 1887, and the suffragettes.)

The reasons for the upsurge of reactionary-economic violence in England during the second half of the eighteenth century are not difficult to discern. The Industrial Revolution was already eroding a countryside still in many respects unchanged since medieval times. It was a landscape of empty, quiet acres, dotted with small hamlets and villages, each linked by cart track or lane to market towns which were themselves little more than overgrown villages. Rural occupations differed little, if at all, from those of Shakespeare's, or even Chaucer's, time. Weavers, woolcombers, village craftsmen, farm labourers, small tenant farmers, and in some counties colliers and miners, lived out their lives among the community they were born into. In turn each cottager would be elected to serve his year in the office of village constable (often paying a deputy to act for him), and in every hundred a man of similarly humble standing would be appointed as high constable, once an office of importance, now an obsolescent survival from forgotten times. These minor officials possessed little authority, unless they occasionally emerged from obscurity as riot leaders. For practical purposes 'authority' was represented by the squire, a local landowner of means, and the merchant. The squire would probably be a magistrate, closely involved with village affairs, and in nominal charge of the constables; and with him the chain of authority virtually stopped. Remote from the life of the village and knowing little of it but what their servants slipped in salacious gossip, lived the country gentry from whose ranks came the Members of a Parliament at Westminster which was far removed from the countryside. Moreover, as a matter of deliberate policy, it refrained from interfering in provincial matters.

Thus the villagers lacked elementary democratic rights. They had no votes, no trade unions, and no-one to represent their interests. Local government, such as it was, lay in the hands of the magistrates. But these magistrates were also the main employers of local labour, so that, inevitably, their interests clashed with those of their work-people. Under the protective laws of the Tudors the magistrates had had a duty to settle fair prices for food in the neighbourhood, but by the middle of the eighteenth century these laws had lapsed into disuse. Consequently the village people, permanently living near the bread-line, were at the mercy of a free economy. This they failed to understand, deluding themselves that 'justice' still existed. In that, however, they were often disappointed. The alliance of squire and merchant was invincible, and the price of corn was liable to leap, particularly when, in the interests of the ruling classes, Orders-in-Council had permitted its export. The villagers could either starve or help themselves; no-one else would help them.

So, faced with such a calamity, bringing close the prospect of starvation for their wives and children, the craftsman, labourer, weaver and miner took the law into their own hands, and who is to blame them for behaving like the Russells' monkeys? Fortified by home-brewed ale or cider they poached game and stole firewood from the squire's estate and banded together to invade the market town, bent on a course of calculated but discriminating violence. There they looted warehouses and shops and carried off wheat, flour, butter, cheese and meat, which they commonly sold off at 'normal' prices, returning the proceeds of sale to merchant, shopkeeper, or farmer. In a bad year such local activities would extend over wide areas of the country, so that riots took on a national character and earned a place in the history books. Communications at that time were slow, and concentrations of counter-force (soldiers or militia) were sparse, so that riots tended to persist for long periods. Sometimes, thoroughly alarmed, the local magistrates would step in and lay down a 'fair' price, thus relieving the rioters of further pretext for direct action. Generally, however, the policy was to repress disorder rather than alleviate distress; and starving mobs, enraged by hunger and the indifference of authority, would turn brutish. In Birmingham, Norwich, Derby and Nottingham shops and warehouses were plundered and burnt, the houses of the 'enemy' destroyed, and the whole town terrorised by violent mobs. On such occasions the magistrates would order out householders armed with staves, or even firearms, and the market square became a battle-field from which the dead and dying would later be carried off.

To bring such riots to life almost any volume of the eighteenth-century issues of the annual publication, *The Political State of Great Britain*, may be picked from the shelves at random. Let us select that for the six months from July to December, 1740. In July there were severe riots in Norwich and the West country; in December, Edinburgh suffered. The Norwich riots are probably as typical as any. Here, 'a rabble began to be very tumultuous'. The rioters started by attaching a note to every baker's door which declared bravely, 'Wheat at fifteen shillings a Comb.' Fearing disorder the magistrates called in the Dragoons, and ordered them to distribute handbills which claimed that the Government would be petitioned to prevent the export of corn. But the crowd was in an angry, disbelieving mood. At about 8 o'clock in the evening a few rioters were arrested and committed to prison. The mob went wild. They smashed their way into the prison and released their comrades. Soon houses and shops were blazing, and the troops opened fire. Three men, two women, and a boy were killed, and many others wounded. They deserve sympathy; more, at all events, than a 'mealmonger' who killed himself five months later in that violent year in the West of England, where there had been very severe rioting. To suppress it the Government licensed the import of oats, thus failing, as Governments must, to please everybody: the action overcame the threat of violence, but disappointed the mealmonger, who had planned to make a fortune by selling off a hoard of grain dearly during the shortage. This tragedy he took 'so much to Heart, that he cut his Throat, and expired in Forty-eight Hours after in most dreadful Agonies. Those wicked Fellows are so accustomed to cheating', the author concludes philosophically, 'that they will cheat the very Hangman at last.'

The typical early rural rioters, then, were hungry men, outraged by a sense of injustice, and unable to make their voices heard in any other way than by direct action. Much the same motives and methods characterised their behaviour when attacking enclosures that were seen to threaten common grazing rights (or the 'social space' of the zoologist), when fences and palings would be uprooted and used as missiles against the intruding 'enemy'. Similarly turnpikes, which taxed freedom to travel, would be dismantled and bits of their masonry hurled at their instigator if he dared to interfere. On the evidence of George Rudé (*The Crowd in History*) they seem, on the whole, to have been honest, sober, hard-working fellows, not particularly prone to violence, and rarely associating with thieves and robbers. They were not irresponsible young hooligans: their average age was nearer 30 than 20. The fact that the Settlement Acts were applied more harshly to married than to single men meant that a high proportion of them were married. If well led and united in a common cause they could behave with restraint, even dignity, when carrying out the common act of burning or pulling down and pillaging the house of a known 'enemy' of the common folk, whether he dealt in enclosures or turnpikes or factories. *The Annual Register* for the year 1766 records, for example, that a body of Cleehill colliers 'entered the town [Ludlow] in a very orderly manner, proceeded to the house, pulled it down, and then returned without offering any other violence to any other person whatsoever'. But the situation would no doubt have been different if soldiers had been at hand.

The crowd, particularly if it was leaderless or its leaders were weak, was a creature of impulse. It was a prey to mass hysteria, and hence liable to panic. On 10th June 1843, headed by a band, some 2,000 rural workers on foot and 300 mounted farmers entered Carmarthen. Their purposes were reactionary-economic. They deliberately left behind any arms they held and made a quiet, orderly procession through the town. Arrived at the Guildhall, they deposited a resolution protesting against tolls, tithes, the Poor Law and Church rates. Then local towns' people joined in. They led a faction of the crowd to the workhouse, broke it open, and started smashing things. The magistrates called in troops, who took sixty prisoners. Violence had broken out, despite the original restraint of the demonstrators, because they failed to reckon with the unexpected. In this there is perhaps a moral for our own times.

'Economic' rioters rarely took life, though they were not infrequently shot down themselves. Their object was to destroy property, and this destruction they sometimes accomplished on a massive scale. Luddism, in particular, was a destructive movement of great force, though its reputation, as Professor Darvall has pointed out, has suffered from the fact that the movement provided a convenient cover for criminals: 'The Luddites proper rigidly confined themselves to their specific offences, breaking machinery and (in the North) collecting arms. . . . They were not to be held responsible for ordinary robberies which were clearly the work of different groups of men, gangs of common thieves using the Luddite name, knowing that it saved them from all danger of resistance or pursuit.'

The times were, indeed, confused. Not only did rioters and criminals mingle, but rioters and the agents of law and order sometimes took turn-about also, so that it was hard (for the authorities, not the workers) to know whose side a man was on. During the Luddite troubles, when there were no regular police, the part-time parish constable, an ordinary worker in field, factory, mill or mine, had as much reason as anyone else to resort to violence. Earlier, during the eighteenth century, attempts by the Government to pass Militia Acts as a means of conscripting men for duty in a sort of compulsory police force provoked the very riots the force was intended to prevent, and a militia from one part of the country would be despatched to subdue, sometimes with heavy loss of life, men determined to resist enrolment for similar service elsewhere. And sometimes the militia were no more willing to turn against their own folk than were the parish constables. In their home districts they would support rioters in their attempts to force down food prices, with the added advantage that they were able to bring to bear on the side of lawlessness the superior weight of the musket and shot with which the landed gentry had naively entrusted them. This, clearly, was no way to conquer violence.

In turning now to examine the nature of reactionary-religious and political violence in Britain we enter scenes of excitement and danger that set these riots in a class apart from the local economic disorders we have so far discussed. They take on a national character, and most centre on London. Not all, however: the appeal of religion, idealism, even mysticism, touches movements of popular protest at every point. In Britain it is perhaps not fanciful to regard the voice of the saint or prophet as that of the Celtic component in so many of us, mingling with, and edifying, the practical common-sense of the Anglo-Norman. At all events it is refreshing to discover how many popular movements of the past have been touched by a sense of the sublime, when men have experienced for themselves, untaught by literary artifice, a dawn when ' 'Twas bliss to be alive, and to be young was very heaven.'

'Human insurrection, in its exalted and tragic forms,' writes Albert Camus in *The Rebel*, 'is only, and can only be, a prolonged protest against death, a violent accusation against the universal death penalty. . . . The rebel does not ask for life, but for reasons for living.' The men who marched with Wat Tyler and dreamed with John Ball, Cade's men, Aske's men, Roundheads and Cavaliers, fought and died as they did because they were loyal to a cause beyond themselves. They were often exalted by a nostalgia for the past, a sort of golden age it would surely be possible to recapture. Why else should English radical peasants in the 1790s dress up in Saxon clothes and enrol in Saxon tythings? Folk memory and myth preserved an ancient dream of English justice and liberty which it was the duty and right of common folk to restore. 'Here', as Rudé says, 'was a constant appeal to precedent: to the glories of a distant or imaginary past rather than to the prospects opened up by the present. Magna Carta, the Popish Plot, the Bill of Rights, and the "Glorious Constitution" of 1689 were all reminders that these "liberties" had constantly to be fought for against tyranny from within; but one of the most remarkably persistent beliefs of all was that perfect "liberties" had existed under the Saxon kings, and that these had been filched, together with their lands, from "freeborn" Englishmen by the invading Norman knights under William the Bastard in 1066.'[4]

A spirit of exaltation, especially when generated by religious fervour, reinforced many popular protest movements in Britain that had their direct cause in simple economic stress or social grievance. Such a spirit offered an emotional appeal to violence that in some would work even more powerfully than greed or want; and here is one clue to the reasons why the behaviour of an orderly crowd could degenerate into the violence of a rabble. No great understanding of crowd psychology is needed to recognise that moral fervour, playing into the hands of fanatics, can inflame a mob to excesses; and London, with the radical traditions and restless riff-raff common to any great city, was especially vulnerable to situations of this sort. Primitive violence lay near the surface, and the notorious apprentices could always be relied on to reduce an orderly crowd to a rabble long before the soldiers appeared.

It is worth pausing on the Wilkes and Gordon Riots (strictly speaking the former have no place here since they were forward-looking rather than reactionary, but the characteristic features of urban violence were common to both) in order to point the striking contrast between the behaviour of the London mob and that of the sullen, bewildered countrymen whose company we have so far kept. Not surprisingly, the city rioters were younger: many of those involved in the Gordon Riots, for example, were youths and boys, with a fair sprinkling in the 15–18 age group. They would have been apprentices and journeymen, artisans, pedlars and servants. Most seem to have come from good, settled homes. Whether some, or many, were hooligans is debatable. Rudé has pointed out that only a handful of the 160 people brought to trial after the Gordon Riots were shown to have had previous convictions, but this may mean no more than that the policing arrangements and criminal records of the time were rudimentary. When one takes a broad view of the violent character of life among the lower orders, and our long history of turmoil, it would be astonishing if the young people of the eighteenth century behaved decorously, given the chance of a night or more on the town. They inherited all the worst features of the 'London mob' that had terrorised earlier generations, and left its mark on countless foreign visitors to Britain. (And if hero-worship is a rough index of aspirations, it is perhaps worth making the further point that the heroes of the time were very different from the pop-singers and stars of stage and screen of today; prize-fighters and highwaymen were the 'pin-ups' of the youths who mauled London when Wilkes and Gordon gave the sign.)

Whatever view one may take of their inclination towards hooliganism it is clear that these young city rioters behaved quite differently from the rural rabbles. Inspired by a colourful national leader they would set off from shop, bench, yard, kitchen and basement with a great sense of holiday and high spirits, their girls on their arms. And now the contrast is, in its way, a little pathetic. We pictured the countryman in a quiet empty countryside making his sullen way in orderly fashion to the predestined target, swilling home-brewed beer as he tramped the dusty roads to set about the work of destruction he had solemnly promised to undertake, and then (if he were lucky) tramping the long road home again. The risks he had taken were sometimes appalling in their possible consequences for himself and his family: while the Londoner enjoyed a field-day. He drank gin, not ale. He had a public to play to with a captive audience, even Parliament itself. It was in his power to intimidate the Government. His demonstration needed noise, slogans, pennants, cockades, drums and banners. He gave it style, and dash, terrifying to the middle-classes. He would have welcomed the aid of televison cameras. If property was earmarked for destruction (as the houses of Catholics were during the Gordon Riots) they were duly destroyed, and the rabble proceeded on its gay, rumbustious course. Its moral fervour and excitement mounted, and the danger would increase: for when enough men cry for the moon of 'No Popery' or 'Wilkes and Liberty' (or 'Keep Britain White'), and go on and on crying for it, they set themselves on the collision course with authority that ends in violence. For a vivid impression of the reality of such violence we have Dickens's own account, in *Barnaby Rudge*, of the Gordon Riots –

> The detachment who had been sent away, coming back with an accession of pickaxes, spades, and hoes, they, – together with those who had such arms already, or carried (as many did) axes, poles, and crow-bars, – struggled into the foremost rank, ready to beset the doors and windows. They had not at this time more than a dozen lighted torches among them; but when those preparations were completed, flaming links were distributed and passed from hand to hand with such rapidity that, in a minute's time, at least two-thirds of the whole roaring mass bore, each man in his hand a blazing brand. Whirling these about their heads, they raised a loud shout, and fell to work upon the doors and windows. . . .
>
> The besiegers being now in complete possession of the house, spread themselves over it from garret to cellar, and plied their demon labours fiercely. While some small parties kindled bonfires underneath the windows, others broke up the furniture and cast the fragments down to feed the flames below; where the apertures in the wall (windows no longer) were large enough, they threw out tables, chests of drawers, beds, mirrors, pictures, and flung them whole into the fire; while every fresh addition to the blazing masses was received with shouts, and howls, and yells, which added new and dismal terrors to the conflagration. Those who had axes and had spent their fury on the moveables, chopped and tore down the doors and window frames, broke up the flooring, hewed away the rafters, and buried men who lingered in the upper rooms, in heaps of ruins. Some searched the drawers, the chests, the boxes, writing-desks, and closets, for jewels, plate, and

money; while others, less mindful of gain and more mad for destruction, cast their whole contents into the court-yard without examination, and called to those below to heap them on the blaze. Men who had been into the cellars, and had staved the casks, rushed to and fro stark mad, setting fire to all they saw – often to the dresses of their own friends – and kindling the building in so many parts that some had no time for escape, and were seen, with drooping hands and blackened faces, hanging senseless on the window-sills to which they had crawled, until they were sucked and drawn into the burning gulf. The more the fire crackled and raged, the wilder and more cruel the men grew; as though moving in that element they became fiends and changed their earthly nature for the qualities that give delight in hell.[5]

So much for primitive and reactionary violence. It is at about the end of the eighteenth century that we begin to notice the influence of the third of the main objects of public violence we described earlier: men are looking forward to a better future, not gazing hopelessly back into the past. Gradually, between about 1790 and 1840, working-class consciousness was influencing, shaping, and finally dominating the simple economically motivated protests of earlier times. But what was hope to the workers was sedition to their rulers; and the nature of public violence changed accordingly. The new thinking advanced more rapidly in some areas than others, but wherever it took root men no longer felt compelled to burn down ricks, wreck machines and pull down houses in order to seek revenge against an employer, baker or oppressive landlord. As Rudé puts it, 'It was only by gradual stages that this personal target was replaced or eclipsed by principles or causes and, correspondingly, that the old methods of "natural" justice began to disappear.'[6] The underlying reason for this significant change is not hard to discover: 'Both in England and France, the Revolution of 1789, by posing sharply in their multiform aspects the new concepts of the "rights of man" and the "sovereignty of the people", added a new dimension to popular disturbance and gave a new content to the struggle of parties and classes.'

Under these influences the crude motive of hunger was reinforced by aspirations towards a more just and egalitarian society. The wild and whispered talk that flew between factory workers, craftsmen and labourers about the rights and brotherhood of man ennobled the causes of protest. The radicals of the 1790s, from Tom Paine to the early Romantic poets, all played their part in importing from France, and marketing cheaply and attractively in Britain, the stuff of which revolutions are made, enkindling the popular imagination with talk of a millenium. Southey, who was 15 in 1789, wrote years later: 'Few persons but those who have lived in it can conceive or comprehend what the memory of the French Revolution was, nor what a visionary world seemed to open upon those who were just entering it. Old things seemed passing away, and nothing was dreamed of but the regeneration of the human race.'[7] The outbreak of war with France in 1793 caused Pitt's Government to clamp down on free speech and hence drove the radicals underground. But with the return to peace violence, forward-looking and militant, broke out on a grand scale, bringing new forms of protest – the march and 'monster meeting' – thus opening up fresh hazards, as in the classic instance of Peterloo. 'The riots of the eighteenth century', write Sidney and Beatrice Webb, 'had been, almost exclusively, the mere impulse of an untamed people, born of their impatience of suffering or restraint, the habitual licentious disorder of the individuals gathering itself up from time to time into mob outrages on a large scale, excited by some local or temporary grievance . . . with no intermixture of sedition. From 1812–1832 a new spirit may be detected in the riots . . . an unmistakable consciousness among the rioters, demonstrators, machine destroyers and rick burners, that what they are in rebellion against is the established order of society, laid down by Parliament, upheld by the courts and enforced by a standing army.'[8]

All this is no more than an over-simplification of events described in detail in Chapters 3 and 4. It may be sufficient, however, to indicate broadly the manner in which the reactionary food riot of early times, transcending its simple economic cause, had by the early decades of the nineteenth century taken on a forward-looking, political aspect which is recognisably modern. The constant demand of the radicals (they had others, but none was pressed with greater vigour) was 'One man one vote'; and by the time the Reform Bill was before Parliament, with modest success tantalisingly close, the form of protest had achieved a rare degree of sophistication. Its nature is well presented by Joseph

Hamburger (*James Mill and the Art of Revolution*) in charting the delicate path the radicals of 1831 trod in pursuing their ends by talking 'the language of menace', while yet proclaiming a fastidious disapproval of the use of violence.

In founding the National Political Union as an extra-Parliamentary body, Francis Place sought by peaceful means to intimidate Parliament into enacting the Reform Bill. The object of the Union was 'to put the wishes of the people at large in organised array, to give them, by union, so imposing an appearance, that denial of their demands should be hopeless, and direct oppression dangerous'. The radicals feared violence, the Whigs revolution. As for the Government, the evident orderliness and discipline of Place's followers so alarmed them that they declared the movement illegal, fearing it to be a para-military organisation. This was an exaggerated view, though a Birmingham romantic, haunted by dreams of his Saxon past, planned to set up a 'national guard' in units of ten, led by a tythingman, every ten of which were to be led by a 'constable of a hundred', as in remote times.

At all events Place refused to disband his movement, relying on the Englishman's ancient 'rights' of free speech, the right of public assembly and the freedom of the press; and according to the French historian Halévy, 'A free press and the right of rebellion, ultimate guarantees of popular liberty against the encroachments of any department of Government, were a very real part of the British Constitution.'[9] Thus Place put himself outside the law and embarked his followers on the road to violence. And now, to quote Hamburger, 'The fate of social order depended on an estimate of imponderables. Timidity on either side – among the Radicals or the Parliamentary politicians – might assure civil peace, but at the sacrifice of other goals. On the other hand, boldness on either side would bring the risk of violence and perhaps revolution.'[10] The continued obduracy of the House of Lords in refusing to pass the Reform Bill brought close the prospect of a civil contest, but the radicals still played a cool, sophisticated game. Mill devised the novel tactics of brinkmanship. The people, he declared, 'should appear to be ready and impatient to break out into outrage, *without actually breaking out*'. But Mill was a philosopher, not a realist. His policy could only have succeeded if the radical leaders had been able to control their followers, but they were not. Attitudes having been struck, rioting was inevitable; and its scale was determined not by the leader, Place, but by the opposing strength of the authorities. In London, where the first Metropolitan Police had appeared on the streets two years earlier, riots were easily dealt with. It is arguable that these original 3,000 policemen saved the country from revolution, even civil war. In Derby and Nottingham, which were un-policed, old-fashioned attempts to suppress disorder with the aid of soldiers led to fierce rioting which caused Melbourne to write to the Prime Minister: 'Such violence and outrage are I believe quite new and unprecedented in this Country; at least I never remember to have heard of Country homes being attacked, plundered, and set on fire in any former times of political ferment.' Even so it was in Bristol, where the rabble resorted to traditional methods of destruction, that violence reached its peak. That episode, which has a general interest to the main theme of this book, is dealt with in Chapter 4.

It remains to touch briefly on the causes of disorder in more recent times – from, say, the end of the Chartist disturbances until the present day; and for the moment only two preliminary points need be made.

The first concerns the remarkable upsurge of public violence in this country during the years immediately before 1914, when after generations of relative tranquillity three great movements welled up together to confront the Government with problems of disorder from which they were rescued only by the outbreak of war. These groups, as G. D. H. Cole and Raymond Postgate put it, 'whose grievances and aspirations were not after all new, began about 1910 to demand what they wanted in a violent fashion that had been well-nigh forgotten in British political life'.[11] The violence was forward-looking, and on the part of the men involved mostly unintended; but on the part of the suffragettes it was deliberate. The circumstances of this relapse are described in Chapter 5. The point to be made here is that the violence was due to a breakdown in the confidence of large sections of the community in the ability, or even the will, of Parliament as it was then constituted to concede their demands. The lesson in this situation is too obvious to need spelling out.

The other point to be made as we bring the story of public

violence in this country nearer to the present day is that, despite the interlude of 1910–14, violence never again broke out on a scale approaching that of the Wilkes and Gordon Riots of the eighteenth century, the Reform Bill Riots of 1831, or the Chartist disorders. The reasons for this will be discussed in later chapters; here they can be summarised quite shortly.

The general reason, which begs more questions that it answers, must come first. The British, once like the French amongst the most ungovernable of peoples, for long habituated to violence as a national pastime, settled down: constrained, though, not so much, like the Germans, by the imposition of state authority, as by a native self-discipline which was rooted in antiquity, and which flowered – perhaps the flowering will be seen to have been only an interlude? – during part of the twentieth century. Second, the economic and social motives for violence diminished as most of the demands of the Chartists were met. Third, the work of Huxley and Darwin reinforced social changes that led to the disappearance of religious differences as a motive in English politics; and racial prejudice, that other cause of dangerous rioting, was virtually absent from Britain. Fourth, the forces of law and order were belatedly strengthened with the spread of professional police forces throughout the country. Fifth, the unique character of our police (as a force of unarmed civilians, in contrast to the soldiers who had in earlier times provoked as much violence as they repressed) enabled a rapport to be established between police and trouble-makers that has been of incalculable value – so long, that is, as the police have not themselves been disaffected. Sixth, the growth of trade unions, and the use of strike action as a means of protest, led to confrontations in which violence has been incidental rather than, as in former times, deliberate. Finally the spread of the franchise, together with growing literacy and the penny Press, gave increasing numbers of men and women a sense of involvement in their own destinies that earlier generations lacked. Thus the prime causes of public violence in Britain had, by about the year 1900, been largely (though not wholly) eliminated; and it is significant that it was left to women, the single remaining disenfranchised group in the community, to resort to deliberately violent methods of protest during the first decade of this century.

This last point is perhaps as good as any with which to conclude this discursive introductory chapter, since it illustrates a truism that cannot be repeated too often. Whenever in a civilised state a substantial section of the community has reason to feel, on racial, social or religious grounds, that it is under-privileged, or otherwise deprived of elementary political rights, its protest is likely to take the form of direct action. Here is one answer, not the only one, but possibly the most cogent today, to the question posed in the title of this chapter.

Tradition has it that long ago there really were 'good old days', when England was free from violence. The seventeenth-century lawyer and romantic Sir Edward Coke, writing of Anglo-Saxon times and Alfred's laws on tythings, claimed: 'By the due execution of this law, such peace . . . was universally holden within this realm, as no injuries, homicides, robberies, thefts, riots, tumults, or other offences were committed, so as a man with a white wand might safely have ridden before the conquest, with much money about him, without any weapon throughout England.' Coke, embattled against King Charles to establish the ascendancy of the common law, may be guilty of special pleading; but Sir Arthur Bryant, in our own day, adds substance to the tradition. 'The English', he writes of the years immediately before the Conquest, 'were in many ways a more civilized people than any in northern Europe; they seem to have been gentler, kindlier and more peaceably governed.'[1]

This, on the face of it, seems an astonishing state of affairs. How is the persistent legend of a peaceful people to be reconciled with all that we know of the barbarity and cruelty of early times? Trevelyan offers an interesting explanation: 'So long as the Viking battle-axe was crashing through the skulls of monks, and the English were nailing to their church-doors skins flayed off their Danish enemies, the hatred between Anglo-Saxon and Scandinavian was profound.' (And the same would be true two centuries later of relations between Anglo-Saxon and Norman.) But 'in days before the printing press, the memory of inter-racial wrongs

27

and atrocities was not artificially fostered. Green earth forgets – when the schoolmaster and the historian are not on the scene.'[2] In this good company it is perhaps possible to accept that the legend of an orderly people is well-founded, and that the English were driven to fits of violence only in self-defence against Scandinavian and Norman invaders.

The means of preventing disorder were primitive, but the principle they relied on has endured, more or less, to this day. Traceable back at least to King Alfred's time, the principle was that of placing a personal obligation for helping to keep the peace on every adult male member of the community, and providing means to enforce the obligation. Before the Norman Conquest the law encouraged everyone over 12 (except members of the aristocracy) to enrol in groups of about ten families, which were known as tythings. Every such group had to guarantee that none of its members broke the law; if any did so, the group either had to produce him for judgment or, if the offender escaped, pay a collective fine. Tribes of about ten tythings were formed into a hundred. The head man of these groups was, respectively, the tythingman or borsholder (i.e., pledge-holder) and the hundred-man, or royal reeve. Above the hundred-man in each county was the shire-reeve, or sheriff, who was directly responsible to the King for the conservancy of the peace in the shire. Thus in theory the fugitive from justice was the prey of the whole community, every adult member of which was supposed to stop what he was doing and pursue the wanted man with 'hue and cry'. If they failed to catch him he was declared to be an outlaw and was expelled from the whole system of collective security. As an outcast from society he enjoyed no protection from the law, and his property was forfeit. We do not know whether these arrangements worked well or not, but there is no reason to think that they were ineffective in early times.

This, at all events, was the primitive system to which men were looking back nostalgically a thousand years later, for enough of its elements still survived to tantalise a society in transition. It promoted good order and made for a disciplined society. By involving everyone in the business of keeping the peace it taught English people from early times to accept that everyone had a stake in it. This is an attitude of mind that, much later, probably helped to shape the character of the professional police forces which had to be set up during the last century: there was no need for Peel's police (or for their successors today) to be authoritarian, for they could rely on the instinctive co-operation of a people who for generations – admittedly not always very successfully – had policed themselves.

During the three centuries before the Norman Conquest England was constantly under the threat of foreign invasion. To meet it a military system was developed that grew into an important means, in default of regular police, of combating civil disorder. The Anglo-Saxon system relied mainly on calling out a local citizen army, known as the fyrd, whenever danger threatened. It comprised all the able-bodied freemen in the shire, and its operations were limited to the shire. Unlike the territorial army of modern times the fyrd was an army of temporary conscripts who received little, if any, training. It was officered, and to some extent professionally commanded, by a body of trained warriors, each of whom was paid, supported and equipped by the wealthier residents in a locality. These 'officers', like the fyrd, were only called out for duty when danger threatened, but they might then serve for long periods, as they had to during the Danish raids on the East coast. Above the 'officers', yet again, was a *corps d'élite* of highly trained professional fighting men known as housecarls. These mercenaries were maintained both by the King and by the aristocracy. Thus the English forces at the Battle of Hastings comprised all three elements of the military system, the fyrd in this case comprising the men of Sussex.

Modern historians dispute the precise steps by which these arrangements developed into the military-feudal system of the Normans, and the matter need not be pursued here. What is clear is that Duke William the Bastard abstained from unnecessary interference with the local Anglo-Saxon laws and administration, still pivoting, as in ancient times, on the shire, the hundred and the tything; and the means of preventing crime and disorder emerged from the turmoil of conquest changed in only one important respect: enrolment in a tything, hitherto permissive, became compulsory. Every freeman was now obliged to act, so to speak, as his brother's keeper in his own locality, with an additional obligation for fyrd service (or military feudal service) when danger threatened from outside. These twin obligations of very early times are the roots from which grew two important branches of our administrative arrangements for preserving the peace. During the three centuries that followed the Conquest the citizen's liability for 'police' duties as a tythingman evolved into an identical liability for service as a parish constable. At the same time the duty for fyrd service evolved into a liability for service in the medieval militia. Both these ancient forms of public service remained essential parts of the machinery for dealing with public disorder until as recently as the last century. How characteristic it was of the British habit of cherishing old forms and old ideas that when the Government, faced by Hitler's threat in 1939, resolved on conscription, the institution in which the 20-year-olds found themselves was called the Militia; and the liability of every able-bodied man (not specially exempt) to serve as a parish constable survived on the Statute Book until as recently as 1964.

We must return, however, to the eleventh century, when these institutions were taking root, to note the importance of the change which the Conqueror and his son had effected in the old Anglo-Saxon arrangements for keeping order. 'Between the voluntary pledging of a man by his neighbours in 1030,' writes Professor W. A. Morris (*The Frankpledge System*), 'and the duty, in 1115, of every man in a tything to serve as a surety for every other man . . . is a break that can be explained only by governmental action of a deliberate and rigorous nature, prompted by the imminent danger to which the public peace was exposed from the ordinary freeman of the realm.' To the arrogant race of Anglo-Saxons, the Conquest came as a national catastrophe. Completing it in 1069 by teaching the north of England a lesson in frightfulness, William confiscated most of the great Saxon estates and handed them over to his new warrior aristocracy. These few thousand invaders were efficient and cruel. They replaced Saxon sheriffs by trusted Normans, whose task it was to travel about the country and hold special courts to ensure that the tything system was enforced, and that none evaded his social obligations. The tythingman (or chief pledge as he was coming to be known in Norman times) as head of his group would be required at these courts to 'present' any offender against the peace. And the grey, stark castles, with round towers rising above hamlets and towns, lording it even over London's own wall, awed and terrorised the populace. When the Lincolnshire outlaw Hereward the Wake showed a talent for amphibious warfare in Fenland he provided material for legend rather than a focus for counter-revolution. Most of his compatriots went no farther than to allow their beards to grow as a sign of protest against the occupying forces. Some, with lengthening folk memories of a golden age of freedom under the Saxon kings, were still doing so as late as the thirteenth century.

But this sullen peace of conquest, temporarily imposed by tyranny, did not endure. For two centuries intermittent private war ravaged the land, and generations were habituated to violence. The maelstrom of Stephen's reign, imperilling the Conqueror's achievement in hammering England into a nation, must have coarsened her people. We hear no more of men riding from one end of the land to another with a white wand. The legends are dark with the cruelty of Geoffrey de Mandeville and his rival gangs of thugs. Men are tortured, cast into dungeons, maimed and murdered. But then, later in the twelfth century, the sky lightens. The coronation of the intelligent autocrat Henry II opens up a new chapter of concern for justice and the dignity of man. Henry replaced the worst of the Norman sheriffs by Englishmen – or Anglo-Normans – and by the Assize of Clarendon, a century after the Conquest, he laid the foundations of the rule of law, that, together with the supremacy of Parliament, were the bases on which the seventeenth-century lawyers and statesmen were to build English liberty. At the same time the Assize of Clarendon brought up-to-date the principal means of combating disorder. Hitherto the tythings had merely been required to bring to judgment known criminals who were wanted by the authorities. Clarendon took matters further. It required the villagers, in addition, to report any suspicions they might have about one another. The chief pledge (or tythingman) would be put through an interrogation designed to discover, for example, such suspicious persons 'as sleep by day and watch by night, and eat and drink well and have nothing'.

During the early decades of the thirteenth century the harshness of this inquisition relented. Central law enforcement gave way to local enforcement, as conditions relaxed. The damp, echoing castles of Stephen's misrule were being replaced by the first of the stone manor houses, and the manor itself was emerging as a unit of local government. Anglo-Norman country gentry, lovers of archery and all out-door sports, inheriting something of the French delight in dancing and the fine arts, emerged as a middle class; and it became increasingly common for the local lord of the manor to be delegated, or to usurp, the function of the royal sheriff in supervising the local courts at which the tythingman (*alias* chief pledge, soon also to be *alias* constable) presented his reports. Often delegation went further, and the lord's steward acted in his place. And this gentler regime was bringing with it a breath of the Merrie England of which William Morris dreamed in the nineteenth century and fought the police in Trafalgar Square to restore. Probably that England really existed, for the barbarism of the age was sweetened by the caress of a Church that was remote, in that relatively tranquil time, from the oppressive institution later generations were taught to fear. For now the Church cast its embracing cloak about township and manor, protecting rather than suffocating, and giving in the promise of eternal life an infinitely valuable reward for the loving care with which craftsmen and masons were building the marvellous country churches that still survive to awe our own generation with aspects of feudalism that no history book can recapture.

Twice a year, at Easter and Michaelmas, the folk of the manor would drop tools for the summons to a manorial court (or court leet as it was alternatively known) to hear the tythingman report. These gatherings were in part judicial, in part administrative, and for generations they helped to educate the new middle class of lords of the manor and their stewards in the business of law and local government. Equally important, they required local people to participate in their own self-government, so encouraging open speaking and respect for justice and fair dealing. By developing this early habit of debate and common-sense compromise the courts did much to shape our native institutions, and to imbue the national character with tolerance. Acting in its judicial role the court imposed collective fines on the community for the lawlessness or other misdeeds of its members. During the reign of Henry II these could be severe: the minimum fine was set at half a mark (6/8*d*), then the equivalent of an average labourer's wages for three months. In its other, administrative, role the local court dealt with such matters as roads, bridges and grazing rights, and appointed the principal officers of the manor for a year's conscripted and unpaid service in such offices as churchwarden, ale-taster, bread-weigher, and tythingman. And the tythingman, at about the time we are now considering (the middle of the thirteenth century), was variously being known by the title 'tythingman' or 'borsholder' (from the Saxon), 'chief pledge' (from the Norman), or, more commonly as the century advanced, 'constable', a title also brought to England by the Normans which rather rapidly descended the social scale, having been originally attached to a high official of the King's court. For centuries, however, the ancient Saxon titles of tythingman and borsholder continued extant in some parts of the country as synonyms for the constable – as the ubiquitous parish officer was generally known by the time of the Tudors, when the new unit of local government, the parish, assimilated the remnants of feudalism.

Again there is no reason to doubt the effectiveness of these modified arrangements for keeping the peace, and in times of danger they were strengthened by a partial or general mobilisation, at the command of the sheriff (later on of the justices) of the whole forces of the shire, known as the *posse comitatus*.* Henry II's Assize of Arms, in 1181, laid down in detail what weapons and armour men of every rank, from the lowest artisan to the knight of a shire, were required to keep for time of need. Thus the whole people were obliged to keep dangerous weapons for the public good; not, as now, forbidden to do so lest they misuse them for private harm. Henry's object was to create, or re-create, a militia on the lines of the old Saxon fyrd. There is little point in trying to distinguish between its civil and military purposes: the militia was available at the command of the sheriff (though only within its own county) to deal with invasion from Wales or Scotland, threats from the Continent, insurrection at home, outlawry, or local rioting. Experience of self-policing thus went hand in hand with growing experience of self-government.

* In Norman-French, *pioar del comtee* – described by Littledale, J., in R. *v.* *Pinney* as 'only the calling out of the people to assist the magistrates'. The concept of the *posse comitatus* seems, however, to have ante-dated the coming of the justices during the fourteenth century.

These wise arrangements were not, however, proof against a tyrant. John, defying the rule of law instituted by his father, systematically withdrew the 'ancient and accustomed liberties': not, of course, those of the common folk, who at this time had none to speak of, but of the Barons. His humiliation at Runnymede was a declaration that ultimate power lay in the hands of 'the people' (which meant different things in different ages) not the Crown, and that it was ruled by law. The design was simple, selfish and temporary, but in the context of history grand. Centuries afterwards the banner of the 'glorious charter' was unfurled time and again as men marched in protest against alleged wrongs. It became a convenient focal point for half our national violence. The snarling John, at bay at Runnymede, would have been astonished to read Trevelyan's description of the significance of his charter during the eighteenth century: '... worshipped by Blackstone, Burke and all England. It had become the symbol for the spirit of our whole constitution. When, therefore, with the dawn of a more strenuous era, the democracy took the field against the established order, each side put the Great Charter in the ark which it carried into battle. Pittites boasted of the free and glorious constitution which had issued from the tents on Runnymede, now attacked by base Jacobins, and Radicals appealed to the letter and the spirit of "magna charta" against gagging acts, packed juries and restrictions of the franchise. America revolted in its name and seeks spiritual fellowship with us in its memory.'[3] In all this, of course, there is much of legend and expediency. All the froth of a brave charter can be reduced by the unromantic to an attempt by an aristocratic ruling class to extort from a greedy and half-mad king their feudal privileges. The first instalment of its legacy of violence was immediate. The cornered king hit back, aided by an army of French mercenaries. For six months England suffered civil war and the fate of the charter hung in the balance. Then, as luck had it, John died of a surfeit of peaches and new cider. The French were driven out. The charter was re-affirmed by his successor, to be put away until Charles I's subjects re-discovered it 400 years later at the beginning of another civil war.

These violent convulsions, like the anarchy of Stephen's reign, made nonsense of the machinery for keeping order, or rather they

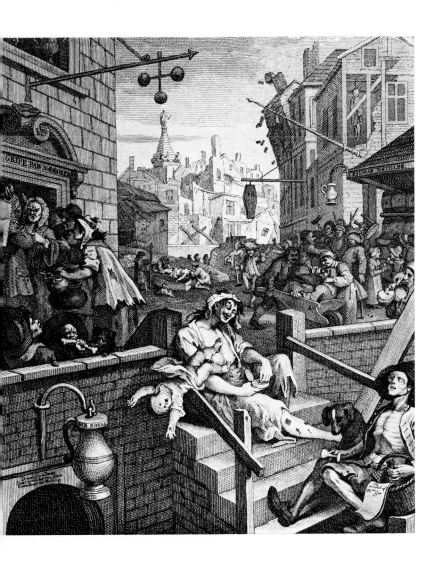

Gin Lane. Centuries old primitive violence in London
as depicted by Hogarth

The Gordon Riots. London 1780.
The sack of Lord Doscat's house in Bloomsbury Square

dwarfed it; and they provided poor soil in which to grow the new concept of the rule of law. The bonds of society were breaking down, and throughout the thirteenth century violence increased. Brigandry, outlawry and armed bands menaced a nascent civilisation, as throughout human history emerging nations have often been at the mercy of the worst elements in society; and the compulsory enrolment of folk in tythings as surety for one another became a thing of the past. This was the deteriorating situation that Edward I sought to remedy in 1285 by the famous Statute of Winchester, an enactment that was to remain in force for over 500 years. As the only public general measure of any consequence to regulate the policing of the country between the Norman Conquest and Peel's Metropolitan Police Act of 1829, it deserves notice. At all events it helped to carry the nation through centuries of violence, and its fundamental principles, inherited from Saxon times, are alive yet.

To a large extent the measure consolidated much that had gone before, gave it fresh currency, and re-advertised it. The Statute brought up to date the list of weapons and armour which every male between 16 and 60 was to keep in instant readiness at his house, for service with the militia. According to a nicely graded scale of wealth these ranged from a simple bow and arrows to 'a hauberke and helme of iron, a sword, a knife and a horse'. Two high constables were to be appointed in every hundred to make a half-yearly inspection of arms. (Three hundred years later, in Queen Elizabeth's time, this systematic inspection of arms at periodic musters was still being practised; from them derives the phrase 'to pass muster'.) The high constable of the hundred, successor of the Saxon hundred-man, combined military and civil functions. He was an unpaid officer appointed by the hundred court. Responsibility for keeping the peace was thus localised, and the Statute of Winchester reaffirmed this by reviving the ancient Saxon obligation on all freemen in a community to take up arms and join in the 'hue and cry' after an offender, fugitive, outlaw or rebel. Today it is sometimes said that every policeman is a citizen in uniform; then it might have been said that every citizen was a policeman in plain clothes. By all these means fresh life was given to the early principle of personal involvement in, and responsibility for, maintaining the peace. And the value of the ancient

D

principle of communal responsibility, too, was recognised in this great Statute. If a hundred failed to keep the peace, or to arrest an offender, the whole hundred was to be 'answerable for the robberies done and the damages', which were to be paid before the next following Easter. Finally, Edward I recognised, in this Statute, the special danger of riots and crime among the turbulent apprentices in the towns, where a system of watch and ward was introduced to supplement the work of the parish constable. All adult male citizens were to be placed by the constable on a roster for regular service as watchmen for duty at every gate of a walled town from sunset to sunrise. How enduring are the strands in our history! – more than 500 years after the Statute of Winchester, when means were needed to deal with the Luddite Riots of 1811–12, Parliament passed another (temporary) Act enabling the Nottingham magistrates to require the constables to conscript watchmen for day and night duty from among all the male rate-payers over the age of 17. Indeed the draftsman of the Act of 1811, in his choice of nomenclature, looked even further back into the mists of antiquity, to an era twice as remote as that of the Statute of Winchester, in putting the duty of conscripting men not only on the constables, but also on 'every headborough, borsholder or tythingman' of Nottingham.

Growing in prosperity and in the freedom of her peoples, England, in the century that followed the Statute of Winchester, remained a characteristically turbulent child of a shifting and insecure environment. Violence was commonplace, reaction severe. A glimpse of affairs comes down to us in the Statute of Northampton, 1328 (it remained in force until 1967), which made it an offence to bring force 'in affray of the peace' or to go 'armed by night or day in any fair, market or elsewhere in such a manner as to terrify the sovereign's subjects'. Robbers and murderers were too numerous to be traced. Instead the law recognised its impotence by declaring them to be outlaws, so that they were free to roam the countryside, wreaking further violence. However, in time of war an outlaw could secure the king's pardon and have his crime expiated by enlisting in the local militia, or enrolling as a mercenary in the pay of the king or one of the noblemen serving in the wars against France. Many of these were the riff-raff who fought in the Hundred Years' War and won the famous victories of Crécy and Poitiers (1346 and 1356). Their conduct on returning home can be imagined: and to the inability of the obsolete system of tythings, manorial courts and parish constabulary to cope with their armed violence can be ascribed, at least in part, one of the most famous of all our laws for dealing with disorder – the Justices of the Peace Act, 1361.

The Act introduced the era of the country gentry as principal agents in keeping the peace, an era that survived until the last century. The justices, Coke claimed in the seventeenth century, provided England with 'such a form of subordinate government for the tranquillity and quiet of the realm ,as no part of the christian world hath the like'. Coke, of course, was their ally during the seventeenth-century struggle for the rule of law and the supremacy of Parliament. Even so, he did not exaggerate. For nearly 500 years, until the professional police took over, a handful of English magistrates in every age determined with variable success the outcome of innumerable outbreaks of violence. Secure in their stone-built and sometimes moated manor houses the gentry had already, for several generations back, supervised the manorial courts that appointed the parish constables and dispensed justice to minor offenders. Their class had filled the office of high constable of the hundred, inspecting the arms at half-yearly musters, and calling out the people of the shire, under the sheriff's lordly authority, in time of danger. To them were granted the charters of independence for borough and city that successive sovereigns (in particular the avaricious John) were always anxious to sell for ready cash. Thus they had acquired skills in local government as well as in the law; and at a time when men were turning away from the authoritarianism of the church they emerged as the natural local leaders in this pious, raucous, optimistic and vigorous age, exercising an easy and on the whole good-humoured authority that their successors would eventually acquire from public school, university and club. Their breed was still well to the fore in local affairs in the nineteenth century. Today's foreign tourist in rural Britain can no doubt recognise some still.

Numerous experiments, starting in 1195, paved the way for the historic Act of 1361. Knights, known as *custodes pacis*, had been appointed during the thirteenth century to take security to keep the peace from everyone over the age of 16. An Act of 1327 required every county to appoint 'a good and lawful man' to keep the peace. The calamitous consequences of the Black Death (1348–49), which reduced the population from some four million to two-and-a-half million in sixteen months, no doubt brought home the need for more systematic means of preventing disorder. The 1361 Act grafted onto the old Saxon idea of giving pledges as sureties for the peace (implicit in King Alfred's system of tythings) the principle of preventive justice, by empowering a magistrate to bind a person over to keep the peace in a determined sum of money, in default of which he could be arrested – as many have been in our own times under this hallowed Statute of Edward. A powerful and enduringly useful weapon against public violence was in this way forged out of primitive origins.

The year of the Justices of the Peace Act, 1361, is an apt time at which to take stock of the state of public order in England. To people then living, Chaucer's contemporaries, the way of life, for all its violence, was secure. The old manorial system, with its solid, closely protective society, had served the generations well, even though now its force was nearly spent. For two centuries English society had quietly mellowed. Undisturbed by foreign invasion, it had evolved organically its own natural balances. The language had taken shape, civilisation was flowering marvellously in a riot of soaring spires, and common folk were discovering the natural delights of England's unspoiled fields and woods. Yet it was the end of an era, for the people were growing up. In manor court, town mote and trade guild they were learning to think.

The aristocracy, too, had been growing up after its fashion. It made much of the seemly gamesmanship of chivalry (the Order of the Garter was instituted in 1348) and a streak of the early puritanism that chivalry implied seeped downwards. To encourage the manly and socially useful sport of archery a proclamation of Edward III prohibited, on pain of imprisonment, 'handball, football or hockey, coursing and cock fighting, or other such idle games' which enticed men from the butts. The proclamation was characteristic of the age. The grace, sweetness and good humour of England's springtime were far from being products of a permissive, let alone a free, society. Liberty was rationed. It meant freedom to delight in the dawn chorus, the greenwoods, the maypole, the fresh gathering of daisies on a May morning, but it meant little more. Magna Carta was not for the masses. The stable conditions in which the arts flourished in Chaucer's England had been won at the cost of enslaving whole generations of her subject peoples. Progress had stopped. The grip of the Church over men's lives and souls was total. England was slowly fossilising: but for the whispering voices of hundreds of thousands of peasants in south-east England, daring to talk of freedom. To this classical situation, it may be remarked, how inadequate is the Russells' analogy between violent behaviour in men and monkeys (page 9). The two and a half million inhabitants of England in 1361 lacked neither living space nor food, yet because man is a political animal the old order was about to crack up in a century of violent lawlessness that is difficult to match in any other period of our history.

The Peasants' Revolt, 1381, marking the beginning of this age of violence, was the first and in some ways the most menacing, as it was the most inspiring, rising in English history. Its causes were partly social, partly economic. Similar forces were breaking into revolt all over Europe as for the first time in the history of western mankind we see the glimmering of a political awareness among the working classes, stirring, as it were, out of a slumber that stretched back to the beginning of time. The social motive of the revolt, holding much in common with the motives of the Chartists some five hundred years later, has already been noticed. Thoughtful peasants were daring to peer beyond the prison wall of custom that had confined their ancestors to the feudal manor. Some labourers contrived to bargain for their freedom by commuting the work they owed their lord by paying rent to till his land for themselves. Clandestine unions sprang into being to resist old manorial customs, and some chose the fugitive life of outlawry rather than submit to the slavery previous generations had accepted without question. Hence was born the revolutionary idea of peasant freedom, fixing its primary hatred on the church, now the greatest landowner in the country – and certainly the most unpopular, since the Papal court at Avignon had begun to extort mounting taxes from its subjects overseas. The Church's preaching was thrown back in its face as the chanting peasants asked awkward questions –

> When Adam delved and Eve span
> Who was then the gentleman?

This first stirring of a political consciousness among the peasantry was shaped and given coherence by the far-reaching consequences of the Black Death, which shattered the whole primitive economy of the country. The sudden disappearance of rather more than one-third of the population doubled the market value of labour. The pestilence depopulated whole townships and tore great gaps in manors, fields remained untilled, food was scarce, and the country was wasting away. Meanwhile, with the economy collapsing, no-one thought to terminate the idiotic French wars. Instead the Government resorted to a freeze of both prices and wages, as Governments have done in modern times; but the Statute of Labourers of 1357 was imposed arbitrarily on a people who did not understand its purpose. Its attempt to limit wages, combined with the aristocracy's stubborn determination to preserve feudalism, were the underlying causes that paved the way to the upheaval of 1381. A crusading spirit was sweeping across England, and by 1380 a situation had developed which, in a more advanced civilisation, would have been revolutionary.

The rulers were caught napping – not surprisingly, for no working-class movement had ever been known before. They chose this particular moment to impose a special tax on the poor to help finance the French wars with which they deluded themselves that England would found a continental Empire. The situation blew up in their faces. From all over East Anglia and the Home Counties, in June 1381, men converged on London, inspired by a revolutionary of considerable genius, John Ball, and led by Wat Tyler, a man with a talent for organisation. They marched, as Trevelyan puts it, with a 'Robin Hood' programme demanding the end of feudal dues in exchange for a rent of fourpence an acre, together with the abolition of game laws and outlawry, the division of church property, and other lesser demands. They burnt the manor rolls as they marched, so destroying the hated evidence of servility and appealed, instead, to ancient charters of the Saxon kings that had long ago guaranteed their liberties. London apprentices and a few radical aldermen opened the gates of the capital and the peasants flocked in. Soldiers back from the wars joined them, and Richard II was held a prisoner in the Tower. But now the behaviour of the peasants seems to have been a model of restraint, considering the violent nature of the times. They singled out the King's 'evil advisers', the Archbishop of Canterbury, who was Chancellor, for summary execution, together with a few other notorious oppressors, and that was about all. Yet the peasant army could, had they wished, have taken over the country, for the Government's situation was now as appalling as had been their earlier behaviour. It was as though a Government today, having dismissed the police and disbanded the army, proceeded to impose a wage freeze and a crippling tax on the poor, banned football, closed down the bingo halls and television, and ordered everyone to obtain a rifle or pistol and spend his Saturday afternoons at target practice: a siren-song to revolution. And the peasants of 1381 were angry, they were well armed, and by the Government's own prescription they were the most skilful people in Europe in using the most powerful weapon of the day, the English long bow.

They were, however, completely untutored politically. They recognised injustice when they saw it, but the rising was doomed before ever it started because its few leaders would not have known what to do with victory had they won it. They were unfamiliar with the Latin and Anglo-Norman in which the law and government business were conducted. They could not have run the country even if they had wanted to, and it is unlikely that they did. Their violence was thus a pathetic futility, and their cause hopeless. Indeed it was hardly a cause at all, for the movement was made up out of a mass of little local demands for ancient 'liberties', such as a concession from a particularly oppressive landlord to hunt in his warren, or to grant a fresh charter for his land. But incomprehension in that early time was total. Kill the King's 'evil advisers' and revive ancient freedoms, the word went round, and all would be well.

Against this massive threat the Government could offer nothing but a few private armies maintained by a handful of nobles and knights. Their real defence lay in treachery, and in exploiting the awe with which common folk regarded the person of the King.

Richard II appealed to the mob in person, offered himself as their leader, and appeared to concede their demands. His Ministers, however, had no intention of granting anything. In the confusion Tyler was slain and the leaderless bands dispersed, happy in the delusion of victory. The revolt spread to distant parts of England, while in London came reaction. The concessions were withdrawn and an attempt was made to restore feudalism. But the peasants would hardly realise that they had been duped, for just as the movement itself lacked coherence because its parts wanted the means to communicate with each other, so its aftermath went unpublicised in a manner that would be impossible today. The fruits of victory therefore went unharvested.

Some tentative conclusions may perhaps be drawn from this pathetic rising. First, it brings out a component of the English character that we have already noticed in Chapter 1 and shall come across many times again: the restrained and selective manner in which men driven to violence in search of 'justice' set about singling out individual targets or individual victims. Second, and related to this, the rising showed that an English Government, too, could behave with a degree of moderation that came near to matching that of the peasants. Admittedly some 150 people were executed, but they were given proper trials, and in the following year, 1382, a general amnesty was proclaimed. Here is evidence of a political wisdom at work that was careful to reject provocation to further acts of violence. Third, the rising serves to remind us that it is a measure of the rottenness of a society when a substantial section of the community reject 'the system', deliberately put themselves outside it (as outlaws, or revolutionaries as we would call them today), arm themselves, and win widespread popular support. Only the chance that the peasants of 1381 had more faith in their King than their cause staved off further insurrection. The situation would have been very different in a modern, sophisticated state, as it was in Russia in 1917, and came near to being in England in 1817–19 and again in 1831.

Finally, the rising provided a reminder to contemporaries that the law about public order had to be kept up to date. The first statute to deal with 'tumultuous assembly, rout and riot' seems to have been passed in 1381; a second, in 1393 (which provided for the sheriff 'with the strength of the county' to arrest and imprison such as made 'assemblies, riot or rumour against the peace'), was evidently directed at the Lollards. These statutes were early predecessors in a long line of legislation that led to the Riot Act of 1714 (page 73). Some of the early justices must have been reluctant to enforce them (or it may be that the king was simply looking for new ways of raising money for the French wars) for in 1411 an Act of Henry IV introduced a penalty of £100 on any justice found negligent in suppressing riots. Then three years later, in 1414 (the year before Agincourt), an Act of Henry V gave statutory form to an ancient principle of the common law by making it an offence punishable by imprisonment and a fine for ordinary persons to fail to assist the justices. This Act, and the principle it enshrined, enjoyed a long life. Referring to Henry V's statute, Chief Justice Sir Nicholas Tindal declared 400 years later, in giving judgment in a case that arose out of rioting in Bristol in 1831 (pages 123–5), that it was an error to suppose that the citizen had a free choice whether or not to come to the aid of the magistrates to suppress rioting – 'Every man is bound, when called upon, under pain of fine and imprisonment, to yield a ready and implicit obedience to the call of the magistrate, and to do his utmost to assist him to suppress any tumultuous assembly.' Thus King Henry V's Act of 1414 was of more enduring importance, though of less renown, than his victory in the following year on the field of Agincourt: a fact that shows how misguided historians can be in their scale of values.

The non-revolution, meanwhile, continued to work itself out quietly during succeeding generations, inspired by the folk-memory of a day when London's Bastille had fallen to the masses. Wycliffe's Lollards tunnelled away at the foundations of the Papal Church, sowing the early seeds of protestantism in England, and everywhere, with growing prosperity, men were buying their freedom from the old manorial bondage. Thus the emancipation progressed throughout the fifteenth century, until under Queen Elizabeth it was complete and an open labour market with fluid employment paved the way to public disorders of a different kind.

Long before this, however, weak rulers and the onset of religious intolerance provided the conditions in which the intellectual ferment of the late fourteenth century spilled over into the senseless violence that marred much of the fifteenth, perhaps the bloodiest period in our history. That century opened, appropriately, with a statute of 1401, which required heretics to be burned. The Church, resorting to brute force to defend its prestige, wealth and power, availed itself of persecution to impose the obedience earlier generations had willingly accepted. The new middle class, inspired by Wykeham and coaxed by innumerable humble parish priests, took up the challenge. Totalitarianism, whether of Church or state, was repugnant to men who were tasting freedom for the first time. The tightening of the law against public disorder made little impression against a swelling spirit of rebellion that occasionally burst into flames, as in 1450, when Jack Cade raised all Kent in arms with a following that straddled the social classes as widely as had Chaucer's pilgrims, for here was no mere peasants' rising. The rebels marched on London with a manifesto that combined political as well as social grievances, reinforced with patriotism outraged at the loss of all England's French empire save Calais. The traditionally radical City was as sympathetic to Cade as it had been to Tyler, and he made his headquarters across the river at the White Hart Inn, in Southwark. On Friday, 3rd July, his forces crossed London Bridge and entered the City. Here, more specifically than Tyler's men seventy years earlier, they declared the 'legality' and limited nature of their objectives: 'We blame not all Lords, nor all that is about the King's person, nor all gentlemen, nor all men of law, nor all bishops, nor all priests; and we will not rob nor reve, nor steal, in order that these defaults be amended; and then we will go home.'[4] There is no suggestion whatever of indiscriminate violence, but rather of the cool determination of an oppressed people to achieve by a show of force and unity aims that they were unable to advance by political means. Having stated their objectives, Cade's men retreated; and then, on the following Sunday evening, advanced again. This time, however, they met the King's men in the middle of London Bridge, and a furious battle raged on the bridge all that night, when, as John Paston (who was wounded) put it, 'many a man was slain or cast in Thames, harness, body and all'. Cade was then treated to Tyler's fate. He was duped with promises of pardon and an undertaking that the rebels' grievances would be considered. He withdrew his forces and was at once declared a traitor with a price of a thousand marks on his head. He was captured, beheaded and quartered. The head was then thrust on a spike on London Bridge to face Kent, and bits of the body were sent as grisly warnings to all the towns implicated in the rising. It is thus arguable that the King and his ministers discriminated as nicely in the pattern of their retribution as Cade had done in his declaration of intent.

Here, at least among the commoners, great principles were at stake: which is more than can be said of the gang warfare that now broke out among their rulers, as rival families embarked on the mutual slaughter known as the Wars of the Roses. Following only two years after the end of the Hundred Years War with France (1338–1453) this tribal warfare provided ideal conditions in which the returning soldiers who had been licensed to plunder French towns and villages were able to continue their profession. Fighting nobles hurled their retainers at one another, sparing no quarter. The remnants of the age of chivalry were blasted to pieces by new-fangled gunpowder. Men invaded their neighbours' land on trumped-up law charges to increase their own estates, and in this chaos the arts and crafts languished.

Modern scholarship has drawn attention to the dangers of exaggerating this situation. In his book, *The Yorkist Age*, P. M. Kendall has observed that widespread disorder shook the country for a space of perhaps eighteen months scattered over a period of several years, and he suggests that our vision of events has been widely distorted by the genius of Shakespeare, who, 'eager to command his audience, zealously crammed the most violent happenings of more than half a century into a dozen theatrical hours. . . . Your average Englishman living through these times would probably have been amazed to learn from a subject of Queen Elizabeth the First that he had endured a generation of horrors.'[5] Each battle lasted for only a few hours, and the numbers engaged were small. Commoners who survived were allowed to slip quietly away; only captured nobles were put to death. However, if the fighting put ordinary people to little personal inconvenience its debasing effects on public behaviour cannot be doubted. Men were offered a continuing spectacle of violent lawlessness, brutality and ritual butchery. Corruption, moreover, in this society in dissolution, was general. Protection had to be bought. Justice was a mockery. Judges and jurors alike were open to bribery and intimidation. The recently introduced justices of the peace were no exception. 'The records of the period', says Trevelyan, 'sometimes give a curious picture of a set of country gentlemen now enforcing the King's Peace and the Statutes of Labourers, now charged with robbery, piracy and murder, now sitting on the Bench, now sent to prison.'[6] It was at this time of weird contrasts, when old, feudal England was finally breaking up, that Chief Justice Fortescue, exiled on account of his association with the Lancastrians, was nevertheless contrasting English liberty with the servility still endured by the lower orders in France. In the eternal battle for freedom and order, freedom at least survived after a fashion, though at this early date it was freedom from oppression rather than freedom of speech.

It is not difficult to deduce, from this relapse into anarchy, the lesson which is relevant to our theme. It is as necessary in modern times that a Government should command superior force as it was in the time of the Plantagenets. The Government failed then in its primary task of maintaining social order not so much because it lacked the will as because it lacked the means. The King was unable to assert his ascendancy over the warring nobles and their retainers. To this situation the purposes of justices, high constables, parish constables and militia were irrelevant; and a civilised, well-disciplined society was a prey to the law of the jungle. When the victor of Bosworth Field emerged to found the Tudor dynasty, order was again restored. Henry the Welshman disbanded the armies of retainers that had done so much damage, reduced the power of the nobles (so, incidentally, paving the way for the rise of the justices of the peace who did much to pacify England during Elizabeth's reign), and provided the strong central authority without which order in an emerging state is impossible and freedom worthless.

In this relatively more tranquil society the machinery for keeping the peace was found to have survived intact, so sound were the principles of Saxon England, long ago fused with the Norman, and embodied in Edward I's great Statute of Winchester. In 1511, two years after ascending the throne, Henry VIII reaffirmed the Statute; and during his reign and the reigns of his successors, when the stranglehold of the Church over men's minds and lives was relaxing and the last remnants of feudalism were disappearing, men still served their turn as parish or high constables under the authority of the local justice, accepted their service in the county militia, and turned out twice yearly for the muster at which their arms were inspected on behalf of the sheriff. The manuscript letter of an unknown Italian who visited England during Queen Mary's reign, recently discovered in a Spanish monastery, attests contemporary evidence of the deep roots which our native self-discipline had by this time struck, proof even against civil war:

> In this country the reputation and respect for the law is so great that even a man of very high standing, if he be summoned by the Court by a plain Messenger, will raise no difficulty and go with him. Whenever a man refuses to go, or puts up any resistance by word or deed, they pursue him until they have him under arrest, and the offence, even if it was a minor one, immediately becomes criminal.[7]

In all this we can see the principles of the Statute of Winchester still very much alive. But were these principles any longer adequate to the needs of a new age? Did the experience of the Wars of the Roses suggest that more regular means of keeping the peace were needed? Was the militia adequate, and reliable? The Tudors were strong rulers but, at all events until the later period of Elizabeth's reign, they continued to preside over a turbulent land. Attempts by Henry VIII to impose new taxes sparked off rebellion. Rural rioters protested against the devaluation of the coinage and the enclosure of land that from time immemorial had been held in common. Giustinian, the Venetian ambassador to the court of King Henry, reminds us, in vivid despatches to his monarch, how brutal a force was the London mob. Above all, although in England religious fanaticism never reached the intensity that it did in France and the Netherlands, the bitterness of religious factions and Henry VIII's intolerance threatened the nation with renewed anarchy and civil war. The 30,000 men who in 1536 so honourably marched as Robert Aske's Pilgrimage of Grace, fought a dictatorship oppressive of freedom, as well as a religious policy they loathed, and like Tyler's peasants in 1381 they had overwhelming force on their side. Henry, like Richard II, had only one weapon to combat it. He resorted to treachery. Aske, joining company with Tyler and Cade, was duped, and paid the terrible price. Moreover, in this time of violence Henry showed none of the moderation of Richard II. To the Duke of Norfolk he issued an order whose ruthlessness is worthy of the twentieth century:

> Our pleasure is that before you close up our banner again you shall in any wise cause such dreadful execution to be done upon a good number of the inhabitants of every town, village, and hamlet that have offended in this rebellion, as well by the hanging of them up in trees as by the quartering of them, and the setting of their heads and quarters in every town, great and small, and all such other places, as they may be a fearful spectacle . . . which we all require you to do without pity or respect . . . cause all the monks and canons that be in any way faulty to be tied up, without further delay or ceremony, to the terrible example of others. Wherein we think you shall do unto us high service.[8]

These great protest movements of the mid-sixteenth century were growing increasingly sophisticated, thanks partly to Caxton's invention, in 1476, of the printing press; and such insurrections as the Pilgrimage of Grace, Kett's rising in East Anglia in 1549 (whose causes, mainly agrarian, were not unlike those of the Peasants' Revolt) and Wyatt's rebellion in 1554 caused thinking men to turn their minds to the novel idea that England might need a professional police force, or army, to maintain order at home. Feudal society had been tightly knit, and social discipline was an integral part of it. But when feudalism collapsed its in-built disciplines fell apart too, so that the state was no longer able to command the authority that had previously been delegated, in nicely attenuated degrees, right down the social hierarchy. It was precisely the same situation that caused France, and other formerly feudal countries that were still influenced by the vestiges of Roman rule, to fill the 'power vacuum' in the state by instituting a system of military police – in France the *maréchaussée* (1544) which later developed into the *gendarmerie*. Awareness of this, and of the dangers of incessant public violence at home, was the background to a great debate that took hold of late sixteenth-century England: and England chose, perversely, to go her own way.

The dilemma was very clearly seen. 'Without civil order there can be no true commonwealth,' wrote Thomas Starkey in 1584, and others expressed a similar concern. Without order there could be no real liberty, and order must rest, ultimately, on force. Yet might not force in the end prove to be a greater evil than disorder? The debate, initiated during Elizabeth's reign, was to continue for centuries, at first battening on the evils of a standing army, later on the supposed evils of a police force. The dilemma as seen through the eyes of contemporaries comes out plainly in a Discourse published by William Stafford in 1581:

Knight   In France they have diverse Bandes of men in Armes, in diverse places of the Realme, to represse such Tumults quickely if any should arise. If wee had the like heere, wee might bee boulde to have as many Artificers as they have.

Husbandman   God fworbote that ever wee shoulde have any such Tyrauntes come among us; for, as they say, such will in the Countrey of Fraunce take poore mens Hennes, chikens, Pigges, and other provision, and paye nothinge for it, except it bee an ill turne, as to Ravishe his Wyfe or his Daughters for it . . . that woulde rather bee an occasion of Commotions to bee stirred, then to bee quenched. For (as hee sayd) the Stomaks of Englishe men woulde never beare to suffer such Injuries and Reproaches, as he heard that such used to doe to the subjects of Fraunce, which in reproche they call Pesaunts.

And the Husbandman concludes:

> I would not have a small sore cured by a greater griefe, nor for avoydinge of populer sedition, which happeneth very seldome and soone quenched, to bring in a continuall yoake.[9]

This was the prevailing opinion. People had not forgotten the sufferings of their forebears in not so distant times when nobles had been permitted to keep retainers; and there can be no doubt that long memories of that lawless era lay behind the extreme reluctance with which men in later centuries approached the idea of a standing army or professional police force. As we shall see later these early experiences conditioned the character of our police when they were eventually set up.

In default, therefore, of a regular police or army the Tudors contrived to scotch the more dangerous political and religious riots and rebellions by calling on the sheriff to order out the *posse comitatus*, or militia. They also instituted a secret service as an attempt to forestall trouble, introduced into England the practice of intercepting mail, and, *in extremis*, employed the statecraft of terror and treachery. But the turmoil of the age was not confined to political or religious-motivated disturbances. Widespread popular risings from economic and agrarian causes brought into play a new remedy against violence that was to achieve great importance in later times. A Statute of Edward VI in 1553, building on the fourteenth-century laws dealing with riot which have already been mentioned, anticipated many of the provisions of the more famous Riot Act of 1714. Under this Statute it became high treason for twelve or more persons, being assembled together, to continue together for the space of an hour after being ordered by a magistrate to depart. Even so it seems doubtful whether this early version of the Riot Act had much effect, for it merely tinkered with a problem of growing dimensions. Throughout much of the Tudor period the countryside was terrorised by bands of tramps, beggars, thieves, ex-soldiers and unemployables. The closure of the monasteries added to their number. Together with the homeless, unemployed from decaying manors and villages and the riff-raff of towns, they constituted a formidable and continuing threat to the peace, which would undoubtedly have led to much more violence had not the wise Government of Elizabeth I realised what no Government had realised before, and not all were to realise later: that social problems have a national as well as a local concern, and that they cannot be overcome by repression alone.

Here was a discovery in the art of conquering violence which was of the first importance. Until the development of the English Poor Law, between 1549 and 1601, the task of dealing with tramps and vagabonds had taken a prominent place in the day's work of the parish constable. To him fell the duty of arresting the stranger in town or village, placing him in the stocks, shackling and maiming him as required by the barbaric laws of the time, branding him with hot irons so that he should in future be recognised for the pariah he was, and then whipping him out of the village or town 'until his or her body be bloodie'. By these means the outcasts from monastery or manor were provoked to further violence and to aggravate matters the honourable medieval idea of giving alms to the poor virtually lapsed with the

The 'Peterloo' massacre. Manchester 1819.
The Yeomanry charging the mob

GRAND PROCESSION
ON MONDAY NEXT,

MARCH 14, 1842, IN HONOR OF FEARGUS

O'CONNOR
ESQ.

THE UNFLINCHING ADVOCATE

Of the Toiling Millions.

All Persons wishing to join the PROCESSION, and to do honor to that unjustly persecuted

FRIEND OF THE PEOPLE!

are informed that the DARLASTON & WALSALL ASSOCIATIONS will meet the BILSTON and WOLVERHAMPTON Associations

A Chartist Poster of 1842

disappearance of the great monastic houses. A huge nomadic society was thus created with no alternative to a life of violence. It was the achievement of Elizabeth's ministers that they both recognised the problem and installed machinery to solve it by providing for the appointment of overseers of the poor in every parish, with power to levy a compulsory poor rate. This timely government intervention, in the form of obligatory local social services, proved a much more effective means of staving off social disorder than any strengthening of the law or of the machinery for its enforcement – constabulary, justices and militia. Thus a lesson of great value was learned which unfortunately was subsequently lost to sight until more recent times. Elizabeth's ministers minded the interests of the poor because they realised that the interests of public order are bound up with them.

The justices, by late Tudor times, had emerged as the pivot round which the whole of this machinery turned. Exercising central authority, they promoted a degree of local liberty. Increasingly they were taking over from the manorial courts and parish vestries the duty of appointing the village constable. They sat on the Bench in the courts of law and they supervised the overseers of the poor in working the Poor Law. Under Elizabeth they became the local agents of the central government not only in social affairs and in administering justice, but in regulating prices and wages also. Thus in times of depression, when corn was scarce, as in 1587 (the year before the defeat of the Armada), they were instructed by the Privy Council to enlist the co-operation of local people in preparing food rationing schemes. They ordered the removal of grain from one area to another and settled 'fair' prices for food. A typical report is that to the Privy Council from the Justices of Gloucestershire in 1587:

> We have visited the marketts, searched the barnes, store-houses and granyers of farmers and others and have in discretion appointed them a certeyne quantytie to be brought weeklie to the markett. And we have sett downe several prices upon everie kind of graine ... we will hereafter have care to see the same solde as may be beste for the relief of oure poore neighbours.[10]

The Elizabethan justices must share with the Queen and her ministers, who recognised and exploited their value, the great credit for having put at least a temporary halt to the turmoil of centuries. A contemporary observer, Sir Thomas Smith (*De Republica Anglorum*), summed up their role admirably in 1589, when the justices were probably at the peak of their effectiveness:

> There was never in any commonwealth devised a more wise a more dulce and gentle nor a more certain way to rule the people whereby they are always kept as it were in a bridle of good order, and sooner looked into that they should not offend than punished when they have offended.[11]

Yet if the key to the relative tranquillity which the England of Shakespeare enjoyed is to be found in the rule of the country gentry, it must not be overlooked that this benevolent state of affairs was backed by very considerable force. Set firmly against a professional police or army, Elizabethan England nevertheless tightened up service in the militia. 'Immoral' games such as cards, bowls and dicing had long replaced archery as the popular (and at one time compulsory) amusement: Elizabeth, with an eye on external enemies of the state rather than internal, put the clock back. Everyone over 17 had to keep a bow and arrow, and trained archers were forbidden to use firearms. The gentry were required to increase their own armaments beyond the scale laid down in the Statute of Winchester. The sheriff of each county (still subdivided as of old into hundreds, townships and parishes) was replaced in 1559 by a prominent member of the county aristocracy, entitled the lord lieutenant. Once or twice a year under his authority, the deputy lieutenant, having consulted the county magistrates, issued orders to the constables for the time and place of a muster of arms. Each parish constable was then responsible for producing men, arms, and equipment for inspection. Frequently the arms and armour were maintained by the parish as a whole, and stored in the church. At least one of these small armouries still exists in the Suffolk village of Mendlesham. Together with the arms of the gentry they would be cleaned and polished for what was as much a social as a military occasion. In times of emergency over 100,000 men might be kept in a state of alert for months at a time. After 1573 a small daily wage was paid to compensate them for their loss of earnings.

In course of time the militia became further refined, as the Government saw the danger of insisting that the lower orders should be armed with the increasingly powerful weapons that were becoming available. As a result, in 1573, a change was introduced. Musters were ordered to select for special training a limited number of the wealthier and more able men, loyal citizens 'well-affected to her Majesty and the State', who were expected to pay for their own arms and training. Typically these were farmers, tradesmen and artisans. The change is important, for it came at a time when parish constables were increasingly opting out of their duties and paying deputies to serve in their place, with the result that the office of constable, once so proud in the Norman hierarchy, had fallen into the object of contempt that Shakespeare depicted in Dogberry, Verges and Constable Elbow. But now these same farmers, tradesmen and artisans found themselves again enlisted for obligatory public service, this time in a *corps d'élite* of the militia which came to be known as a trained band. In this capacity they were to play an important part in dealing with the social disorders of later periods.

Thus the old idea of involving men of good-will and good sense in the maintenance of the public peace persisted unbroken from Saxon times and, in turning their backs on the idea of a state army or police force as being incompatible with individual freedom, the national instinct proved sound. When these institutions were eventually set up, after agonising struggles, society had matured to a degree that enabled it to invest them with the character of a service rather than a force. Here was luck indeed. Our sixteenth-century civilisation was not ripe enough to contrive the delicate balance between order and liberty that the English concept of 'police' implies, and it is our lasting good fortune that (unlike other states at the time) our ancestors did not attempt to strike it. As it was, the end of the Elizabethan era, so glorious in so many ways, saw a welcome abatement in the terrible record of violence in our public life. The genius of native art, architecture and literature again flourished, as squire, parson and brick-built country house took the place of the long defunct line of feudal lord and knight in castle or fortified manor. A gentle tolerance, rooted in antiquity, had for the moment transcended religious squabbles. The enlightened age of Shakespeare, like that of Chaucer two hundred years earlier, was something of a calm before the coming storm. During those two turbulent centuries, moreover, society had acquired the beginning of the political maturity which alone can reconcile order with true liberty. Nevertheless, it would falsify history to suggest that in either interlude wealthy men were ever again safely able to ride the length of the country with no protection other than a white wand – if indeed they ever had done.

Britain entered the turbulent seventeenth century with social defences still aligned to the conditions of the middle ages; she entered the nineteenth with the same defences modified to take account of the temporary needs of the seventeenth. In this chapter an attempt will be made to show how the means of combating disorder constantly lagged behind its causes, with the result that the country faced the onset of the Industrial Revolution at the very time when she was least equipped, politically as well as administratively, to deal with social and economic upheaval: an upheaval, moreover, during which the nature of collective violence was itself changing, as the labouring classes confounded the familiar pattern of local rioting with a struggle to establish a national political movement of their own that would make local rioting unnecessary. The tensions implicit in this situation explain why the number of regular soldiers required to suppress violence at home in 1812 exceeded the number Wellesley was permitted to take to the Peninsular. The balance sheet was not, however, without its credit side. Experience in using the military for civil purposes, and in particular the moderate way in which the use of soldiers was regulated by the law, directly paved the way for the eventual establishment of a mild system of police whose character owed everything to native manners, nothing at all to foreign influences. This system of police, in turn, was to be a major influence in pacifying Britain.

In any history of popular protest movements in Britain the century and a half that followed the age of Shakespeare presents an odd contrast. The seventeenth-century processes that hammered out the constitutional principles which were to govern the country for three hundred years were accompanied by civil war, rebellion, and the violence of religious persecution. The age abounds in famous plots: the Gunpowder Plot, the Rye House Plot, the Popish Plot, the Derwentdale Plot, and many others. The Secretary of State was assiduous in perfecting the means of espionage and counter-espionage. Much of the century is characterised by religious prejudice working on mob violence, with its climax about the year 1685, marking the onset of the persecution of the Huguenots in France and the savagery of Judge Jeffries in dealing with Monmouth's rebellion – 'the last popular rising in the old England'.[1] Then the bloody century ends 'not with a bang but a whimper' in the bloodless revolution of 1688 and the Toleration Act of the same year. The domestic background to it all is a pattern of ascending degrees of violence in private as well as public behaviour. Duelling and the baiting of foreigners were commonplace, fights and rough-houses were everyday scenes, the London mob could terrorise the City whenever the apprentices chose, and the turn of the century saw the advent of hooliganism among the young rich as well as the young poor. Lawlessness, by 1750, had spread to all classes.

The point of contrast is this: if we except Monmouth's rising the violence of the age was never effectively harnessed to a popular cause. Cavaliers and Roundheads exploited it, as did Catholics and Anglicans, but, for reasons to be discussed later in this chapter, the common people attempted nothing on the scale of the Peasants' Revolt or the insurrections of 1536 and 1549. There are plenty of recorded instances of riots against enclosures and rising food prices, but these, dangerous enough for a few hours to a few people, were local, sporadic and ineffectual. It was not until the Industrial Revolution was well advanced that common people gave the authorities cause for serious concern.

The violent episodes of the seventeenth century were motivated in the main by political and religious causes (social and economic influences came both earlier and later); and they were directed by the upper and upper-middle classes. For once the poor were victims of violence rather than its cause. The parliamentarians, lawyers and squires who blew the dust off Magna Carta probably inspired as little popular enthusiasm for their high and inscrutable purposes as the Barons who had obliged King John to sign it 400 years earlier. The battle for the rule of law against the divine right of kings, like the fight against John, was undertaken by men of property defending privilege. The principles bandied about by Charles's fanatical yeomanry from the west of England and Cromwell's fanatical yeomanry from East Anglia meant nothing to the overwhelming mass of the population, who could see little in it for them from either side.

Nor, as it happened, was the outcome of the struggle entirely to the advantage of ordinary people, at all events for many years. The defeat of the political and religious tyranny of the monarch paved the way for a practical balance between freedom and order that provided an example to the world, as it still does. But the drawbacks in the settlement came later. It was more than a century afterwards, when the challenge of organised violence was beginning to assume a characteristically modern form, that two unforeseen consequences of the Civil War emerged as decisive factors, and nearly another century elapsed before the lessons of this situation were taken to heart. One of these consequences (to which we return later in this chapter) was the growing insubordination, in relation to the Crown, of the magistracy, bringing with it the necessity of government by *laissez faire*. A result of this was that for many years national social and economic policies ceased to be enforceable, and the poor were often unprotected. The other was the institution during the reign of Charles II of a standing army. The two changes worked in contrary directions: the first towards a localisation of the social and economic problems that increasingly lay at the root of disorder, the second towards the centralisation of the most effective means of repressing it. The situation was thus the opposite of our present one, where economic and social problems are tackled nationally and the means of preventing disorder are local. It was not until nineteenth-century governments began to realise the importance of getting the balance of the administrative arrangements right that the first steps could be taken in conquering violence.

The immediate effects of the Civil War on the populace ought not to be exaggerated. Most people, like their ancestors two hundred years earlier during the Wars of the Roses, carried on with business as usual. Out of a population of some five million not more than 150,000 were under arms, and a high proportion of them were serving in the militia. The 'New Model' army which Cromwell created in 1645 comprised some 22,000 men compulsorily enrolled. After the war it absorbed other parliamentary armies to a total of some 70,000 men, the infantry being drawn from the lower agricultural and urban classes, the cavalry from county families. Much of this army was kept in being during the interregnum, and its expense was borne by a tax on the estates of Royalists on the old principle that those responsible for disorder should pay for the re-establishment of order. Then, for eighteen months during 1657–58, Cromwell gave the nation a taste of military dictatorship. His twelve 'Major-Generals' replaced sheriffs, justices and lords lieutenant as the principal officers of the peace, stretching their sinews to combine responsibilities for law and order, tax collection and public morals. The experiment, however, was short-lived, so ludicrously ill-adjusted was it to the national character.

On Cromwell's death in 1658 Britain's first-ever army was virtually disbanded, but it was not long before what had been accepted as a temporary necessity for waging war was seen also as an indispensable aid in the maintenance of peace. Social conditions were deplorable. Hoards of vagrants and disbanded soldiers roamed the land. The reaction to puritanism swept over the country in a wave of licence. Large areas of London succumbed to vice. The political and religious hatreds that had caused the fighting were by no means extinguished when it stopped. Protestants continued to glower at Catholics, Royalists at Roundheads. If ever a sovereign needed an army to maintain order at home it was Charles II, but experience of Cromwell had left behind an abiding distrust of standing armies, and members of the Restoration Parliament were in no hurry to provide him with one. They preferred to set about patching up the traditional means of keeping the peace. The Statute of Winchester was re-examined, and from time to time orders went out from the Privy Council requiring a sheriff to call out the *posse comitatus*. The ramshackle paraphernalia of justice, constable and sheriff, however, had long been obsolescent, and many courts leet had forgotten their feudal obligations to appoint parish constables. So, to remedy their negligence, a statute of Charles II provided that, in default, constables were to be appointed by justices in quarter sessions.* A second statute enabled magistrates to swear people in as special constables, not for a specified term, but for a particular emergency. The facility was little used for many years, but later on it was to become an important ancillary means of keeping the peace. The King, meanwhile, complained that the strength of the nightly watch in London was inadequate to deal with its mounting problems, and the Court of Common Council responded by authorising the appointment of 1,000 watchmen, or bellmen, who, with their familiar staves, rattles and lanterns were for generations the favourite butt of hooligans. All this, however, was mere tinkering. The Restoration Parliament was soon obliged to go farther, and in doing so they paved the way for the gradual eclipse of the old arrangements. First they turned their attention to the militia. Then, with evident reluctance, they faced up to the fact that the country was now in such an abject state that a standing army would again have to be created. This time it was to be permanent.

The militia, descendant of the old Saxon fyrd, had during Elizabeth's period constituted an effective territorial force, based on the county and the hundred, and available to be called out in time of danger. Charles I had tried to build it up to even greater perfection, quaintly hoping (as the Plantagenets had done) that people would enjoy drilling and training as a form of recreation. Some may; all, as ratepayers, grumbled at the cost of maintaining arms, as later generations were to complain about the cost of the police. The Government issued drill books and ordered the names of defaulters to be reported. Oaths of allegiance were sworn and the trained bands, in particular, were built up in the towns as a *corps d'élite* for internal defence. As a result the county militias, under lords lieutenant, emerged as potentially powerful forces in the state, and an important issue in the Civil War was whether they should be controlled by King or Parliament. One of the first

* It has been argued by some historians that this change is of great constitutional significance in marking the final subordination of local to central government in rural districts, and of the conversion of a local administrative officer (the constable) into a 'ministerial officer of the Crown'. The circumstances in which the Act was passed tell convincingly against this view. It was almost certainly a move of pure expediency.

enactments of the Restoration Parliament, in 1662, reorganised the militia under the formal authority of the Crown, and placed the lord lieutenant under a duty to order it out not only to suppress insurrection or rebellion, but also to aid the civil power when a local riot threatened to get out of hand. The officers of the militia were local landowners, whose rank depended directly on their wealth; it thus formed an exclusive county club for the aristocracy. At the same time trained bands were abolished, with the exception of those for the City of London, which kept order after the Great Fire of 1666, having earlier demonstrated their value by sheltering the Five Members (they included Hampden and Pym) whose abortive arrest by Charles helped to precipitate the civil war. It may have been in a deliberate attempt to compensate for the abolition of the remainder of the trained bands that Parliament provided for the appointment of special constables.

Finally, the militia reorganised, the Restoration Parliament set about the anxious business of re-creating an army; and the Articles of War of 1668 by which it was constituted leave no room for doubt about its purpose. This was declared to be to maintain 'the security and peace of our Kingdom'; and that its continuance was to be 'no longer than the minds of our subjects shall be composed to unity and due obedience'. These lofty thoughts proved in the event to offer a short-sighted view of the future of the British Army. Laws were soon enacted authorising its use against religious dissenters and on many other 'police' activities; and its usefulness to Charles II was such that by the end of his reign the original force of 5,000, which were all that Parliament allowed, had risen to 16,000. Regular soldiers were not ordinarily used to suppress local riots: they were too sparse to cover the country effectively, and most were concentrated in London or the coastal forts. In London, however, they were occasionally employed to overpower the mob – much to the annoyance of the trained bands, themselves some 20,000 strong. Typical cases were the riots of 24th and 25th March 1668 (page 11) to which Pepys refers in his diary – possibly the first instance of the use of soldiers against a rabble:

> ... To Lincolne's Inn-fields, thinking to have gone into the fields to have seen the 'prentices; but here we found these fields full of soldiers all in a body, and my Lord Craven commanding them,

and riding up and down to give orders, like a madman. . . . And we heard a Justice of the Peace this morning say to the King, that he had been endeavouring to suppress this tumult, but could not; and that, imprisoning some of them in the new prison at Clerkenwell, the rest did come and break open the prison and release them; and that they do give out that they are for pulling down the brothels, which is one of the great grievances of the nation. To which the King made a very poor, cold, insipid answer: 'Why, why do they go to them then?'

Next day everyone was:

Full of the talk of the 'prentices, who are not yet put down, though the guards and militia of the town have been in armes all night, and the night before; and the 'prentices have made fools of them. Some blood hath been spilt, but a great many houses pulled down; and, among others, the Duke of York was mighty merry at that of Damen Page's, the great bawd of the seamen.

The use of soldiers against rioters at this period, however, was exceptional. Like the militia, the army was instituted primarily to protect the security of the state against insurrection, rebellion or invasion inspired by political or religious motives; and for several years it and the militia represented an internal balance of power, a sort of equipoise in the state, the one under the King's control, the other obedient to the county aristocracy. Key figures in maintaining this balance were the two Secretaries of State for the Northern and Southern Departments. Between them they employed about forty 'king's messengers', or 'messengers in ordinary', a body of hard-working spies who seem to have enjoyed unlimited powers of search and arrest, and who kept their paymasters in touch with a multitude of informers. The Secretaries of State, indeed, were regarded by Macaulay as 'little more than superintendents of police'; and Max Beloff has commented on their 'enormous amount of work in connection with the unravelling of plots, the suppression of seditious publications, and the control of the movements of suspicious persons', to the neglect of economic and social issues. On their advice the Privy Council issued a constant stream of directions to justices, sheriffs, mayors and lords lieutenant about the precise means they were to employ to maintain public order, sometimes, for example, telling a lord lieutenant to bring the militia to the aid of a hard-pressed civil authority. The council were vigilant in seeing to it that a mayor or justice who failed in his duty was heavily fined under the Act of Henry IV that we noticed in the previous chapter. A defaulting borough might even forfeit its franchise.

Twenty uneasy years passed in this fashion; and then, in 1685, the combined power of the state, army as well as militia, was used to put down Monmouth's rebellion. It was a turning point in the struggle of the British people in learning how to live with an army. Monmouth's defeat at Sedgemoor, the last battle to be fought on English soil, provided James II with an excuse to increase the number of troops to some 30,000. The equipoise was upset, the King's design instantly suspect. With good reason men feared that he planned to govern the country with a standing army, using troops to restore it to catholicism. Events followed logically. James's flight sparked off violence in London, and the trained bands had orders to fire on the mob if necessary. But in general the bloodless revolution, and the manner of its accomplishment, testifies to the calm and common sense of the people; and at last the Bill of Rights, the Act of Settlement and the annual Mutiny Acts brought the army (in 1689 some 17,000 strong, including 7,000 Dutch troops) under effective Parliamentary supervision.

In this way the army became an accepted and permanent institution, but during the reigns of William and Anne its activities were viewed cagily. The Dutch soldiers were sent home, and the army was reduced by Parliament to some 8,000. The Privy Council was abstemious in issuing warrants to allow soldiers to be used to coerce or repress the people, so real and recent were the fears James II had aroused. Justices turned to constables to maintain order, or, if a threatening situation developed, looked to the sheriff to call out the *posse comitatus*, or the lord lieutenant to call out the militia – procedures which may well have had the same result, since the local officer responsible was in either case the high constable of the hundred. The records of the War Office show that for nearly thirty years – until January 1716 – troops were scarcely ever again called out to suppress riots on any substantial scale. Thereafter, however, soldiers were seen to be so useful that their employment became increasingly common.

Before leaving the seventeenth century and turning to examine the fresh causes of violence during the early part of the eighteenth, we may now pause to bring into focus the means available to deal with it, noting once again how ill adjusted were the means to the ends. The first line of social defence, comprising parish constables, justices and sheriffs backed by the ultimate force of the *posse comitatus* of the county, was in an advanced state of decay. The second, the county militia, like the first, was a part-time force only. Nevertheless it could be rapidly mobilised to deal with local disturbances – which its officers, the squirearchy, had a vested interest in suppressing, partly as employers of labour, partly because they were liable to be punished by the Privy Council if they failed. During the reigns of William and Anne, when the regular army was at its weakest, the militia (totalling some 93,000 men, including 6,000 mounted) undoubtedly provided the most effective 'police' force in the country, and it is no exaggeration to say that it provided the key to the maintenance of public order, for the use of the third line of social defence, the regular army, was still viewed, except perhaps in extreme court circles, with disfavour. Moreover, the legal basis on which soldiers were used had yet to be defined by the courts, and at best they could offer only a rigid weapon against disorder that, from the start, was liable to provoke more violence than it repressed. Finally, it is to be noted that the ascendancy of the army and the militia as primary means of putting down disturbances, frequently acting on orders of the Privy Council, had been the direct outcome of the political and religious struggles of the seventeenth century, but these particular convulsions were virtually at an end. To the socially and economically motivated riots of the eighteenth the new means were ill adapted, but successive governments, enervated by luxurious living at home and agreeably distracted by war overseas, long remained as blind to this situation as they were indifferent to the nation's growing domestic problem. Max Beloff has noted that John Bellers was virtually a lone voice crying in the wilderness in 1699: 'Foreign Wars waste our Treasure but Tumults at home are a Convulsion upon our Nerves . . . what can awe the misery of the Starving?'[2] To the alert, critical and informed public of today such a view would be seen as material for a 'Panorama' programme, or its equivalent in America, where Bellers's observation has a certain contemporary point. The differences between then and now is the difference between an immature, largely illiterate nation, unaware of its problems, let alone of the means for their solution, and a nation sufficiently grown up to be able to debate its problems openly, even though it cannot always solve them.

Such views as those of Bellers went unheeded in 1699 not so much because they were novel as because they were out of joint with the times. The Elizabethan magistrates, it will be recalled, had been subservient to the Privy Council: the Council sent out to them a stream of orders to regulate the local economy by settling fair food prices and even, occasionally, by rationing food. These arrangements survived until the Civil War but became obsolescent when the squires conquered the King. After 1660, more particularly after 1688, government paternalism ceased to be practicable, since the authority required to give effect to it was no longer available. Mayors and county magistrates were obliged to accept directions in matters of public order, but they resented interference by the Privy Council in the local domestic issues with which their private interests were bound up. The Council was still able to regulate social and economic affairs in the capital and in parts of Middlesex – it had to, to prevent the London mob from tearing the City apart – but provincial Britain was no longer effectively governed from London. It was not until events in the nineteenth century again obliged governments to recognise that the cause of public order is bound up with concern for the poor that the virtues of the Tudor system were heeded. The point was only taken, however, after violent struggles.

It is, in a way, surprising that the consequences of this transformation in the roles of central and local government were not to be perceived for so many years. Part of the explanation lies in the apathy of the lower orders during the seventeenth century and the early part of the eighteenth to set about improving their condition, but this merely shifts the question a stage further. Why were they apathetic? It cannot be said that their condition was particularly good, for it was actually declining. The Settlement Acts retained an echo of feudalism, tying men to the land; and the economic drift of the century was 'towards a sharper demarcation of classes and towards depriving the poor of such economic protection as the Tudor and early Stuart governments had managed to keep up for them'.[3] How, then, are we to explain their

64

relative tranquillity – faced with as combustible a recipe for violence as could well be devised – religious fanaticism, social tension and economic distress?

Part of the answer lies, no doubt, in the fact that there failed to emerge for many years any philosopher, man of letters or politician sufficiently sympathetic to the condition of the labouring classes to bother to publicise it. The disjointed riots of seventeenth- and eighteenth-century Britain were observed with detachment as a sort of natural phenomenon easily repressible by force; and it occurred to few to connect them with the collapse of effective machinery for imposing national economic policies. In any case the lower orders lived for generations in a perhaps enviable state of political lassitude, in a succession of seemingly endless Augustan summers. So long as the outward form of things seemed stable the labourer was content enough, and permanence was everywhere about him in the countryside. Most Tudor, Elizabethan and Stuart manor houses were still occupied by squires and their descendants, open-handed generosity was still common, and the villager who looked to the squire for support, as his ancestors had done for generations past, was not to know that the old order was slowly passing away. He only discovered by chance, during bad periods, that the squire was no longer protecting him from economic distress; nor would he have realised what it would mean to his children when the manor house changed hands and a new squire moved in, with interests in trade and industry rather than the land, lacking any tradition of paternalism.

All these were little local changes that were slow to build up into a national pattern, and to obscure them were entrenched forces of conservatism. In many areas the old relationship of squire and peasant survived even the Augustan age, and men could still say without a trace of irony –

> God bless the squire and his relations
> And keep us in our proper stations.

Everywhere there was a remarkable absence of class antagonism. A spirit of tolerance seems to have seeped through society after the upheavals of the seventeenth century, and despite an increasingly savage penal code county magistrates were confident enough of their own secure way of life to be lenient in dealing with offenders brought before them. It is against this superficially stable social background that the discriminating and even genteel behaviour of such rioters as those at Cleehill becomes intelligible (page 16): it is almost as though an unspoken pact existed between rioters and authorities that neither side would use more force than seemed necessary to establish their respective points. Certainly there was no enmity between them. Class consciousness was a nineteenth-century discovery. It would be wrong, however, to romanticise this situation. Sometimes, as we saw in Chapter 1, very considerable force was used to crush these sporadic agricultural riots of the eighteenth century, and as that century advanced the force to which the justices increasingly turned was that provided by the county militia or the regular army. To understand why, we need to look more closely at the state of the civil arrangements.

The civil power remained, right until 1829 (and for years after that in many parts of Britain) an inheritance from medieval England, and at the root of the system still lay the ancient Saxon principle of involving all men as part-timers in the business of maintaining the peace. The principle had been long out of date, had been long unworkable, and was totally inadequate to the novel problems of the Industrial Revolution. Nevertheless successive governments cherished it because it offered a form of policing on the cheap. Consequently each county continued nominally to rely for its first line of social defence on the medieval phalanx of parish constables and high constables of the hundred under the authority of the sheriff. All was still governed by the elderly Statute of Winchester, and ancient forms jostled oddly with modern realities. The *posse comitatus* was called out as late as 1839. The Saxon titles of tythingman and borsholder were solemnly bestowed by courts leet (sometimes by justices in quarter sessions) on astonished citizens of the growing industrial towns in the North and Midlands. Elsewhere constables were still selected on rota by house row to serve their annual period of unpaid service, as their predecessors had been soon after the Norman Conquest.

The system creaked badly in the seventeenth century and broke down completely in the eighteenth. Everywhere respectable citizens were opting out of the office of constable by paying deputies to act in their place. Most such professional deputies were as useless as the watchmen many towns were beginning to appoint towards the end of the eighteenth century under local Acts of Parliament. And the high constable of the hundred, once the proud inspector of the assize of arms under the Statute of Winchester, still in useful employment as a peace officer even in Stuart times, had by the time of George III declined to the status of a minor local government official whose main task was to collect rates. All was in transition; and to complete the story of decay in the primary means of preventing disorder the office of magistrate, too, was falling into the hands of corrupt practitioners, a process speeded by the disaffection from the Crown, in the years following the Revolution of 1688, of a number of county families who for generations had filled the office of justice. The total situation by, say, 1760 is thus a striking one. The nation's first line of defence against disorder was crumbling at the very time when the onset of the Industrial Revolution was bringing the threat of violence nearer. All therefore depended on the success of the second and third lines: militia and army; and here, too, subtle changes were taking place.

The army was being forced into prominence as an aid to the civil power because by the middle of the eighteenth century the value of the militia had declined. An attempt was made by Parliament in 1757 to reinvigorate it, but the new arrangements worked badly. They introduced the idea of compulsory service in the militia by ballot. A quota was laid down for each county, and all men between the ages of 18 and 45 were liable for service in what was, in effect, a part-time infantry force drawn from the lower classes. However, just as a constable was able to pay a deputy to serve in his place, so also could a reluctant militia-man pay £10 to have a substitute named, and these substitutes tended to be of inferior quality. The loyalty of the militia, too, like that of the parish constables, naturally inclined towards their own local people. The ballot was commonly attended by rioting, and there were occasions when a body of militia was ordered to shoot its own comrades for siding with rioters against authority. Moreover the militia were largely untrained, and it was difficult to call them out at short notice from their normal work. They had provided

F

the key to the maintenance of order in pre-industrial Britain during the half century that followed the Restoration, but for the next hundred years, say from 1740 onwards, their role was very largely taken over by the regular army.

It is, indeed, no exaggeration to say that early industrial Britain was policed by soldiers: they put down virtually every serious disturbance. Often they would be called in, as in the instance described on page 15, after 'economic' rioters had already resorted to violence in the presence of magistrates who were otherwise powerless. Such operations must have imposed a severe strain on the loyalty and discipline of the men, for by the time they arrived there was little they could do but open fire on the crowd, often inflicting fatal injuries. And sometimes those who suffered were the very people with whom the soldiers had been living on intimate terms in billets. Consequently, in order to put a distance between troops and people, strategically placed barracks were erected throughout the country. The first was built at Berwick-on-Tweed in 1722, and at the end of the century there were over forty of them, accommodating some 20,000 troops. They took over, after an interval of 600 years, something of the purpose of the Norman castles, as centres from which to subdue a turbulent population. So remote had become fears of a standing army by this time, and so valuable was it now seen as a means of combating violence, that Pitt was warning Parliament quite openly in 1793 that 'A spirit had appeared in some of the manufacturing towns which made it necessary that troops should be kept near them.'[4] As we shall see in the next chapter the situation worsened after the turn of the century, when for several years parts of the North and Midlands resembled a country under military occupation.

Even so soldiers could not be everywhere at once. In many areas readier and more local means were needed to crush a riot before it got out of control. To meet this demand governments throughout the eighteenth century encouraged the formation of private voluntary associations composed of well-armed members of the upper and middle classes. Such bodies trained themselves, they could be rapidly mobilised, and, acting in their own self-interest, they could be highly effective against rioters – even, if necessary, against the militia. The obvious danger that their growth threatened the country with class warfare seems to have been slight during that period so remarkably free from class antagonism. It was not until 1819, when volunteers in the more formalised Yeomanry attacked demonstrators in the so-called massacre of Peterloo, that this danger became a reality.

The increasing readiness to call in the military to suppress riots during the 1740s and 1750s did not go uncriticised, and it is at this time that we find the first serious thinking about the case for setting up a professional police force in England. To the novelist Henry Fielding must go the credit not only for drawing attention to 'the very large and peaceful body which forms the fourth estate in this country, and have been long dignified and distinguished by the name of The Mob', but also for pointing the way towards the creation of a police force to deal with it. Fielding was appointed to the office of Chief Magistrate at Bow Street in 1748, and two years later he published a celebrated pamphlet, *An Enquiry into the Causes of the Late Increase of Robbers*, declaring an intention, 'to rouse the civil power from its present lethargic state'. In the pamphlet he posed, in contemporary terms, the identical dilemma that had baffled the sixteenth century (page 48). His design, he claimed, was to be one which 'alike opposes those wild notions of liberty that are inconsistent with all government, and those pernicious schemes which are destructive to true liberty'. His practical proposals, however, failed to measure up to this prospectus. He contented himself with appointing to the Bow Street office half a dozen 'thief-takers', a nucleus which his blind half-brother John later expanded into a corps which, by about 1785, were coming to be known as the Bow Street Runners. Even so, by the end of the century London still had only about 120 full-time 'policemen', rather more than half of whom were Runners, the remainder being attached in groups of half a dozen to each of seven Metropolitan Magistrates' offices which were created in 1792. This paltry force was, of course, totally irrelevant to the problem of the London mob, and we may assume that they kept well out of its way in times of trouble. As for provincial Britain, most towns of any size obtained powers under local Improvement Acts to appoint a few paid night watchmen or day constables. These, too, were powerless in the face of a mob, and were not intended to deal with one.

Henry Fielding died in 1750, his grand design largely un-accomplished, and for nearly three-quarters of a century after-wards the idea of instituting an effective police force in Britain gained little ground. Public opinion was hostile to it. Only with the greatest difficulty had the nation learned to control a standing army, and few were now prepared to risk traditional English liberties at the hands of a system of police which continental experience, so it was widely held, proved to be incompatible with freedom. A repressive *maréchaussée* or *gendarmerie* was all very well for the French, and the creation of a Berlin state police in 1742 would have occasioned no surprise at the characteristic behaviour of the Germans, but to the English these were sinister institutions. So closed was this attitude of mind that it was not until after the Gordon Riots, in 1780, that the adequacy of the available means of dealing with popular disturbances was seriously called into question; and even then the idea of police aroused no more than a flicker of interest.

A direct result of this continuing absence of a police system in eighteenth-century England was the increasing barbarity of the criminal law against violence. Arson had traditionally been punishable by death. In addition, numerous Acts of Parliament during the century were specifically aimed to curb acts of violence arising out of social unrest. With the advance of the Industrial Revolution they were directed particularly at machine wrecking and the destruction of equipment and manufactured articles such as wool and silk. Most added to the already formidably long list of offences which carried the death penalty (in the period between the Restoration and the death of George III they rose by about 190); although it is refreshing to find the early influence of the criminal law reformers in 1788, when Parliament substituted transportation for death as the penalty in a Bill which sought to make it a capital offence to destroy knitting frames. It is also worth noting that, just as the rioters were generally discreet in the objectives of their violence, so also the law, keeping pace, defined new offences with nice precision, so cherishing an old tradition that the criminal law should operate no more widely than the particular circumstances required.

We can now begin to sum up, in a context, say, of 1760 or 1770, the responses which 'authority' was making to the growing challenge of violence during the second half of the eighteenth century. Most prominently, it had now discarded the old system of constabulary as virtually useless. Yet it continued with a sentimental attachment which is perhaps typically British to pay lip-service to the Statute of Winchester, holding that the old Saxon principle of personal unpaid service as a peace officer still had enough life left in it to match the new circumstances. The authorities on the ground, of course, and in particular the magistrates, knew very well that the old system was impotent, and they had grown to rely for the suppression of violence on the use of regular soldiers together with (decreasingly) the militia and (increasingly) voluntary armed associations of the upper and middle classes. They also sought to make an occasional example of offenders by taking advantage of the savage penal code, although in practice compassion often influenced a court to award a sentence of transportation rather than death. And finally, having come to terms after agonising struggles with a standing army, the country had no disposition to tinker with experiments to introduce a standing police force.

The clear and inevitable result of this situation was that the violence of rioters was opposed, in the main, by the violence of soldiers. Here was a stark confrontation. Had it continued for any length of time on a national scale it could have led to as disastrous a breakdown of order in this country as France was to witness later in the century. A principal reason why it did not was that the collective violence of eighteenth-century 'economic' rioters was far from representing any national movement. It was local, reactionary, and in national terms, leaderless. A second reason is to be discovered in the saving grace of the principles of law which in Britain regulated the use of troops in aid of the civil power. The dangerous state of affairs that was developing in the late eighteenth century, as the dissatisfaction of multitudes was gradually shaping itself into a political programme, could well have exploded into a revolutionary situation here as well as in France had not these principles of law been wisely interpreted by the courts in setting about the delicate task that only they could perform, that of maintaining a balance in the state between force and counter force. It is this crucial role of the judiciary that we must now examine.

The essential principles of the law against public violence during the eighteenth century, as it developed in a series of decisions by the courts, may be briefly summarised as follows. First, every 'civilian' peace officer (sheriff, magistrate and constable) was obliged to do all in his power to suppress a riot. Second, a peace officer was entitled to call on the help of every available citizen, and anyone who failed to respond was liable to penalties. Third, no more force was to be used in suppressing a riot than necessary. Fourth, a community was liable to a collective fine if it failed to prevent disorder. The situations at which these principles of law were directed were varied.* At one end of the scale came 'unlawful assembly' – a meeting 'of great numbers of people with such circumstances of terror as cannot but endanger the public peace . . . as where great numbers complaining of a common grievance meet together, armed in a warlike manner'. To make such an assembly unlawful actual violence was not necessary: its threat was enough. Next up the scale came riot – 'a tumultuous disturbance of the peace by three or more persons . . . with an intent mutually to assist one another against any who oppose them, in the execution of some enterprise *of a private nature, and afterwards actually executing the same* in a violent and turbulent manner to the terror of the people'. Lastly came an insurrection, differing from riot in that it contemplated an enterprise not of a private nature, but of 'a general and public nature', savouring of high treason and involving, technically, an intention 'to levy war against the sovereign'. In addition to setting himself at risk against these crimes against public order any individual in a mob was also, of course, liable to be charged with specific offences such as murder, robbery, stealing, arson, and the many other offences that carried the death penalty.

Clearly a heavy responsibility lay on the magistrate on the spot to make up his mind swiftly what, under these broad legal heads, was the nature of any particular outbreak of violence, what the mob was after, and what force, if any, to summon in order to disperse it. In this task he was well served by two legal hand-maidens. The first was the Justices of the Peace Act, 1361, with

---

* To put these definitions nearer to their historical context I have taken them from the Manual of Military Law of 1884. The modern versions differ only slightly – see *The Law Relating to Public Order*, I. Brownlie, 1968, Appendix I.

its power to bind over potential rioters to keep the peace: court records of the period show this to have been extensively employed. The second was the Riot Act, 1714, whose predecessors we noticed in the previous chapter. The Act, which fell into disuse only in this century (it was repealed in 1967), was largely a repetition of these earlier statutes. It seems to have been introduced largely in response to popular rioting in disapproval of the House of Hanover at a time, it will be recalled, when the regular army was small and soldiers were rarely, if ever, called out to deal with riots. (Its cause was thus political and not economic.) Like its predecessors the Act in no way limited the powers of the magistrates under the common law to call on force to suppress rioting (misunderstanding on this point was one of the reasons why the Gordon Riots got out of hand); but, in a characteristically British way, it offered (as had Edward VI's statute of 1553) a 'cooling off' period before the possibly deadly force of soldiers was used. In other words it offered an opportunity for magistrates to put an end to a threatening situation before any actual outrage was committed; and, similarly, it served as a warning to bystanders to get out of the way. The Act provided that where twelve or more persons were 'unlawfully, riotously, and tumultuously assembled together, to the disturbance of the public peace' and having been required by a proclamation read by a magistrate to disperse ('reading the Riot Act'), had still refused to do so one hour later, they were to be adjudged felons. This was no mere technicality. It made the demonstrators liable to arrest, and indemnified constables, justices or those who came to their aid (including soldiers) for killing or injuring rioters. Moreover, such as survived and did not escape were liable, on conviction, to the death penalty.

These principles of law, together with the Riot Act itself, were all well established long before it became customary for magistrates to turn to soldiers to suppress violence, and when this happened they had somehow to be applied to the military. The manner in which this was done provides a classic example of the British talent for adapting old ideas to new institutions in such a way as to provide a muddled but on the whole effective compromise. Soldiers were given (are still given) no special privileges, exemption or indemnity which was not enjoyed by everyone else.

73

To them were applied two ancient and fundamental principles of the common law: like every other citizen they were bound to come to the aid of the civil power when a magistrate requested their help to maintain law and order; but like every other citizen they were allowed to use no more force than was necessary. Thus in the eyes of the law a soldier's duties and liabilities in dealing with riots were identical with those of a civilian.

The eyes of the law, however, are myopic; and these principles only begin to make sense if we recognise that, unlike civilians, soldiers form part of a disciplined organisation; and unlike a civilian body, the organisation is armed with deadly weapons. This wider view distorts the simple principles of law. The first (that the soldier merely acts *qua* civilian in coming to the aid of the civil power) had from early times to be reconciled with the fact that soldiers came under the orders of the Crown. If therefore magistrates wanted them to be moved from one place to another to suppress disorder they were obliged to seek the Crown's authority. The first recorded instance of such a petition is in August 1717, in response to which an Order of the Privy Council directed the Secretary at War to make soldiers available. Other instances follow, in each of which the Secretary at War issues a warrant directing the troops 'to repel force with force in case the Civil Magistrate shall find it necessary' or similar words. Given the slowness of communications at the time the intervention of soldiers generally came too late to have any effect, and the Government relaxed its tight control over their use. 'Poor Men out of Employment,' the Secretary at War wrote confidentially to the Commanding Officer of the dragoons at Manchester and Warwick in 1766, 'especially when they are in large Numbers, generally grow riotous, and too often are above the Management of the Civil Magistrate, unassisted by Military Force. The safe and usual Method of the War Office has been to defer any Orders until Application should be made for it, in form, but there are Occasions when Men in Public Employment should venture for the Public Good, and prevent Delays when Delays might be dangerous. I have therefore unasked, but not uninformed of the present State of your Neighbourhood, sent you an Order, herewith enclosed, which I desire you will keep entirely to yourself, till the Civil Magistrate shall apply to you for Assistance. If that never happens the Order had better never be known. . . .'[5] Soon the need for secrecy disappeared, and the practice became common for the Secretary of State to issue standing orders to the military authorities that, on the requisition of the magistrates, they were to give help in suppressing disturbances. It follows that the law and the civil and military authorities have taken a rather different view of the status of troops called in to deal with disturbances. To the one they are merely citizens armed in a particular manner, to the other they are soldiers under military discipline.

The confusion in the situation is evident. It is heightened when we set the second of the principles mentioned above (that, like civilians, soldiers are not allowed to use any more force than is necessary) against the fact that a soldier can only act by using arms and that the weapons he carries are deadly. The soldier enjoys no special privilege or exemption. He cannot excuse himself if without necessity he takes human life; and this necessity, too, is defined narrowly. It extends to the necessity for protecting persons or property against various forms of violent crime, and the necessity of dispersing a riotous crowd which would otherwise be dangerous. The dilemma for the soldier is therefore painful. If he fails to come to the aid of the civil power on the requisition of a magistrate he is liable to be punished by the civil courts. If he fails to use adequate force to quell disorder he is liable to be court-martialled for negligence. If he uses too much force he is liable to be tried for murder or manslaughter. A private soldier might even be at risk for having obeyed an order to fire which the cool judgment of a court later declared to be illegal in the particular circumstances. This predicament was vividly summed up as late as 1835 by Major-General Sir Charles Napier, who was afterwards to play a prominent part in dealing with the Chartist disturbances. The principle 'reduces the soldier to a choice between the hanging awarded to him by the local law for obeying his officer, and the shooting awarded him by the military law for disobeying his officer! In such law there is neither sense nor justice and (being one of those unlucky red-coated gents thus agreeably placed between hanging and shooting) I beg to enter my protest against this choice of deaths. If such is the law, the army must become a deliberative body, and ought to be composed of attorneys, and the Lord Chancellor should be made

Commander-in-Chief.'[6] Shrewdly, Napier went on to suggest – 'It has been convenient for ministers to leave things undefined, so that if circumstances demand it, they may cover themselves by sacrificing the officer' – an early variant of the quip, 'I'm all right, Jack.' The situation was thus confusing and could have calamitous consequences for some. Yet, for all its muddle, it preserved and handed on the ingrained British principles that, in dealing with rioters, soldiers were only civilians in uniform (just as, later on, policemen were to be regarded as only civilians in uniform); that they were subject to the civil law; and that they were allowed to use no more force than was necessary. Thus in principle respect for the rights of the individual triumphed over bureaucratic institutions. This was the impressive achievement of the eighteenth-century lawyers.

These important principles were not, of course, simply handed down like tablets of Mosaic law. They had to be hammered out in the heat of riots and then appraised coolly by the courts, and in this process many suffered. Four important trials serve to mark the course of events: those of John Porteus, a soldier, in 1737; Samuel Gillam, a magistrate, in 1768, and Donald Maclean, another soldier, in the same year; and Barkley Kennett, Lord Mayor of London, in 1780. (Two other trials in which these principles of law were further developed are mentioned in the next chapter.)

Severe rioting broke out in Edinburgh in 1737 following the public hanging of a notorious smuggler. After the execution, when the magistrates had gone, the mob attempted to seize the corpse from the gibbett. Captain Porteus, the officer in command of the troops summoned to attend the execution, gave the order to fire. As a result seventeen people were killed or wounded, and Porteus was put on trial for murder. He was convicted and sentenced to death, but he appealed. The mob, fearing that the appeal might be successful, broke into Edinburgh gaol. They lynched Porteus and hanged him from a home-made gibbett amid further riots, during which neither magistrates nor soldiers this time dared to intervene. So, all local authority vanquished, it was left to Parliament to assert itself. This it did by passing a special Act which provided for the Provost of Edinburgh to be dismissed, and the Corporation to be fined £2,000 for the benefit of Porteus's widow.

This incident served as a warning to the military that their duty in dealing with rioters was hazardous. The next served a similar warning on the magistrates. This was the trial for murder at the Old Bailey of Samuel Gillam, a Surrey magistrate, arising out of his conduct at a riot in 1768 that became popularly known as the 'massacre' of St. George's Fields.

The episode was the culmination of several years of sporadic rioting in London provoked by the radical John Wilkes, a man who doubted everything on principle and had no other principle. Five years earlier, in 1763, he had been a Member of Parliament. A rakish cynic of colourful personality, charm and audacity, he contrived to focus within himself a surge of popular discontent. Wilkes came from the upper-middle classes, and for some time was a colleague of the notorious Sir Francis Dashwood in the Hell Fire Club, and also as an officer in the Buckinghamshire Militia, which for a short time he commanded. Then, in 1762, he published the first issue of a political newspaper, *The North Briton*, as a riposte to Smollett's *The Briton*. Number 45 was published on 23rd April 1763, and Pitt's Government chose to regard it as libellous. Wilkes was arrested and committed to the Tower. Proceedings on a writ of *habeas corpus* followed soon afterwards at Westminster Hall, during which Wilkes declared, 'The liberty of all peers and gentlemen, and, what touches me more sensibly, that of all the middling and inferior set of people, who stand most in need of protection, is in my case this day to be finally decided upon a question of such importance as to determine at once whether English Liberty shall be a reality or a shadow.' With these challenging words Wilkes stepped forward as the idol of the masses and the cry 'Wilkes and Liberty' was born, the blue cockade its emblem. The prisoner was discharged on account of his privilege as a Member of Parliament, and he proceeded triumphantly to have the whole of *The North Briton* reprinted. This the Government saw as a further affront. Parliament ordered the volume to be publicly burned by the Common Hangman at the Royal Exchange. The impressive ceremony took place on 3rd December 1763, but the crowd rallied to Wilkes. Riots broke out and the sheriff and hangman had to run for their lives to the safety of the Mansion House. The constables very sensibly disappeared too, save for a few who tried to burn *The*

North Briton before the crowd made off with it, and burned
effigies of unpopular Ministers instead. Wilkes was now master
of the London mob, able to exploit its violence whenever he
chose. He and his followers introduced the weapon of public
meetings as a means of bringing pressure on the Government.
The Government, alive to the danger, levelled charges of criminal
libel and blasphemy at him, and he was manœuvred into a duel.
Wounded, he fled to Paris. The Commons promptly expelled him
for libel and purported also to outlaw him for blasphemy. In
exile, however, he remained the idol of London, and the cry
'Wilkes and Liberty' was heard everywhere. Within a couple of
years economic distress caused by increases in the cost of living
had reinforced the slogan's political appeal, and there were
countless riots and processions in London as Spitalfields weavers,
coal heavers and apprentices joined forces with craftsmen, small
traders and even City merchants, all proclaiming a common
interest that centred on the absent hero.

Wilkes returned in March 1768, having spent four years
abroad, and at once offered himself for re-election to Parliament.
He won the seat for Middlesex and the mob celebrated riotously
for two nights. Every householder was obliged to put a candle in
his window for Wilkes, and the windows of any house found to
be in darkness were smashed. The Mansion House was attacked
and the City Council offered a reward of £50 to any informant
who secured the conviction of an offender; but the mob now held
Londoners in terror, and the appeal failed. Wilkes had demonstrated the total incompetence of the civil power, and it began to
look as though the only way to protect London from disaster
would be to call out the military. The Government hesitated to
take so appalling a risk. Once again, in April 1768, Wilkes was
summoned to Westminster Hall for the hearing of the outstanding
charges of outlawry and blasphemy, and he was committed to the
King's Bench prison at St. George's Fields, in Southwark. The
case was over at 6.30 p.m., and when Wilkes left Westminster
Hall immense crowds were lining Palace Yard and Westminster
Bridge. As the prisoner drew near to the Surrey side of the river
the mob detached the horses from the carriage in which he was
being conveyed. Then they reversed the carriage and dragged it
along the Strand and Fleet Street to The Three Tuns Tavern, in

Spitalfields. They drove off Wilkes's guards and gave the hero an ovation when he appeared at an upper window. During the night he slipped away in disguise, and next morning knocked on the gaol door, demanding to be let in. These antics endeared him to the mob and the Government were wringing their hands. The incident, declared the Secretary of State, was 'a disgrace to civil government'. Rioting continued every night for a fortnight as crowds gathered round the prison. The Surrey magistrates applied to the Secretary at War for troops. The Government's concern is manifest in a reply that gave the clearest encouragement to the magistrates to use them: if the peace was not preserved the blame would be attributed to 'the want of prudent and spirited conduct in the Civil Magistrate'. The proper occasion to use troops 'always presents itself when the Civil Power is trifled with and insulted. Nor can a Military Force ever be employed to a more constitutional purpose than in support of the authority and dignity of the Magistracy.' Samuel Gillam may have reflected on these brave words when, a few weeks later, he stood in the dock at the Old Bailey to stand his trial for murder.

The tenth of May was the day of the opening of Parliament, and the air was full of rumours that Wilkes was to be escorted from prison to take his seat, or that the mob would break the prison open. From early in the morning crowds converged on St. George's Fields from all over London. By noon they were estimated to be some 40,000 strong. Gillam and three other Surrey magistrates hastened to the scene and ringed the prison with soldiers. A section of the mob broke through the cordon and someone pinned a saucy rhyme on the prison wall. The magistrates ordered it to be torn down, and tempers burst. Revolutionary slogans were shouted, and Gillam read the Riot Act, once, and then again. The crowd jeered and stones began to fly. Gillam ordered the troops to open fire, and five or six people were killed and fifteen wounded. In the tumult a soldier named Donald Maclean, accompanied by an officer and two other privates, chased a rioter off the Fields, lost him, entered a cow-shed next to the Horse Shoe Inn, and bayoneted and then shot dead William Allen, the publican's son, mistaking him for the fugitive. The evidence about the behaviour of the troops is conflicting. Some observers thought that they had been reluctant to fire, but a constable later testified at the Old Bailey that the Horse Guards occasioned the 'whole disturbance . . . the people huzzaed and hissed, but no further riot. The soldiers fired at random. A great number of them fired three times, and seemed to enjoy their fire; I thought it a great cruelty.' At all events the mob now had its martyrs, and riots went on all that night and continued unchecked for several weeks afterwards.

The troops, however, were publicly congratulated by the Secretary at War, thus adding to the sense of public outrage, which was exacerbated when the Surrey Assizes acquitted Private Maclean after a coroner's inquest had found that he had wilfully murdered Allen. For good measure the Secretary at War then awarded Maclean thirty guineas compensation, taking in Parliament an equivocal line that the soldier's action had been indispensable to prevent mutiny, but he was nevertheless innocent, 'his piece having gone off by accident'. Gillam, meanwhile, was defended at the Old Bailey by both the Attorney General and the Solicitor-General, for the Government were leaving nothing to chance. The court held that he had been justified in resorting to force to quell a riotous mob, that he had done his duty, and that he would have been answerable to the public had he failed to do so. He was accordingly acquitted, but the danger in which he had been placed made a profound and enduring impression on all his brother magistrates.

Much of this leaves a nasty taste of high politics at work, and the continuing struggle between Wilkes and the Government is unedifying. He was fined £1,000 and sentenced to twenty-two months' imprisonment on the charges of libel and blasphemy. While he was in prison Parliament again expelled him, Middlesex re-elected him, and Parliament declared the election void. After his release, in 1770, amid scenes of tumultuous rejoicing, he became in turn alderman, sheriff, and then Lord Mayor of London, and once more returned to Parliament, fully accepted by the Establishment. Of more direct concern here, however, are the lessons of the riots Wilkes had provoked. One was the jolt London had given to Ministers who rode rough-shod over traditional British liberties and the elementary democratic right of electing a Member of Parliament. Another was a reminder that a state whose only effective force in support of the law is military runs the risk of either over-straining the loyalty of its soldiers, or over-straining the law in their defence. A third was that soldiers could be no substitute for civil police in dealing with violence. This point, however, went unheeded until the Gordon Riots forced it into the open. Contemporary thinking evinced little but bewildered frustration, well reflected in a comment by the Duke of Newcastle – 'We must be either governed by a mad, lawless Mob, or the peace be preserved only by a Military Force; both of which are unknown to our constitution.' An equally baffled Parliament did, nevertheless, set up the first of a long series of Select Committees in 1770 to review the arrangements for policing London. The Committee expressed surprise that the assorted parishes which formed the metropolis were 'under no particular Act of Parliament, but exercised their authority under the Statute of Winchester [which], being very obsolete, is a very improper regulation'. However, the Committee left it at that, merely recommending a tightening up of the old system. A lesson more attentively regarded at the time was that learned by the magistracy when they read of Gillam's trial, a lesson that was to cause Barkley Kennett, the Lord Mayor of London, to follow Gillam to the dock at the Old Bailey twelve years later: not, this time, because he had used too much force, but because he had failed to use any.

The riots that Wilkes provoked were directed to serious, forward-looking purposes. They mark a transitional stage in the education of the masses in the radical thinking that was to grip the nation thirty years later. The Gordon Riots, by contrast, were an anachronism. 'No Popery' was a cry from the heart of the seventeenth century, but in a hundred years it had shed none of its emotive power. Generations had been fed on illustrated editions of Foxe's *Book of Martyrs*. They had been brought up to revile the Pope as a fiend and see all Catholics as enemies. The rising of 1745 still outraged popular thinking. For years Catholics had constituted an under-privileged minority, and among their many deprivations was a rule that a man could not enlist in the army without making an attestation of Protestant faith. It was this particular handicap that led, indirectly, to the most savage riots in British history. In 1778 the American war was going badly and the Government needed more recruits – even Catholics – for the army. After taking soundings of popular opinion they prevailed on a private member, Sir George Savile, to introduce a non-party Bill to relieve Catholics of the bar to enlistment, and also of a few other minor disabilities. This Bill was enacted without controversy in 1778.

We now move forward two years, to Friday, 2nd June 1780, for London the first day of a hot, terrible week. During the morning a crowd estimated to have numbered 60,000 assembled in the notorious St. George's Fields, excited, no doubt, by recollections of boisterous times with Wilkes. Their object now was to petition Parliament to repeal the Act of 1778. At the head of the vast parade was a half-mad fanatic of thirty, Lord George Gordon, the president of a body which called itself the Protestant Association. He was playing with fire, setting out to emulate Wilkes in manipulating the London mob. For 'Wilkes and Liberty' there was now substituted the cry, 'No Popery'. Much organisation had backed the demonstration. Blue cockades were again issued, and three great bodies of marchers crossed the river, descending on Parliament with a petition which is said to have contained 120,000 signatures. The timing was meticulous: the arrival of the marchers at Westminster coincided exactly with that of Peers and Members of Parliament. The crowd was well briefed. Many Members were roughly handled, and when minutes later the Commons assembled most were in a bedraggled state, wigs gone, hair ruffled, clothes torn and spattered with mud. Yet, in this early stage of disorder, the crowd was civil, composed of well-dressed folk, dissenters, even old-fashioned Puritans. Soon people were beating at the doors of the Chamber, and the Lord Chief Justice, Lord Mansfield, ordered a magistrate to disperse the mob. The magistrate replied that it was much too big for him 'with the help of any constables I should be able to collect together'. Towards evening Gordon presented his petition. The Commons indignantly rejected it, and Gordon went outside to inflame the crowd. Inside the Chamber tension mounted, as the Commons realised that they were prisoners. A Member suggested that they should draw swords and fight their way out, and others murmured agreement. Then, about 9 o'clock, a detachment of troops arrived. The cavalry charged once and then retreated. The mood of the crowd was fickle. Some jeered and threw stones, others cheered. The troops marched away, and by 10 o'clock all seemed to be over. Members of Parliament slipped quietly away to their homes. Gordon, wearied out, went too.

This was the overture. A little before midnight a rabble carrying torches and armed with crowbars, blacksmith's hammers, chisels and pick-axes assembled silently outside the Sardinian Embassy in Lincoln's Inn. At a given sign they set about smashing windows and doors, hurling furniture, skirting-boards, window-frames, floor boards, rafters, books, papers, anything combustible, into the street, tumbled it all into a huge bonfire, and then set light to the house and its adjacent chapel. It was a technique that during the next six days was to be perfected. The Bavarian Embassy in Golden Square suffered the same fate a few hours later. On the following morning, Saturday, Members of Parliament made their way to Westminster armed with clubs and blunderbusses, but the week-end passed off quietly. The rioters, exhilarated by early success and emboldened by the evident feebleness of the civil power, needed a breathing-space to draw up a list of victims. Then, as dusk fell on Sunday, 4th June, the work of systematic destruction began in earnest. It started in the slums of Moorfields with the sacking and burning of Catholic houses and chapels, and during the night the mob surged west to destroy Sir George Savile's house, arming themselves with his iron railings for weapons. Edmund Burke, also marked out for violence, was luckier, since someone had thoughtfully despatched a platoon of sixteen soldiers to guard his house in Charles Street. Throughout the whole of Monday the work of destruction and looting continued unhindered. That day Sir John Fielding, the magistrate at Bow Street, was bold enough to commit a few rioters to Newgate, an act that brought savage retribution. Scarcely another magistrate in the whole of London dared to show himself. Platoons of soldiers marched hither and thither, but no-one could be found to give them orders, let alone to read the Riot Act, and their commanding officers were docile. They had all been well schooled not to act without orders from the magistrates. Their understanding (not all lawyers shared it when the great inquest took place later, and which was afterwards held by the Law Officers to have been mistaken) was that the common law did not justify the intervention of the military without civil authority, even when felonies

G

were being committed in front of their eyes. No officer, at all events, was prepared to risk the fate of Captain Porteus, just as no magistrate forgot the lesson of Samuel Gillam. So the mob were treated to the farcical spectacle of an officer appealing in cultured tones to their better nature, asking them please to go quietly home, after which the platoon marched off.

By Tuesday every prudent Londoner was wearing a blue cockade and had chalked 'No Popery' on his door. That morning a spirited magistrate named Hyde rode into Palace Yard and ordered the soldiers there to charge the crowd in order to clear the way for Members to enter Parliament. He also read the Riot Act, but to no avail. For this action Hyde, like Fielding, was a marked man. At nightfall the mob turned his house and possessions into a crackling inferno before moving off to Bow Street to tear down John Fielding's house, wrench doors off their hinges, prise up floor boards, hurl furniture, old books, manuscripts that had belonged to both the brothers, all the possessions of their lifetime, down on to the cobblestones below, consigning the lot to a huge bonfire. Then, vengeance done, the cry went up, 'A-hoy to Newgate'. Leaving Fielding's house a gaping ruin the mob smashed their way with sledge-hammers and pick-axes through the prison roof, released 300 prisoners, fired the building, gulped down the governor's gin, and made off to Bloomsbury Square for a prime target, the house of Lord Mansfield, the Lord Chief Justice. Here, before the horrified gaze of his friend the Archbishop of York (he lived next door, and had been warned that his name was next on the list) they set about the well-practised technique of destruction, watched by 300 silent soldiers. Then came a curious interlude. At the height of the blaze, while furniture was still being hurled from gaping windows, a magistrate appeared, read the Riot Act, and ordered the startled soldiers to fire. Within seconds five rioters were dead, others lay wounded. The mob melted away, the soldiers marched off. But it was a freak incident. A quarter of an hour later a drunken, enraged mob roared back into Bloomsbury Square, carrying tarred rope, wood shavings and turpentine to finish off the Lord Chief Justice's house before going on to smash open three more prisons.

When the sun rose on Wednesday the smoking streets of

London resembled a battlefield, and the mob, reinforced by 1,600 convicts, were in complete command. All the more respectable people who had flocked to Gordon's banner on the previous Friday seem to have disappeared, and the rabble was made up of apprentices, journeymen, criminals and prostitutes ready to settle accounts with the rich. Some 7,000 soldiers had been rushed into London from the Home Counties, and more – including regiments of militia from as far away as Northumberland – were on the way. But nobody knew what to do with the soldiers. Burke unhelpfully criticised the Government for 'establishing a military on the ruins of the civil government', and Fox even declared that he would 'much rather be governed by a mob than a standing army'. The magistrates, for their part, remained in hiding, and there is evidence that the radical City authorities, influenced by Wilkes, were in no hurry to bring them out. It was therefore left to George III, at this moment of total collapse of civil government, to take decisive action. During the morning he summoned the Privy Council and insisted that commanding officers should have discretion to give the order to fire; in default, he declared himself resolved to ride out into the streets and give the order himself. Luckily the Attorney General supported the King, even though most of the Council did not. A General Order was immediately issued to the troops – 'In obedience to an order of the King in Council, the military to act without waiting for directions from the Civil Magistrates, and to use force for dispersing the illegal and tumultuous assemblies of the people.'

By that afternoon some 15,000 well-armed troops were encamped in the Royal parks, regulars and militia, and the rioters were known to have armed themselves with stolen weapons. No-one knew any longer what the riots were about. Religious hatreds had long been swamped by class hatreds, and the cry of 'No Popery' was little more than a rallying call for the mob. All the poor, downtrodden, submerged nine-tenths of London were simply out for what they could get from unprotected houses and shops. But, in addition, the house of every Minister, every Bishop, every Catholic, every magistrate, and many others were known to be marked out for the special treatment with which London was now so terribly familiar. As dusk approached many fled into the countryside, and the cost of hiring a coach rocketed beyond the means of all but the wealthy. The horrors of the ensuing night gripped the imagination of Dickens and live on in the pages of *Barnaby Rudge*. The firing started quite early, outside the Bank of England, but the multitude there was too vast to be deterred by a few musket balls. They smashed open three more prisons, and then broke into a long coveted target: Langdale's distillery, in Holborn. A fire engine was ingeniously applied to pump out gin and rum from the cellars, and soon streams of spirits were gushing down the streets, spreading the flames. Men, women and children lapped up the raw spirits, and some drank themselves into a stupor and burned to death. Others looted the burning houses. In the glare of the flames was seen a single, ludicrously pathetic, figure of a watchman, only visible sign that the state retained a vestige of authority, with lantern and rattle 'calling the hour as in a time of profound tranquillity'. Then a party of the Northumberland Militia arrived and opened fire. Alderman John Wilkes, meanwhile, no doubt enjoying the irony of his situation, had assumed command of the troops outside the Bank, and these were now joined by several armed voluntary associations of vigilantes. Here firing continued for the remainder of the night, and several hundred people were killed or wounded.

On the following day, Thursday, the riots gradually petered out and a shocked nation proceeded to hold its inquest. Public indignation centred, of course, on Lord George Gordon, for having, as it was supposed, unleashed the mob by allowing a peaceful demonstration to get out of hand, and on the Lord Mayor and magistrates for their negligence in failing to nip it in the bud. Gordon was tried for high treason and acquitted. The Lord Mayor was less fortunate, although he was lucky not to have appeared at the Old Bailey earlier on other charges than that which he now faced. Barkley Kennett had started life as a waiter in a brothel. Later he owned one, and then worked his way up to respectability through the wine trade to be alderman, and afterwards Lord Mayor of London. It was said at the trial on Kennett's behalf that during the disorders he asked the rioters 'to do no more mischief than was necessary', so neatly turning tables on a good principle of policing; but this seems to have been about the limit of his intervention. He was convicted of criminal negligence and fined £1,000; and in its judgment the court pointed, belatedly, to the error of supposing that troops could not be ordered to fire until one hour had elapsed after the reading of the Riot Act. Attention was also directed, in judgments by Lord Loughborough and Sir James Mansfield, to the mistake of thinking that the passing of the Riot Act meant that 'the King's subjects, whose duty it is at all times to suppress riots, are to remain quiet and passive'. The mistake 'was all the more extraordinary because formerly the *posse comitatus* . . . consisted of military tenants who held lands by the tenure of military service'. It was 'not only the right of soldiers, but it is their duty to exert themselves' in aiding civil power; and it was 'highly important that the mistake should be corrected which supposes that an Englishman, by taking upon him the additional character of a soldier, puts off any of the rights and duties of an Englishman'.[1] The same point was made by Chief Justice Sir Nicholas Tindal in the trials which followed the Bristol Riots of 1831 (Chapter 4).

During the weeks that followed the riots many voluntary associations sprang into being for the defence of property, and innumerable pamphlets appeared arguing for yet more savage criminal laws, the revival of the *posse comitatus* of ancient times, or the modernisation of the militia. By general agreement the use of soldiers was an objectionable way of putting down disorder, and some alternative had to be found. Yet the obvious one, the institution of a system of police, was viewed with universal distaste. On the second day of the riots, when London was blazing fiercely, Lord Shelburne (two years later he was to become the first Home Secretary) dared to speak out in praise of the French system, which he considered to be 'wise to the last degree' in its construction, and only abominable in 'its use and direction'. Britain, he thought, might do well to think again, building a police system adapted to the native love of individual liberty. For some years, however, Shelburne received little support. Parliament was as indifferent to the need for police reform as it remained towards any other social problem. The prevailing view was expressed by the Solicitor-General soon after the riots, who now saw them as 'a single instance of a defect in the civil power which, in all probability, would never again occur'. The riots, he argued, provided no case for destroying the well-tried system of constabulary and justices that had served the nation well for centuries. The enviably pampered persons who occupied a few hours at Westminster between sessions at the gaming tables and their country pursuits found no reason to challenge this view.

At this level of argument the matter rested for several years. No substantial section of public opinion wanted a police force. Some objected to the cost, and most shrank from the danger of imitating the French system (the only one familiar to Britain) which was then the most efficient and ruthless in the world, relying on a highly developed system of espionage and the menace of terror. When, therefore, in 1785, Pitt ventured to introduce a Police Bill into the House of Commons he roused a storm of controversy. The Bill anticipated Peel's historic Act of 1829 by nearly half a century in proposing the creation of a police force to act throughout the whole of the Metropolitan district (including the City) under the control of three salaried Commissioners of Police. The City uttered a howl of anger, and the Middlesex and Surrey justices (surely Gillam would not have joined the chorus?) compained of 'a dangerous innovation and an encroachment on the rights and security of the people'. Pitt gave way and withdrew the Bill, admitting that 'he was not fully master of the subject'. It was a subject that baffled many others, including Dr. Johnson, who declared bleakly: 'The danger of unbounded liberty and the danger of bounding it have produced a problem in the science of Government which human understanding seems hitherto unable to solve.'

The lessons of the Gordon Riots were therefore as backward-looking as the riots themselves. The nation was able to persuade itself that the old system of justices and constabulary still had enough life left in it to serve most purposes, and that in an emergency it could always muddle through with the aid of soldiers, however muddled the soldiers themselves might be. And to support the old system two hallowed principles, derived from Saxon times, could be seen to be still active during the riots. One was the old tradition of self-policing, revived in the many voluntary armed associations that sprang into being when it was evident that the constables, watchmen and magistrates were ineffective. The other was the ancient principle of common law, codified in Henry V's statute of 1414, that all the inhabitants of a district had a duty to exert themselves to suppress riots, and that if they failed they were liable to be fined or to pay out compensation. One aggrieved citizen, Mr. Justice Wilmot, obtained a verdict against the residents of Bethnal Green for £1,355 for the destruction of his property.

People might also have drawn limited satisfaction from the knowledge that, despite the enormity of the riots, the mob behaved during the early stages in the traditionally discreet manner. Victims were clearly marked out for definite reasons, and it was only towards the end, on the Wednesday night, that violence seems to have been indiscriminate. Individual householders were undoubtedly terrorised, but it would be an exaggeration to say that terror was general. There is evidence that the mass of Londoners regarded the whole thing as a great spectacle. Theatres and other places of entertainment remained open, and Dr. Johnson wrote to Mrs. Thrale describing a stroll 'to look at Newgate and found it in ruins, the fire yet glowing'. The mob was then 'plundering the Session House at the Old Bailey: there were not, I believe a hundred, but they did their work at leisure in full security without sentinels, without trepidation as men lawfully employed in full day'. Property was the target, not persons, and only rioters seem to have been killed. A similar moderation emerges in the Government's handling of the matter when the riots were over. A great legal argument developed on the point whether the Order-in-Council had been tantamount to a declaration of martial law, some holding that an order to the military to act independently of the civil power was in the nature of a measure of war, which should be indemnified by special Acts similar to those that had followed the rebellions of 1715 and 1745. The Government, however, insisted that the soldiers had acted within the normal principles of the constitution and under the common law; and they made strenuous efforts to allay rumours that rioters were to be punished summarily by court martial. No doubt they feared further riots if these stories went unchallenged. Burke, similarly, pleaded for leniency in dealing with rioters – a magnanimous gesture, considering that his own home had been singled out for destruction.

Here, in this contemporary evidence of the relatively gentle temper of English society, and the strong revulsion, despite the week's traumatic experience, against any form of police, lies the outstanding interest of the Gordon Riots to this study. Most people shared Fox's view that he would 'much rather be governed by a mob than a standing army'. This long-maturing attitude of mind, national instinct, call it what you will, emerges, towards the end of the eighteenth century, as a point of fundamental importance to a correct understanding of the whole of the later study of public tranquillity in Britain. Its roots were buried deep in history. We have traced them to the great debate in the sixteenth century when England rejected the idea of a standing army to replace the disciplines of feudalism, and we have seen how eventually, when the maintenance of an army became unavoidable, the nation deliberately refrained for years from using it to suppress disorder. Clearly if ever the antagonism to a police force should be broken down the English police would have to be modelled in the exact matrix of the English character. It followed that the force would have to be a very mild one, and quite unlike any other in the world.

We have dealt at some length with the Wilkes and Gordon Riots because they bring into convenient focus the numerous issues involved in the challenge of violence at the end of the eighteenth century – the changing causes of disorder, the evolving principles of law, the substitution of military for civil force, and the slow maturing of statecraft. The dramatic events in London must not, however, distract us from what was happening in provincial Britain, where the social and economic pressures were mounting. During the summer of the Gordon Riots James Watt journeyed to Cornwall with his first forty steam engines to shatter the ancient peace of the tin mines, Richard Arkwright was experimenting with spinning frames in Preston, and country squires everywhere were accelerating the pace of land enclosure. The age of steam engines and of iron smelting by coke was at hand, and within a couple of generations the work of inventive and ambitious men was to transform the face of much of England.

The process of change owed as much, however, to the ferment of new thinking as to the invention of new machines. In 1780 the war with America was in its fourth year, and the heady language of the Declaration of Independence had crossed the Atlantic to France. Rousseau and Voltaire had not long been dead, and the challenge of their heresies was in turn reaching out across the Channel to stir the minds of young people in England out of intellectual torpor. Engineers and farmers and inventors might threaten the stability of the social order, but the propagandists for human betterment were after bigger game. Their challenge was to the whole of society, and so was aimed, ultimately, at the system of government. The King's ministers, however, preferred to devote their attention to the card tables, and it was not until July 1789 that the danger of radicalism at home became a serious public issue; even so three and a half years were to pass before the outbreak of war between England and France brought out its full menace. By that time French sympathisers, seen through the eyes of Pitt's frightened Government, had become an active fifth column, and Jacobin ways of thought were fashionable among the young intelligentsia. When a crowd of French sympathisers smashed his windows the old cynic Wilkes was tolerantly benign, and refused to prosecute: 'They are only some old pupils of mine,' he said, 'set up in business for themselves.'

The French Revolution, at first welcomed by much of middle class and dissenting opinion in Britain, soon divided the nation into opposing camps. As early as 1790 came Burke's reaction, with the publication of *Reflections*, and four months later (in February 1791) Paine replied with the first part of *The Rights of Man*. Paine's iconoclasm came as a gleeful shock to millions, and his book was soon to take its place alongside the *Bible* and *Pilgrim's Progress* in countless cottages where its seditious talk came with all the force of a revelation –

> The time is not very far distant when England will laugh at itself for sending to Holland, Hanover, Zell or Brunswick for men, at the expense of a million a year, who understood neither her laws, her language, nor her interest, and whose capacities would scarcely have fitted them for the office of a parish constable. . . .

Such impious thoughts and many others of the kind, including a programme for social reform which is almost a prospectus for Britain's welfare state of 1969, were followed in 1792 by the second part of *The Rights of Man*, and finally by *The Age of Reason*, in which Paine set out to liberate men from what he saw as the dogma and superstition of religion. Thus, as an *enfant terrible*, Paine outclassed Wilkes. Like him he fled to France, hustled out of the country by William Blake, and (in December 1792) was outlawed. Predictably, *The Rights of Man* was condemned as seditious libel. By this time, however, Paine's mischief was done, and all the machinery of state could not make amends.

The seeds of revolutionary thought were thus firmly implanted in British soil, and they were watered by a confluence of currents that led to momentous consequences. The grievances of the submerged nine-tenths of the population, who for more than a century had been blindly groping after 'justice' (and forever rioting in vain hopes of finding it) were joined by the aspirations of groups of political radicals made up of dissenters, industrialists and tradesmen. The workers wanted 'justice' and food, the radicals, more far-sighted, demanded democracy. The alliance, had it lasted, might have brought about a second revolution in Britain a century after the 'Glorious Revolution' of 1688, whose inadequacies were now apparent to all but the landowning classes.

In January 1792, the first working-class organisation in Britain was set up by a shoe-maker, Thomas Hardy. It was known as the London Corresponding Society, and its programme was limited to a demand for universal suffrage and annual parliaments. Soon many similar bodies sprang into being. Here was a notable point of departure. From now on 'the mob' was no longer a thing to be encouraged or led by theorists like Wilkes and Gordon. It had grown its own self-consciousness and could stand on its own feet. The search for 'justice' need no longer be blind and local. Since the abortive rising of 1381 it had taken the labouring classes 400 years to organise themselves into political groups, but now they made up for lost time. A prescience of popular government inspired them. Reaction, however, was terrified and swift. The Government banned 'seditious meetings', and magistrates and local aristocrats were encouraged to raise fresh mobs as instruments of terror against radicals. Hence Tory 'Church and King' rioters (their banners were so inscribed) burned Paine in effigy in towns throughout Britain, and with running battles between Pittites and Paineites, the threat of public violence reached its peak. A century that had been so happily free from class antagonism was ending with Britain not very far from civil warfare.

Events in France then influenced matters decisively. The September massacres (1792) alienated much British middle-class opinion from the cause of the revolution and frightened it off reform at home, so that the temporary alliance between the radicals and the working classes came to an end. 'If there was no revolution in England in the 1790s,' writes E. P. Thompson, 'it was . . . because the only alliance strong enough to effect it fell apart; after 1792 there were no Girondins to open the doors through which the Jacobins might come.'[8] The outbreak of war with France provided Pitt with the opportunity (or, the charitable might argue, the necessity) for repressing radical thinking at home. There seems to have been some evidence of insurrectionary movements, but the actions Pitt took dismayed many of his contemporaries and continued to outrage the liberal Trevelyan as long as 130 years afterwards: 'In 1794 the government was so far blinded by panic that it sought the lives of the Reformers.' *Habeas corpus* was suspended (the suspense continued for eight years) and the shoe-maker Hardy was arrested by a motley party consisting of the King's Messenger, two Bow Street Runners and the Home Secretary's Private Secretary. He was examined by the Privy Council (that is the Cabinet, including Pitt himself) and charged with high treason. But from the fate of being hanged, drawn and quartered he was saved by the refreshing common sense of an English jury, who acquitted him. Thus thwarted, Pitt's angry Government were nevertheless determined to have their victim. They proceeded with the prosecution of Horne Tooke (a one-time crony of Wilkes) and John Thelwall, later linked in only half-deserved immortality to Coleridge. ('Citizen John,' Coleridge claimed he said when the two walked together in a glade at Alfoxden, Wordsworth's temporary refuge in the Quantocks in the summer of 1797, 'this is a fine place to talk treason in.' 'Nay, Citizen Samuel,' Thelwall replied, 'it is rather a place to make a man forget that there is any necessity for treason.' After this agreeable exchange the Home Secretary, more of a realist than either, sent a spy named Walsh to check up on Coleridge's friend, the gloomy young man Wordsworth, recently back from flirtations in and with revolutionary France, and living with a woman who, Walsh reported, 'passes for his sister'. Wordsworth had to move; and in consequence of the break-up of the Stowey-Alfoxden circle much happened that was of great moment to English literature, but which hardly concerns a study of violence.) The acquittal of both Tooke and Thelwall completed Pitt's humiliation and sent the radicals cock-a-hoop. It seems probable that a genuinely revolutionary spirit was now widespread, but the fact that an English jury had denied the cause its martyrs may have prevented revolution. In October 1795, during a year when food rioting was endemic throughout the country, a crowd of some 200,000 mobbed the King with cries of 'Down with Pitt!' 'No war!' 'No King!' 'No Pitt!' 'Peace!'

Pitt responded with what looks like panic legislation. A Treason Act was passed to deal with 'incitement to disloyalty', and soon afterwards a Seditious Meetings and Assemblies Act required promoters of meetings of more than fifty people to give notice to the magistrates, who were empowered to arrest speakers and disperse the meeting. Defiance of a magistrate's orders was, of course, punishable by death. It required considerable courage on the part of Coleridge to publish a journal, *The Watchman*, to campaign for the repeal of the Acts. The curtailment of free speech was carried further in 1797 after the mutinies at Spithead and the Nore (which were partly inspired by Thelwall), when the Incitement to Mutiny Act of that year made it a felony punishable by death to attempt to seduce any member of the armed forces from his duty. The Act was used against British communists as late as the 1920s. A network of spies, meanwhile, scoured the country, and soldiers were concentrated in barracks so as to prevent them from fraternising with the people. Then, two years later, in 1799, a Combination Act forbade all trade unions, so putting the workers at the mercy of their masters. Meanwhile the press gangs had been told to root out dangerous agitators so that they could be shipped off out of harm's way. By all these measures the voices of protest were effectively silenced for the duration of the war. The problem of social disorder was shelved and the revolutionary forces driven underground, as menace held all radical England in check. But pent waters gather force, and when the challenge of violence was renewed after the war it came on a scale that could not be ignored.

4: The Great Struggle

In the year 1800 a world was passing away; by 1850 it had gone. The fifty years spanned the struggle of a society in transition, a struggle to prevent the unrest of swift social evolution from degenerating into the violence of revolution. The dominant influences at work were Wesleyism and (to use a general term) radicalism. Opposing them was the determined reaction of the Whig and Tory ruling classes. One eventual result of the encounter was a tempering of the spirit of the whole of society as, after bitter clashes, the enforcement of the law governing free speech and public assembly was relaxed in a way that helped rulers and ruled to come to terms with one another and work towards an understanding. From this sprang the recognition that to curb violence it was necessary to relieve distress and conciliate popular opinion – principles of enduring importance that paved the way to the state regulation of industry in the late nineteenth century, and the establishment of the welfare state in the twentieth. A second far-reaching result, so important that it must be seen as a condition of the first, was the replacement of the old means of maintaining order, under the threat of continuing violence, by a uniquely mild system of professional police. The support of this system enabled the nation to grope its way, more or less confidently, without major disasters, out of an age when collective violence was local and reactionary, into a new era when violence was expressed in forward-looking and political contexts that were incipiently much more dangerous.

Wesleyism gathered together many of the strands of the great tradition of English dissent, infused it with moral discipline, and shaped every moment of the waking lives of millions of poor folk whose only education was derived from pulpit and Sunday School, and whose reading was mainly confined to the Old Testament, *Pilgrim's Progress* and, after 1792 perhaps, *The Rights of Man*. It conditioned their habits, their attitude towards employment, their use of the little leisure they had, and the upbringing of their children. It encouraged a spirit of charity, fortitude of mind, and submissiveness towards authority. It was thus a stabilising influence. It could also, as Blake, Southey, Hazlitt, Matthew Arnold and others recognised, be a grim, joyless, unlovely religion, narrow and fiercely intolerant, a force to brainwash and twist the minds of its adherents. It was this dark side that horrified the historian Lecky: 'A more appalling system of religious terrorism, one more fitted to unhinge a tottering intellect and to darken and embitter a sensitive nature, has seldom existed.' Yet again, by providing opportunities for common folk to air their consciences and share their compassion in chapel and pub, Wesleyism taught men how to organise themselves, and to stand on their own feet – in short, self-help. From the time of the Corresponding Societies of the 1790s, right through the period of Chartism and down all the later years of Queen Victoria's reign these influences of Wesleyism worked powerfully to counter trends towards violence, yet were always supplying, in association with radicalism, the moral fervour that nevertheless goaded men to violence through frustration.

We glanced at some of the early propagandists of radicalism in the last chapter. Most were as good puritans as any Methodist, though they were uncompromisingly irreligious. They lived austere lives, argued incessantly, and wrote dull books. Their influence, however, in encouraging the growth of working-class movements and in shaping their objectives, was prodigious. And they were brave men, for during the whole of the first twenty years of the nineteenth century radicalism was a dangerous trade, undertaken at the risk of imprisonment, transportation or death. Propagation of radical views was possible only by straining at the leash of the law of seditious libel – 'written censure upon public men for their conduct as such, or upon the laws, or upon the institutions of the country'. Such a restrictive principle, as Sir

James Stephen and other legal historians have pointed out, was incompatible with the concept of the freedom of the Press, and 'wholly inconsistent with any serious public discussion of political affairs'. At this time, it is evident, British 'liberty' embraced the liberty of the Press only on the sufferance of the rulers. The concept of seditious conspiracy, together with the offence of unlawful assembly, provided the authorities with limitless opportunities to prosecute the organisers of public meetings.

These two influences – that of Wesleyism among the lower orders and the bottled-up radicalism of intellectuals and middle-class dissenters – worked abrasively on a nation that, by 1810, was economically impoverished by war. The combined effect of Napoleon's Continental System and the American Non-Intercourse Act (which came into force in 1811 and closed the important American market to British manufactured goods) was to precipitate a severe industrial depression. British exports fell by one-third from 1811 to 1812. The result was catastrophic. Thousands, particularly in the North and Midlands, were thrown out of work, prices soared, and a succession of bad harvests (1809, 1810, 1811 and 1812) made matters worse. Acute and unrelieved distress was widespread, and Britain had her first lesson in the interdependence of industrial nations, and in particular her dependence on the lost American colonies. The situation, it might be supposed, would have called for the immediate and energetic intervention of the Government, but it did not. The connection between distress and disorder, so clearly perceived by Elizabethan statesmen, had gone unrecognised for more than a century. To Perceval's government of 1811 the distress of the labouring classes in the North and Midlands was a natural phenomenon, beyond the reach of state action. It would cure itself, or not, as the case might be. Social reform, in any case, was too risky a matter for the contemplation of ministers who were obsessed by the fear of bloody revolution at home, and who regarded radicals and all the working class as natural enemies. Moreover the radical intelligentsia, secure in their middle-class incomes (or, as the case might be, in their prisons) also held that the troubles of the country were due not to too little government but to too much. All government, in their view, was an evil, corrosive of individual liberty, as had been amply demonstrated by twenty years of oppression. The authority of the state should be replaced by the free and responsible citizenship of everyone, acting together in the public interest, and free under the rule of law and the free inter-play of the market to strike their own bargains with one another. This doctrine of individualist radicalism, elevating to its teachers, was of no help to the multitudes who were thrown out of work in 1811.

In this lies the explanation of the outbreak of mass violence known as Luddism, a movement that was precipitated in 1811 by real want, but whose motive force also owed something to the revolutionary groups that were driven underground during the 1790s. The war years were the years also of the greatest intensity of the Industrial Revolution, and Thelwall had written truly: 'Every large workshop and manufactory is a sort of political society, which no act of parliament can silence, and no magistrate disperse.'[1] A new working class was taking shape in the shadow of Blake's 'dark satanic mills', and its mood was as ugly as its environment, bitter with a sense of political oppression and economic exploitation, and forbidden even to combine in trade unions for self protection. Class hatreds were generated, and relations between master and men became distant, even cold. Everywhere there was a sense of loss: the craftsman was losing his status, the villager his common rights, the weaver his liveli-hood, whole communities the simple pleasures of country life, and everywhere men were losing their self-respect. It is arguable that a second revolution, even accompanied by violence, would in the long run have spared Britain much misery, for it would at least have given the workers an opportunity to participate in shaping the outcome of their catastrophe. Instead the ugly new pattern of life was imposed on them from above, and in this process, as Trevelyan puts it, 'The mass of unregarded humanity . . . were wholly uncared for by church or state; no Lady Bounti-ful visited them with blankets and advice; no-one but the non-conformist minister was their friend; they had no luxury but drink, no-one to talk to but one another, hardly any subject but their grievances. Naturally they were tinder to the flame of agitation. They had no interest or hope in life but evangelical religion or radical politics.'[2]

We can picture the gatherings of determined, grim-faced men

The New Police Force, 1854

Metropolitan policemen in 1866

in taverns and chapels throughout Nottinghamshire in March 1811 as news reached them that in the small town of Arnold, just outside Nottingham, men had smashed more than sixty knitting frames in a single night. They had failed in all other means of bringing pressure to bear on employers not to reduce wages and to maintain a high quality of output, so only direct action was left. Machine wrecking was a familiar form of riposte, and within a fortnight more than 200 frames had been destroyed. Years earlier a Leicester apprentice named Ned Ludlam had been reprimanded for failing to use his machine properly. He lost his temper and smashed the machine with a hammer; so in future all machine wrecking was, in the popular vocabulary, Luddism. By the beginning of April all was peaceful again, for all the old resources of authority were concentrated on the outbreak of violence. Dragoons were called out, the magistrates ordered a special nightly watch to be set up, special constables were enrolled, some Bow Street officers were despatched from London, and liberal rewards were offered for the detection of offenders. But public sympathy was with the rioters, and no arrests were possible.

The Luddite attacks brought into play for the first time on a large scale a new weapon that had only been available to the authorities since 1796. This was a body known as the Volunteers, which during the first three decades of the nineteenth century gradually replaced the militia as the only effective and trustworthy police force, ancillary to the army, in repressing industrial disorder. Originally set up for local defence soon after the outbreak of war with France, they comprised the yeomanry, an officer corps of local gentry and farmers, and the infantry, recruited from the labouring classes. So, in rural areas, the system was reminiscent of feudalism: great landowners again enrolled their tenants in troops and companies, so that loyalty and discipline were inbuilt. Enlistment in the Volunteers was attractive since its members were excused from the militia ballot, though they were obliged to assemble for a week's annual training and were subject to military discipline when on duty. By the end of the eighteenth century there were some 11,000 volunteer yeomanry (or cavalry) and 26,000 infantry. (The surge of patriotism after the renewal of war in 1803 added even Wordsworth to their ranks.) As it happened the Volunteers were not needed for home defence, but the yeomanry arm rapidly established its value for home policing. It was used to put down riots among the militia, and the self-interest of its members needed no outside spur to encourage them to deal with local industrial disturbances. The status of the yeomanry was thus an equivocal and dangerous one. In effect the Government had legalised the formation of armed associations of the wealthier classes to put down by force the unrest of the poor. This situation carried within it the seeds of class war; and the lasting notoriety of the confrontation at Peterloo (1819) stems largely from the fact that a charge of yeomanry against unarmed working people was essentially an act of class warfare, happily almost unknown in Britain before or since.

We must return, however, to March 1811. That first episode of machine breaking, confined to a small area of Nottinghamshire, was the start of one of the most widespread and destructive outbreaks of violence in our history. The objects of the Luddites were partly to coerce their employers to grant higher wages, partly to destroy the new machines that they saw as a threat to their livelihood. The motive force was thus economic, not political, and the violence was reactionary. It took the traditional form of direct action against the property (that is, machines or mills) of individual employers who had been carefully picked out as being particularly oppressive or unjust. What distinguishes the behaviour of the Luddites from that of countless thousands of similar rioters in earlier times is the scale of their violence, the evidence of organisation that lay behind it, and the vast amount of property that they managed to destroy. The main period of rioting was confined to rather less than two years (March 1811–January 1813) and it affected parts of Nottinghamshire, Leicestershire, Lancashire, Cheshire and West Yorkshire. In order to suppress it the authorities eventually had to throw in a whole army, root out the ringleaders by employing hundreds of spies and informers, and then make an example of seventeen of them by a public hanging staged at York castle.

A second eruption of machine wrecking occurred in Nottinghamshire in November 1811. Night after night men massed in the forests to draw up lists of victims, then moved swiftly and silently to their several destinations armed with muskets, pistols, axes and hammers. Pickets were placed to give the alarm, then

doors were beaten down and machinery smashed beyond repair.
Each carefully planned raid was completed in the space of twenty
or thirty minutes, and when dawn broke the wreckers had
disappeared without trace, leaving no clue to their identity.
Against these sudden, isolated attacks under cover of darkness the
authorities were powerless, and alarm bordered on panic as
factory owners realised that they had no-one to protect them but
themselves. The ordinary population of the affected districts was
solidly behind the wreckers, and no-one could be found to lay any
information against them. Consequently no arrests could be made
and the Luddites grew bolder, sending out threatening demands
for money for the cause:

> Gentlemen all, Ned Ludd's Compliments and hopes you will give
> a trifle towards supporting his Army as he well understands the
> Art of breaking obnoxious Frames. If you comply with this it will
> be well, if not I shall call upon you myself. Edward Ludd.[3]

As the Luddites stepped up the scale of their violence, so the
authorities built up counter force, but in this they always lagged
behind. The ancient machinery of the county creaked badly as it
rumbled into action. The Lord Lieutenant of Nottinghamshire
and the High Sheriff disputed each other's right to control the
forces of the shire. The magistrates cowered in their lonely,
isolated manor houses, scared to intervene on account of their own
vulnerability to attack by the nocturnal mob. The parish constables were, naturally, loyal to their kind. The magistrates turned
to Charles II's statute of 1668 to enrol special constables from the
'respectable' middle classes, but there was little they could do
either. The whole of the civil power was shown, at the first whiff
of trouble, to be virtually useless. Events therefore followed their
logical course: terrified machine owners conceded a rise in wages
(though a few of the bolder spirits stood out) and, at the same
time, formed themselves into armed voluntary associations to
protect their own and each other's property. The magistrates
requisitioned regiments of militia and yeomanry, sometimes
from distant parts of the country, and implored the Home
Secretary to send regular soldiers. By December 1811 the Midland
area commander, General Dyott, had rushed some 800–900
cavalry to the district, together with 1,000 infantry, and the Home

Secretary told Parliament that the force was larger than any that had ever previously been used to keep order. By February it was even bigger. A vast military camp had been established for 3,000 troops, and *The Times* commented on 1st February that the area had 'the appearance of a state of war'. Parliament, meanwhile, regarded the incident as a little local difficulty, and the Government, for their part, were well content to leave it to the Home Secretary to sort matters out.

Early in February 1812 the local magistrates demanded a further strengthening of their hands. They promoted two Bills, a Frame-breaking Bill to make breaking a capital offence, and a Peace Bill to enable them to conscript all adult males as special constables. Parliamentary opposition to the first was founded not on the argument that the death penalty was too harsh (though Byron, in a brilliant maiden speech, did make this point) but that it would be counter-productive, in that so severe a penalty would be likely to encourage the intimidation of witnesses. Both Bills were passed, but little use was made of either, for they came too late to have any effect. By the spring rioting was beginning to subside, and the Luddites were turning to more regular means of seeking redress by presenting a petition to Parliament and setting up a clandestine trade union. A relieved population in the district raised subscriptions to aid the poor, the masters set about installing new machines, and most of the soldiers were marched off to new trouble areas, the more sensitive among them still smarting, surely, under the lash of Byron's speech in the House of Lords –

> Such marchings and counter-marchings! From Nottingham to Bullwell, from Bullwell to Banford, from Banford to Mansfield! and when at length the detachments arrived at their destination, in all 'the pride, pomp and circumstance of glorious war', they came just in time to witness the mischief which had been done . . . and return to their quarters amidst the derision of old women, and the hootings of children.[4]

The next two outbreaks of violence were caused by Lancashire cotton workers during the Spring and Summer of 1812, and West Yorkshire weavers a few weeks afterwards. The targets this time were steam looms and mills. No doubt the riots were sparked off by accounts of events in Nottinghamshire. The rioters' tactics were similar to those employed earlier, but their organisation was better: some of the later attacks, such as that on Rawfold's Mill (which lived on for years in folk memory and served as material for Charlotte Brontë in *Shirley* nearly forty years afterwards) were very determined. So was the menace in the Luddites' messages –

> We will never lay down arms [till] the House of Commons passes an Act to put down all Machinery hurtful to commonality, and repeal that to hang Frame Breakers. But We. We petition no more – that won't do – fighting must.
>
> Signed by the General of the Army of Redressers
> *Ned Ludd* Clerk
>
> Redressers for ever Amen.[5]

Wild rumours circulated in the disturbed areas, many of which, however, were undoubtedly exaggerated; among the more common were stories that men were drilling secretly on the moors at night, that they were carrying out raids for arms, and that they were planning a general rising, even, some held, plotting revolution. Many of these reports were forwarded to the Home Secretary by spies who had a vested interest in fomenting alarm, since they were in danger of losing their jobs when the situation quietened down. That some, or many, of the Lancashire and Yorkshire Luddites were plotting a major insurrection seems unlikely, but the truth will probably never be known. The Luddites swore solemn oaths of secrecy, and there is a ring of truth in the story of the young man who lay dying in hospital after being shot by the defenders of Rawfold's mill. Having long refused, under great pressure, to disclose the secrets of the Luddites, he at length turned to those gathered round the bed. 'Can you keep a secret?' he asked. They nodded. 'So can I,' he said, and died.

The authorities reacted to these later phases of Luddism in much the same way that they had done in Nottinghamshire. In every case the action was local and *ad hoc*, and it followed a similar pattern. Everything pivoted round the local magistrates, and the upshot depended entirely on the zeal of individuals. First they would enrol special constables, and perhaps appoint a few night watchmen. Then voluntary armed associations would spring into being. Next came the call for contingents of militia – sometimes hesitantly, for fear 'of putting arms in the hands of the most powerfully disaffected' as one magistrate expressed it to the

Home Office – and yeomanry. Finally, and inevitably, came the demand for regular troops. During this escalating process the magistrate would be busy signing warrants for the arrest of suspects and receiving reports from spies on their success in penetrating the enemy's secrets. Their presence would be required at every disturbance so that they could read the Riot Act, for no soldier would dare to use force until this had been done. It is small wonder that the officer commanding the troops in Lancashire, General Maitland, should have complained to the Home Office that there were too few magistrates willing to act quickly and vigorously. It was a cardinal point of policy that troops were not to be made available until a local community had done everything possible to strengthen its civil forces; and the military regarded voluntary armed associations as the proper first line of defence, backed by the enrolment of special constables – in Salford, some ten per cent of the adult male population, 1,500 men, were at one time enrolled. In overall command was the Home Secretary, after June 1812 Lord Sidmouth, whose zeal for repression earned him an unenviable reputation. He virtually ran the whole internal government of the country, such as it was. He gave orders to the troops, sanctioned the employment of the yeomanry and militia, authorised the Postmaster-General to intercept mail, received reports from the lords lieutenant and magistrates, and paid for an army of spies and informers from the secret service fund, which he also drew on to defray the cost of important prosecutions and to reward the few witnesses who were brave enough to come forward. In carrying out all these activities the magistrates and the Home Office did not escape criticism, the former for cowardice and negligence, the latter for inefficiency. There was, *The Times* declared on 1st July 1812, 'less of talent and energy in that office by which our home concerns are chiefly directed than in all the rest put together . . . it is evident to common reason that the Home Office must have become the sink of all the imbecility attached to every Ministry for the last thirty years'.

A combination of regular soldiers and spies eventually put an end to this outbreak of violence. During the summer of 1812 some 12,000 troops were maintained in the disturbed areas, and parts of the North and Midlands resembled a country under military occupation. In September 1812 no fewer than 1,000 soldiers were billeted in public houses in Huddersfield alone. General Maitland in Lancashire and General Grey in Yorkshire acted, however, with patience and restraint; they, more than anyone else in authority, calmed the situation, insisting that troops should be used only as a last resort. At the same time they evolved flexible tactics against the elusive enemy, stationing parties of soldiers in selected villages, posting detachments to guard vulnerable targets, and marching columns by night from place to place in surprise moves that anticipated the Luddites and constantly harried them. A troop of cavalry, from 40 to 100 strong, acted rather as mounted police than as a body of soldiers, and generally succeeded in dispersing a mob by intimidation without recourse to their weapons. But, as with any army at war, the success of these tactics depended on a flow of reliable information from the other side. Spies were the real key to success. Some were recruited by the militia and controlled by its adjutant, others were taken on by the magistrates. The Home Office, exploiting the inheritance of a wealth of experience that went back to Tudor times (though not, perhaps, displayed to full advantage in Walsh's hilarious dealings with Wordsworth and Coleridge in 1797), could infiltrate almost any organisation with its own agents. Without doubt it was this secret activity rather than the marching and counter-marching of soldiers that eventually frightened the Luddites, shook their trust in one another, and undermined their morale. Towards the end of 1812 professional spies sent from Lancashire to Yorkshire had uncovered a number of the more important of their leaders and the end of the trouble was in sight. Thirteen Luddites were executed at Lancaster and Chester, and seventeen more were hanged following a special assize held at York in January 1813; but there some considerate officials in charge of the executions gave the condemned time to sing the Methodist hymn, 'Behold the Saviour of Mankind' before turning them off, in the face of vast crowds, from a couple of hastily erected beams.

The aftermath of the violence presents a familiar picture. Having made an example of the ringleaders and taken the trouble to publicise it widely by distributing leaflets, the Government switched their policy to appeasement. An Act of Indemnity was passed which offered a free pardon to any Luddite who confessed to crimes (a bait to the less militant to abandon the cause), and the death penalty for frame breaking was reduced to transportation (but was raised to death again a year later). Employers who had made concessions under duress withdrew them. In all this there is an interesting parallel with the action taken by Richard II's Government after the Peasants' Revolt. But, in addition, the Government of 1813 showed refreshing enlightenment by publishing pamphlets to explain why the workers had been foolish to destroy machines, and had acted against their own long-term interests. Here is an early indication of the slowly maturing statesmanship that was to play a vital part in the struggle against violence during the Chartist period. There was, however, little sign that the rulers were abandoning *laissez faire* policies, and none at all that they were prepared to recognise a connection between distress and disorder. The old protective laws of the Tudors had lapsed into almost universal disuse, but nothing was put in their place.

Nor, incredible as it seems, was the Government even yet ready to acknowledge the weakness of the civil power, the effectiveness of which at this period Professor F. O. Darvall well sums up as follows: 'The whole machinery of order was so antiquated, and worked so clumsily, that even a restricted local disorder became a matter of emergency and necessitated emergency measures. The hierarchy of order was clear. The system was excellent on paper, provided that the justices could be relied upon to do their duty. But it did not work in practice, and an emergency system had to be improvised *ad hoc* in each crisis by co-operation between the government and the few officials upon whose energy and ability it could count.'[6] During the riots the Generals who controlled troops in the disturbed districts had repeatedly pointed out that a police force would have been much more effective than their soldiers, but Westminster was unimpressed.

The only other demand for police at this time came from Londoners who were shocked not by rioting hundreds of miles away, but by a couple of squalid murders, in December 1811, on their own doorsteps. (These were the Wapping Murders, later lightly treated by De Quincey in his essay, *Murder considered as one of the Fine Arts.*) Interest revived in a book entitled *A Treatise on the Police of the Metropolis,* which had been published in 1797 by a Metropolitan magistrate named Patrick Colquhoun. The author attacked the traditional view that a police force could not be reconciled with individual freedom. 'Police', he maintained, 'is an improved state of society. Next to the blessings which a nation derives from an excellent Constitution and system of general Laws, are those advantages which result from a well-regulated and energetic plan of Police, conducted and enforced with purity, activity, vigilance, and discretion.' Once the shock of the Wapping Murders abated, however, Parliament lost interest in the subject. Soldiers and spies had succeeded, after a fashion, in restoring order, and so they could again; and no police system, it was argued, however perfect, could ever prevent murders from being committed.

But if the lessons of the Luddites' resort to violence were lost on the ruling classes, they were taken to heart by the Luddites themselves. Their striving gave fresh meaning to the idea of self-help. In spite of the hangings at York a victory of sorts had been won, and there was no disposition to squander its fruits, as more simple peasants had done after 1381. Besides, Ned Ludd was a solid, credible folk-hero. The medieval charm of Robin Hood had ennobled the dreams of the fourteenth century, but men of the nineteenth, whose waking eyes looked up every morning to smoking chimneys rather than church spires wanted earthier stuff than dreams. The 'army of redressers' wanted what they had lost, or if that were gone beyond recall they wanted to shape the future. So the old outlaw forfeited his precedence even in his own home county, betrayed, finally, by a spy who sent a Luddite verse to the Home Office as proof of sedition –

> Chant no more of your old rhymes about Robin Hood,
> His feats I but little admire.
> I will sing the Atcheivements of General Ludd,
> Now the hero of Nottinghamshire. . . .

The real 'Atchievements of General Ludd' were the incentives which his followers handed down to the labouring classes to find ways of seeking redress, and an improved standard of living, that were less dangerous than the sort of direct action that led to the gibbet. A boost was given to illicit trade union activities and to the demand for parliamentary and municipal reform: the connection between Luddism and the Reform Bill of 1832 and the Municipal Corporations Act of 1835 is too obvious to need stressing; and, of equally far-reaching consequence, the fighting of 1811 and 1812, by forcing the ruling classes to recognise the importance of domestic matters, paved the way for much of the social and industrial legislation later in the century.

It is worthwhile, before leaving the subject of the Luddite riots, to glance briefly at some of the larger issues they raise. What light do they throw on the development of national attitudes, and in particular on the age-old propensity to violence? On one view Luddism can be seen as a classic instance of reactionary, backward-looking violence whose objects were unattainable. On another view it is notable that an outbreak of sustained disorder on a scale unparalleled (if we discount the Jacobite risings) for more than a century, requiring at its height 12,000 troops to suppress it, more than ever before or since, barely disturbed the surface of national life. The few Parliamentary debates on the Nottingham Framebreaking and Peace Bills were thinly attended. The national newspapers hardly noticed the disturbances. Excitement and alarm were purely local and temporary. Astonishingly enough, during the whole two years of violence the Luddites seem to have inflicted only three fatal casualties. Considering the provocation their moderation and restraint were marvellous. They made no attempt to interfere with the working of justice, or to attack magistrates or constables. They set up no national organisation and seem to have plotted no general rising. With most of the army fighting abroad they could almost certainly, had they wished, have exploited disaffection at home to the point of revolution. But apart from a few alarmists and spies nobody seriously thought they would. Their aims, like those of the peasants of 1381, were local and modest, their methods traditional. They did not want to rule the country, merely to gain a decent living for themselves. In Professor Darvall's words, 'They only wanted to coerce this or that employer, to get this or that particular, local, industrial concession. They used only sufficient force for the limited objects they had in mind, and they used it only when, where, and against whom they had some special grievance.'[7] They leave an abiding impression of moderation, loyalty and self-discipline: men to whom violence, far from being a soft option, was the only option in a struggle against forces they did not understand. Of course if they had understood them they might have seen the real cause of their distress in the cost of the war, the gathering pace of industrialisation, the wickedness of *laissez faire*, and the need for state regulation of wages and the redistribution of industry as old crafts died out. But to have recognised the facts of economic life would have got them no farther than did hammering away sullenly at machines, for the Government was almost as blind. It would not have understood what the argument was about. There was no lack of upper and middle class sympathy for the distressed workers – in 1812 Wilberforce and other philanthropists founded an Association for the Relief of the Manufacturing and Labouring Poor, which gave practical help to paupers. The rulers' attitude from the start, however, was a defeatism that is well summed up in the report of a Parliamentary committee of 1811:

> While the Committee fully acknowledge and most deeply lament the great distress of numbers of persons . . . they are of opinion that no interference of the legislature with the freedom of trade, or with the perfect liberty of every individual to dispose of his time and his labour in the way and on the terms which he may judge most conducive to his own interest, can take place without violating general principles of the first importance to the prosperity and happiness of the community. . . .[8]

For several years following the suppression of Luddism social conditions in many of the spreading industrial areas were turbulent, but it was not until 1816 that the threat of widespread violence again assumed the proportions of a national menace. The end of the Napoleonic wars released unruly elements from the army and navy. The delayed cost of the war, industrial depression, the dislocation of the return to a peace-time economy, and a rapid expansion of the population placed immense strains on society, and reports of rioting and seditious talk flowed into the Home Office daily from all parts of the country. On 15th June a Hampden Club met in London to celebrate the sexcentenary of Magna Carta. For the last time in British history *habeas corpus* was suspended, and the Government turned again to the remedy, a combination of spies and soldiers, that had saved the situation in

1811–12. This time, however, authority's reaction had inconclusive results, for the dangers and weaknesses of large-scale espionage were now fully exposed, and the charge of yeomanry at Peterloo became a *cause célèbre* in the struggle of the working classes, while providing a powerful lesson to the nation that military force was an inappropriate method of countering violence.

It is easy to understand why the Home Office should have come to rely on spies as a primary means of suppressing disorder. They had become, as Professor Darvall reminds us, 'an integral and essential part of the system of internal government . . . one of the most important, and not the least expensive, instruments of government in its attempt to work a medieval system of local and internal government under modern conditions'.[9] Soldiers, as we have seen, were only of limited value to a nation as reluctant as the British to authorise them to fire on disorderly mobs. Lacking a police force, therefore, violence could only be curbed in one of two ways: by appeasing it with economic policies directed to the removal of its causes; or by the operation of swift justice against its ringleaders. *Laissez faire* ruled out the first remedy; spies were essential to the success of the second. Some were recruited by local magistrates, some by the Home Office. From time to time mistakes were made, and the whole system came under severe Parliamentary criticism in 1817, mainly as a result of the activities of an infamous spy named Oliver who, posing as an agent of the London 'physical force party', sought to persuade local radicals that everywhere else in the country men were planning a general insurrection, and that only they lagged behind.

Two of the incidents in which Oliver was involved as an *agent provocateur* occurred in 1817. They make a shameful story. The first, which anticipated the hunger marches of the 1930s, became known as the 'March of the Blanketeers' from Manchester. Its background was partly economic distress caused by low wages, high prices and unemployment, partly a purblind gesture by working people of their right to take power into their own hands, or at least to play a part in shaping their own future. The combination of these two motives resolved itself into a radical programme made up of three principal demands: annual Parliaments, universal suffrage and the repeal of the Corn Laws. Hampden Clubs sprang up all over the country. Posing a threat? To what, and to whom? Nobody knew, but while in London a nervous Government faced up to the possibility that a revolutionary situation might be developing, the Manchester authorities were in no doubt that it already existed. Consequently, when some 12,000 local radicals assembled on 10th March 1817 in St. Peter's Fields (the site, two years afterwards, of Peterloo) the magistrates and soldiers were waiting for them. The intention had been to march to London to present a petition to Parliament. It was a forlorn hope. Mid-way through the morning the magistrates read the Riot Act and ordered out dragoons to clear the fields. Three hundred men had already marched off, but the soldiers caught up with them near Stockport and took them into custody. A few stragglers reached the Midlands and one man actually succeeded in presenting the petition in London, where no more was heard of it, for the Home Secretary was busy cross-examining the ringleaders personally; but no charges could be made to stick. This pitiful incident therefore ended without tragedy, but the next, misleadingly called the 'Pentridge Revolution', did not. In this, a few hundred simple Derbyshire working people seem to have allowed the spy Oliver to delude them into the belief that a general rising of the whole nation was feasible. Their optimism was as boundless as their credulity. They talked glibly of forming a provisional government (which some understood to mean that they would be given provisions after all), and set out on the night of 8th June 1817 to join forces with other columns of workers they believed to be on the march as well. The little band obtained pistols and muskets from farmhouses as they went on their way; but when the sun rose they were greeted not by other marching comrades, but by magistrates and soldiers who had been patiently waiting for them on Oliver's directions. The military rode down as many people as they could, arrests were made, a carefully selected jury worked as efficiently as had Oliver the Spy, and three more hangings went on the record – one of which, however, was deserved, since the ringleader, a man named Brandreth, had in fact killed a servant when obtaining firearms during the night's march.

Oliver had sprung other similar traps before his activities (which were well known to the authorities) came out in public.

When they did so liberal England was outraged, and Parliament set up an enquiry. The predictable result was a demand for an end to such un-English activities. Consequently, since for years spies had been the principal substitute for police, the case for setting up a regular police force was greatly strengthened. Few, however, took this point at the time; and in the following year, 1818, the latest in a long series of Parliamentary committees set up to study the matter concluded that, if it came to spying, police would out-match anyone: a system of police on the continental model would be 'odious and repulsive . . . a plan which would make every servant of every house a spy on the actions of his master, and all classes of society spies on each other'. Britain was evidently as far off having a police force as she had ever been.

It is of interest meanwhile, as a touchstone of contemporary thought, to recall what the writers and intellectuals were making of the events of 1817, the year of the March of the Blanketeers, Pentridge, the unmasking of Oliver the Spy, and the last suspension of *habeas corpus*. Many of the pre-war radicals (not all: Hazlitt is an honourable exception) were the reactionaries of 1817. Wordsworth, having long turned his back on the world, had now re-entered it, and privately favoured an equestrian order of armed yeomanry: 'if the whole island was covered with a force of this kind, the press properly curbed, the poor laws gradually re-formed, provision made for new churches to keep pace with the population, order may yet be preserved and the people remain free and happy.' Coleridge was struggling to repair his own private world before squandering the last gleams of dying genius to irradiate, in attacks on the Reform Bill, his stormy sunset. Only Southey, of that famous trio, flaunted apostasy openly. 'They had turned their faces to the east in the morning to worship the rising sun', he declared of all the radical England that had hailed the miracle of the French Revolution and still, despite its bloody outcome, persisted in their faith; 'and in the evening they were looking eastward still, obstinately affirming that still the sun was there. I on the contrary altered my position as the world went round.' 'In point of reasoning and political judgment', Walter Scott said of the laureate (as he might have done of himself), 'he is little better than a wild bull.' But Hazlitt, Byron and Shelley spoiled for a bull-fight. Someone discovered a poem that Southey had written in 1794 to raise funds for his and Coleridge's utopian scheme of pantisocracy. It was entitled *Wat Tyler*, and was full of wild, republican sentiments, even sedition. Within days 60,000 copies had been printed, and at 3*d.* a copy it was a best-seller in the streets of London. Southey sought a legal remedy for unauthorised publication. He was entitled to expect the court's sympathy, for the case came before Lord Eldon, the arch reactionary who had committed Thelwall to prison in 1794, and who in 1813 had sought to persuade a dangerously progressive House of Lords that it was essential for the safety of the land to preserve the medieval barbarity of quartering the body of a traitor hanged for treason. But to Eldon Southey himself was a radical: 'A person cannot recover in damages for a work which is in its nature calculated to do an injury to the public', he held, quoting good precedent.

Such spirited quarrelling, however, entertaining as it was for the highbrows, had little influence on the undercurrent of radical thinking that was marking out the course of violence from Luddism to Chartism. The main teacher of the humble was himself a more humble man. William Cobbett (1763–1835), the one-time farmer's boy, private soldier, teacher, journalist, political prisoner, and now ardent pamphleteer, was as influential as any in paving the way to Peterloo.

The 'massacre' was the culmination of weeks of careful preparation by radical societies in and around Manchester, resolved to assert their demands by means so impressively massive as to imply the menace of revolution, while yet offering the reassurance of keeping within the limits of the law. For such tactics the time seemed ripe. Years of repression had alienated even moderate opinion from the Government, and the corruption of Parliament had so discredited its legitimacy as to weaken restraints on the use of violence to overturn the established order. The labouring classes had only to organise themselves in an acceptably 'constitutional' framework to emerge for the first time in history as a political force. The ruling oligarchy was, understandably, apprehensive. The reformers were demanding the ancient liberties which, at all great turning-points in English history, 'free-born' Englishmen had always claimed – free speech and freedom under the law – combined, this time, into a formidable demand for a free press, freedom of public assembly, universal suffrage and annual Parliaments; and these claims were given urgency by the need of hundreds of thousands to regain the self-respect the squalor of their new conditions had done much to undermine. Hopes soared, and the working class radicals embarked on earnest sessions of self-education in order to fit themselves for the task of governing Britain. They also felt the need to whip up support at open-air meetings, where noise and pageantry, slogan shouting, and rousing speeches would endow the cause with a visible shape and meaning that would captivate and hold the enthusiasm of the rank and file.

To the Manchester magistrates, to whom the violence of the Luddites was still a recent memory, such plans were dark with menace. They were not prepared to concede that an assembly of working people was possible without implying the threat of insurrection. It was a realisation of this that caused the organisers of a gigantic public meeting to be held in Manchester on 16th August 1819 to prepare something different. The radical Samuel Bamford afterwards explained the intention –

> It was deemed expedient that this meeting should be as morally effective as possible, and that it should exhibit a spectacle such as had never before been witnessed in England. We had frequently been taunted in the press with our ragged, dirty appearance at these assemblages; with the confusion of our proceedings, and the mob-like crowds in which our members were mustered; and we determined that, for once at least, these reflections should not be deserved . . . 'cleanliness', 'sobriety', 'order', were the first injunctions issued by the committees.[10]

During July similar meetings had passed off without incident in Birmingham, Leeds and at Smithfield, and the Lancashire radicals were determined to play their part properly in what was emerging as a great national movement. For several weeks the people drilled in the early mornings or at night, aided by former non-commissioned officers from Wellington's army. Such drilling and evidence of large-scale organisation reinforced the fears of the magistrates. As the day of the meeting approached they worked themselves up into a state of increasing alarm, and their correspondence with the Home Office took on a note of panic. They posted up a proclamation which purported to ban the meeting as

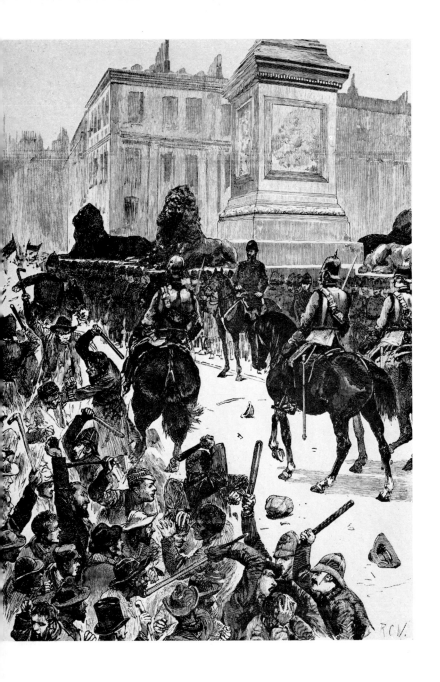

'Bloody Sunday', 13th November 1887. The Life Guards hold Trafalgar Square while the police charge the mob

The arrest of a Suffragette. May 1914

illegal, and in their nervousness made a grammatical slip which the radicals delightedly pounced on: the magistrates, declared the proclamation, 'do hereby Caution all Persons to abstain, AT THEIR PERIL, from attending such ILLEGAL MEETING'. The Home Secretary, meanwhile, discouraged the use of troops, exhorting the magistrates that 'it will be the wisest course to abstain from any endeavour to disperse the mob, unless they should proceed to acts of felony or riot'. The magistrates, however, were in a combative mood. They even disregarded the reports of the leading Government spy in the area, a man named Chippendale, who told Sir John Byng, the Commander of the Northern District, that the orders issued to the people 'are not to break the peace on any account whatever. They are to bear any insult upon themselves . . . they are enjoined not to bring any weapons'. Byng had dispersed the Blanketeers meeting two years earlier without violence, and he now joined the Home Secretary in counselling moderation; so he was told that his presence would not be required on this occasion.

Monday, 16th August, was warm and sunny. From early in the morning tens of thousands of marchers in orderly columns of one hundred each converged on St. Peter's Fields, an open space on the site of what is now the Free Trade Hall. Bands played, men carried banners, and their wives brought the children with them for a day that was to be half demonstration, half festival. By midday some 80,000 people were massed together in the Fields, most wearing their Sunday best; and then, to the accompaniment of music, flags and wild cheering, 'Orator' Henry Hunt took up his place on the hustings, the band struck up 'See the Conquering Hero comes', 'God save the King', and 'Rule Britannia', and Hunt proceeded to address the crowd in terms which, according to the *Quarterly Review*, were reminiscent of Mark Antony's funeral oration on Caesar – 'Good friends, sweet friends, let me not stir you up to mutiny.' The magistrates took up a position overlooking the area, with two rows of special constables between them and the hustings. Meanwhile, out of sight of the crowd, a formidable military force had been assembled – two troops of the Manchester and Salford Yeomanry, 400 men of the Cheshire Yeomanry, two squadrons of the 15th Hussars, and a troop of the Royal Horse Artillery with two six-pounders.

Samuel Bamford gave one eye-witness's account of what followed. 'A noise and strange murmur arose towards the [St. Peter's] church. Some persons said it was the Blackburn people coming, and I stood on tip-toe and looked in the direction whence the noise proceeded, and saw a party of cavalry in blue and white uniform come trotting, sword in hand, round the corner of a garden wall, and to the front of a row of new houses, where they reined up in a line . . . then, slackening rein, and striking spur into their steeds, they dashed forward and began cutting the people. . . . For a moment the crowd held back as in a pause; then was a rush, heavy and resistless as a headlong sea, and a sound like low thunder, with screams. . . . In ten minutes from the commencement of the havoc the field was an open and almost deserted space. . . . The hustings remained, with a few broken and hewed flag-staves erect, and a torn and gashed banner or two dropping; whilst over the whole field were strewed caps, bonnets, hats, shawls, and shoes, and other parts of male and female dress, trampled, torn and bloody. The yeomanry had dismounted – some were easing their horses' girths, others adjusting their accoutrements, and some were wiping their sabres.'[11]

Why did it happen? The magistrates, clearly, were determined to nip insurrection in the bud. Immediately Hunt began to speak they obtained the signatures of some thirty 'loyalists' to a declaration that Manchester was in imminent danger and that 'the array was such as to terrify all the king's subjects'. They read the Riot Act (although it was immaterial that they should have done so, since their common law powers were adequate, if the use of force was justifiable at all, to the situation they had conjured up) and called on the troops to arrest Hunt. The first to go into action were the Manchester Yeomanry, a body set up as recently as 1817 specially to deal with the radical danger, and composed of local manufacturers, tradesmen, publicans and others. They charged the crowd and were soon swallowed up by it. Some were drunk, having spent the morning in taverns while their horses and equipment were being prepared. Some were animated by bitter personal hatred. They slashed about blindly with their sabres and the magistrates ordered the Hussars to go in to rescue them. This second charge swept a mass of people, yeomanry and constables before it. In the event eleven people were killed and some 400 (including 100 women) were wounded, mostly by sabre cuts or by being trampled down by horses.

The shock to the nation was intense. On 23rd August *The Times* said that Manchester 'now wears the appearance of a garrison, or of a town conquered in war'. Soldiers were everywhere, and a new barracks was hastily erected. The Prince Regent sent his congratulations to the Manchester authorities for 'their prompt, decisive and efficient measures', and the Prime Minister, Lord Liverpool, maintained that although the action taken by the magistrates was not 'in all its parts prudent', they had been substantially right, and 'there remained no alternative but to support them'. Canning went to the heart of the matter: 'To let down the magistrates would be to invite their resignations, and to lose all gratuitous service in the counties liable to disturbance for ever.' This line having been settled, rigorous oppression followed. Hunt, Bamford and others were convicted of unlawful assembly, the size of the army was increased by ten thousand additional troops, and in the Autumn Parliament passed the notorious Six Acts. They empowered the magistrates to search houses for weapons, confiscate them, and arrest their owners; drilling was made illegal; seditious meetings were banned, and the courts were given power to seize any pamphlet they judged to be 'a blasphemous or seditious libel'. Probably, like Pitt's measures in 1794, the Acts were intended to terrorise and subdue rather than to bite, and in this they seem to have been effective. For a time coercion silenced the radicals at home, and it was left to Shelley, in Italy, to commemorate Peterloo in *The Masque of Anarchy*:

> I met Murder on the way –
> He had a mask like Castlereagh –
> Very smooth he looked, yet grim;
> Seven blood-hounds followed him. . . .

And 'Men of England, heirs of Glory', were exhorted:

> Rise like Lions after slumber
> In unvanquishable number,
> Shake your chains to earth like dew
> Which in sleep had fallen on you –
> Ye are many – they are few.

The Government, meantime, rewarded William Hay, a leading Manchester magistrate, with the valuable living of Rochdale (worth £1,730 a year) for his work at Peterloo and sought to coax the workers away from the heresy of methodist-jacobin doctrine by granting £1 million for the erection of new Anglican churches.

Yet, for all the repression that followed it, the event was a major turning-point in the long history of public disorder in Britain. For this there are two reasons: first, the consciences of many middle- and upper-class radicals placed them rather gingerly on the side of the labouring classes in the struggle for modest parliamentary reform; second, thinking people could no longer be left in any doubt about the unsuitability of the military as a means of dealing with crowds. Significantly these currents of opinion influenced the thinking of the young Robert Peel. 'Do you not think that the tone of England . . . is more liberal . . . than the policy of the government?' he wrote to a friend in March 1820. 'Do not you think that there is a feeling, becoming daily more general . . . in favour of some undefined change in the mode of governing the country? . . . Can we resist – I mean, not next session or the session after that – but can we resist for seven years Reform in Parliament?' Two years later Peel succeeded the egregious Sidmouth as Home Secretary, and one of his first acts was to set up yet another Parliamentary committee to study the subject of police. It was as nervous as all its predecessors had been – 'It is difficult to reconcile an effective system of police, with that perfect freedom of action and exemption from interference, which are the great privileges and blessings of society in this country' – and its chairman was the astute Peel himself. He well knew, of course, what he was about, and that time as well as abundant political skill was on his side. Moreover the idea of a police force for London had gained influential support in 1820, after a partial mutiny of the Guards. In a memorandum to the Prime Minister Wellington admitted to feeling anxiety about the state of the military in London 'where the Government depend for their protection against insurrection and revolution . . . upon the fidelity of 3,000 Guards'.[12] The Government ought, he argued, to form either a police force in London or a separate military corps, or both.

It was with this support that, in 1829, Peel piloted the Metropolitan Police Act through the House of Commons without opposition; and Wellington, then Prime Minister, saw it safely through the Lords. Peel played the whole thing in a low key. His intention, he declared, was to proceed slowly in establishing a small police force in London, with 'a cautious feeling of his way and deriving aid from experience, essential to the ultimate success of all reforms'. So, quietly persistent, Peel had his way, and the idea of police, so long abhorrent to the English, became acceptable overnight. Of course informed public opinion had to some extent been prepared by the work of the Fieldings, Bentham, Colquhoun and Chadwick. Of course Peel showed patience, unusual in a politician, in biding his time for seven years at the Home Office before bringing forward a measure that he had set his heart on much earlier. Of course he conciliated the Opposition and bought off the City radicals by excluding the City from his new metropolitan police area. All this admitted, it yet cannot obscure the magnitude of Peel's achievement. From 6.0 p.m. on Tuesday, 29th September, 1829, when the first parties of top-hatted 'Peelers' marched to their beats before the gaze of hostile, uncomprehending and at times hilarious Londoners, the rule of the London mob was broken, and the British learned that a system of police need not, after all, be tyrannical.

To Peel, then, must go the credit for having taken the single most important step yet towards the conquest of violence in Britain. Yet the reform could have been a disastrous failure had not the architects of the 'New Police' been scrupulously careful to set up an institution exactly matched to the British temperament. The first joint Commissioners of Police were Charles Rowan, who was 46, and had fought with Wellington at Waterloo, and Richard Mayne, a barrister, thirteen years Rowan's junior. From the start the Commissioners were at pains to present Peel's policemen ('Peelers' or 'Bobbies') as civilians in uniform. They were armed only with wooden batons. They inherited the constable's powers under the common law, and had virtually no other power. Like soldiers and everyone else they were given no special protection by the law. The Commissioners made it clear that they were to be society's servants, not its masters. The pay was fixed at only a guinea a week, and Peel insisted that he would have in the force only men 'who had not the rank, habits or station of gentlemen'. The new recruits were taught that their success or failure would depend entirely on the approval they secured from the public – it could hardly have been otherwise, since they were given neither the authority nor the weapons with which to act by coercion. Prestige and persuasion, not power, were to be the key to success. All these enlightened principles were embodied in a code of instructions which recruits were required to learn by heart – as their successors still do to this day –

> The constable will be civil and obliging to all people of every rank and class. . . .
> He must remember that there is no qualification so indispensable to a police-officer as a perfect command of temper, never suffering himself to be moved in the slightest degree by any language or threats that may be used; if he do his duty in a quiet and determined manner, such conduct will probably excite the well disposed of the bystanders to assist him, if he requires them.
> In the novelty of the present establishment, particular care is to be taken that the constables of the police do not form false notions of their duties and powers. . . .

With the establishment of the Metropolitan Police we move swiftly to the climax of the struggle against violence in Britain. During the ensuing decade, the 1830s, the dam of pent-up radicalism finally burst. Yet outside London England was still, as the French historian Halévy describes her, 'a country without officials and without police, where the executive was weaker than in any other country in Europe, and where the justices of the peace, members of the nobility and gentry, in whose hands the local government of England lay, were obliged to trust for the maintenance of order to the voluntary obedience of the people'.[13] But obedience was not always voluntary. During the Autumn of 1830 a second peasants' revolt fanned out with startling speed from its focal point in Kent, reaching out in weeks to Dorset and Gloucestershire in the west, Oxford and Northamptonshire in the north, and penetrating far into Norfolk and Suffolk in the east. It was the last great reactionary riot in England. The rioters who followed 'Captain Swing' adopted the Luddite tactic of destroying the new threshing machines that were threatening their livelihood, and fired the ricks and barns of any farmer who refused their demand for higher wages. The Government finally put an end to the mounting destruction by concentrating large numbers of soldiers in the disturbed districts and making examples of some of the rioters' ringleaders. During the Winter of 1830–31 nine were hanged, over six hundred received sentences of imprisonment and 464 were transported to Australia for terms of seven or fourteen years, or life – the largest batch of prisoners ever transported from England for a common offence. The rioters, for their part, neither killed nor wounded a single person, and posterity can only lament that this last, despairing gesture of a doomed social class was met by savage reprisals, and not by the redistribution of industry which would be the automatic response of a modern government. The 'Swing' riots also help to remind us of the extent to which the machinery of law and order was still lagging a century and more behind a single generation of swift, even revolutionary, change. Lagging even further behind, and in this lies the dangerous novelty of the total situation, was the machinery of government still rooted in the settlement of 1688; and 'the great cause of revolutions', Macaulay pointed out, 'is in this, that while nations move onward, constitutions stand still'. The mismatch between the causes of violence and the means of dealing with it was, outside London, complete.

It is against this background that, during the two years when the Reform Bill was before Parliament, 1831–32, the nation stood on the brink of mass violence, possibly revolution. In the years since Peterloo radicalism had driven forward with irresistible momentum, and in James Mill (J. S. Mill's father) and Francis Place it had national leaders whose words carried weight at Westminster. A year before his death in 1835 Mill reflected 'with wonder' at the 'shortness of the time in which the spirit of reform in this nation has grown to such a degree of strength'. But the activities of the reformers terrified the uncomprehending middle and upper classes. To them society's foundations were crumbling, and their future was as dark with menace then as ours is now in the atomic age. Every expression of popular discontent appeared ominous, every lack of deference a portent of revolution. 'The year 1831', Harriet Martineau noted, 'opened gloomily. Those who believed that revolution was at hand, feared to wish one another a happy new year; and the anxiety about revolution was by no means confined to anti-reformers. Society was already in a discontented and tumultous state . . . there was every reason to expect a deadly struggle before Parliamentary Reform could be carried.'[14] And Disraeli, remembering these times in 1862, wrote –

Then arose Luddite mobs, meal mobs, farm riots, riots everywhere; Captain Swing and his rick burners, Peterloo 'massacres', Bristol conflagrations, and all the ugly sights and rumours which made young lads, thirty or forty years ago, believe (and not so wrongly) that 'the masses were their natural enemies, and that they might have to fight, any year, or any day, for the safety of their property and the honour of their sisters'.[15]

The reformers, in this climate of fear and distrust, flirted with danger in seeking to bring about changes without precipitating bloody revolution. Denied adequate representation in Parliament, they embarked on extra-parliamentary activities by publishing pamphlets and holding public meetings. But these outlets, too, the Government sought to throttle by prosecutions for sedition; and who but Crown lawyers could be sure, in that formative period, how far the concepts of freedom of the press and of public assembly could be safely stretched?

This was the situation in which, as we noted in Chapter 1, Mill devised the tactics of political brinkmanship: the people 'should appear to be ready and impatient to break out into outrage, *without actually breaking out*'. Using every available organ of propaganda and turning every incident to advantage, Mill embarked on a campaign to implant the conviction in the ruling classes that, unless Parliament was reformed so as to provide a more democratic representation of the people, revolution would be unavoidable. This threat worked powerfully on the Whigs and stiffened them in their resolve to overcome the opposition of the Tory peers. It also worked on the more moderate Tories. Probably it was hollow – Mill himself had no intention of resorting to violence – and it is doubtful whether he could have continued to hold a situation in which his bluff had been called. He was not, however, put to the test, for his tactics paid off. The threat of violent revolution, repeated often enough and made to appear credible enough, did in fact wrest the concession of Parliamentary reform. In this way a lesson of great importance was learned by a relieved nation: that concessions to appease violence, or its threat, are in some circumstances the mark of wise government. Sir James Graham, who was afterwards Home Secretary from 1841–46, summed the matter up in a sentence: there were 'but two modes of dealing with public opinion – either concession, or the suppression of it by force'.

But even the very modest achievements of the years 1831–32 (a modified political outlook among the ruling oligarchy, and a minor extension of the right to vote, which added only half a million to the electorate out of a population of twenty-two millions) were not, as Mill had hoped, won without violence; and it is instructive to compare the manner in which the new Metropolitan Police dealt with Reform Bill demonstrators in London in 1831 with the way in which the authorities in Bristol set about their identical task. In the one case we are already, only two years after the formation of the new police, breathing something of the relatively calm atmosphere of the twentieth century; in the other we return for the last time to the muddle, stupidity and mass violence that disfigured much of the eighteenth.

Severe rioting broke out in Bristol on Saturday, 29th October, 1831, after news reached the city that the Lords had rejected the Reform Bill for the second time. The scale of disorder can be judged from the official estimate of casualties – twelve people were killed and ninety-four wounded. The incident bears a striking resemblance to the Gordon Riots. The mob employed similar old-fashioned but traditional methods in singling out for destruction particular buildings and houses that stood for reaction or oppression; and once again the magistrates did not dare to order the troops to fire, nor did the troops dare to fire without orders. Consequently for three days the mob ran wild, and the nation was again treated to the farce of magistrates and soldiers being brought to trial for their conduct of events. The mayor, a man named Charles Pinney, was charged, along with nine other magistrates of the town, with wilful neglect of duty. It was held that he had refused to order the soldiers to fire, that he had failed to assemble sufficient force to disperse the mob, and that he had refused to ride with the soldiers against them. The mayor's defence was that he had sought to call out the *posse comitatus* by arranging for notices to be posted up on all the church doors (which, it being Sunday, everyone would read) appealing for citizens to come forward as a civil constabulary force, but unfortunately fewer than 150 out of a population of 100,000 had recognised their duties under the Statute of Winchester. In these extenuating circumstances the Judge (Littledale) acquitted Pinney and his colleagues, and in doing so commented yet again on the dilemma which confronted a magistrate: 'If he exceeds his power and occasions death . . . he is likely to be proceeded against by indictment for murder . . . if he neglect his duty, and does not do enough, he is likely to be prosecuted against, as charged in this information, for a criminal neglect of duty.'

The soldiers fared worse. Their commanding officer, Colonel Brereton, was a sensitive and humane man, quite unfit for the duties he was required to discharge. He had available to him in Bristol three troops of cavalry, and there was some skirmishing with the crowd on the Saturday, when one rioter was killed. After that Brereton went to pieces. He gave orders and promptly countermanded them. He refused to allow his soldiers to use violence, with the result that their presence provoked the mob without intimidating it. His hesitancy was partly due to the absence of any magistrate to give firm orders, but nagging away in his mind, as he vacillated between boldness and moderation, would be the lessons of the Wilkes Riots, the Gordon Riots, and Peterloo. During the morning of Sunday, October 30th, a second rioter was killed, and this settled Brereton's course of action. He struck a bargain with the rioters, undertaking to withdraw two of his three troops of dragoons (the 14th, whose members had caused the fatalities) five miles into the countryside on condition that the mob dispersed quietly to their homes. The rioters assented gladly, and that night, with most of the soldiers safely out of the way, got down to work. Following the classic example of the Gordon rioters their first attack came on the local prison, where some of their companions were lodged. Brereton told his remaining troops that they were to defend it, but that they were to use no violence in doing so. The soldiers accordingly stood by as the mob smashed the building, released 150 prisoners, and set it on fire. Thus encouraged the rioters set off to burn down the toll houses, the bridewell, the county prison, and then, setting their sights higher, the Bishop's palace and the Mansion House. A troop of the Gloucestershire yeomanry appeared but could find no magistrates willing to employ them, so they went off again while the work of arson and looting continued till dawn. It was finally checked, on the Monday, when the 14th Dragoons re-entered the city and had no difficulty in restoring order. By that time the more respectable tradesmen and others who had taken part in the demonstration on the Saturday had long ago bolted their doors against the mob of hooligans who had taken over, the original political purpose of the demonstration long forgotten. Brereton and another officer, Captain Warrington, were court-martialled for neglect of duty, but Brereton committed suicide before the verdict was announced; Warrington was cashiered.

Against this sombre background, so reminiscent of the Gordon Riots, it is refreshing to see how the new Metropolitan Police were dealing with demonstrators in London. Their task was far from easy. Agitators worked up public feeling against them. Some of the pioneer policemen were deliberately ridden down in the streets or hurled into the Thames. Inflammatory leaflets appeared – 'Liberty or Death! Englishmen! Britons!! and Honest Men!!! The time has at length arrived. All London meets on Tuesday. Come armed . . . 6,000 cutlasses have been removed from the Tower, for the use of Peel's Bloody Gang. . . .' The story was put about that the true object of the police was to put Wellington on the throne. Faced with a hostile crowd, the police were at first uncertain how to act. In the early days they waited passively to be assaulted, and it was only after some months that they gradually learned the technique of baton charges. The origi-nator of these tactics was the clever radical Francis Place, who had his own reasons for working for the success of the new police, believing that the use of restrained force was the surest way of avoiding a relapse into the vicious circle epitomised by Peterloo – misunderstanding, violence, counter-violence and repression. That leaders of the demonstrators should so quickly have come to terms with senior police officers provided some insurance against the danger of violence; the superb behaviour of the pioneer London policemen underwrote it many times over. Here there is space for only one example of what this meant for London.

In April 1831 Reform Bill rioters, drawing on past experience of the Wilkes and Gordon Riots, staged a great 'illumination' in favour of the Bill, with the announcement that any window that was unlit would be smashed. Superintendent Thomas had at his disposal about 1,200 men, and his subsequent report to the Commissioners speaks for itself.

> 'On the first appearance of riots about the *Morning Post* office, I hastened down with a party of men, and got into the middle of the

crowd, and took occasion to address them immediately around me, entreating them not to persevere in so mischievous and senseless a course . . . for although the police had no wish to interfere, still, they were placed there to prevent further mischief, and that duty should be done at all hazards without reference to any party. At this time I should think there was not less than two or three thousand persons in front of the *Morning Post* office. I was listened to with respect by many round me, and from that time the mischief was greatly lessened. I however got struck by sticks twice, but not of any consequence. I certainly could with a hundred men have completely swept the crowd away, but certainly not without the liability of doing much mischief and incurring considerable opposition and hatred to the Force.' In many instances, the Superintendent reported, his men were 'heartily cheered with cries of "Bravo Police!"' [16]

In October of that year, the month when Bristol's public buildings went up in flames, the demonstrators were again out in the streets of London; and the reports of the superintendents who were in charge of the seventeen divisions into which the Metropolitan Police district had been divided tell their own story. Almost all were in such terms as, 'nothing unusual . . .', everything 'passed off yesterday perfectly quiet and tranquil . . .', 'a party of police was sent . . . and the mob soon dispersed very quietly'. An exceptional report spoke of a 'large mob' which approached St. James' Square being attacked by the police. 'After a short but severe struggle (a number of the mob being armed with bludgeons) the resolution of the Police prevailed and the mob took flight in every direction. The constables had to use their Truncheons freely on this occasion.' [17]

The Whig Government's response to the Reform Bill rioting was to move Parliament to pass another Special Constables Act which empowered magistrates to conscript men as special constables whenever a riot broke out, or threatened. Peel, however, pressed them to go further. Encouraged by the success of the Metropolitan Police, he urged the Government to set up similar forces in every town. But Melbourne was in no hurry. He was content to set up a Royal Commission on Municipal Corporations; and this, when its recommendations were eventually embodied in the historic Act of 1835, required every incorporated borough (there were then 178) to establish a force.

The main object of the Municipal Corporations Act was, of

course, to sweep away the medieval system of town government that had served the thirteenth and fourteenth centuries well, but had stood in the way of progress ever since. In place of flummery it set up democratically elected town councils, membership of which would be open to radicals and dissenters. Flood gates were thus being flung open wide. The requirement to establish a police force, incidental to this main purpose, was intended to secure the formation of borough forces on the lines of the Metropolitan Police, but locally controlled. For many years this intention went largely unfulfilled, as it was bound to have done. The Act was not enforceable, and the people of many towns, naturally eager to oust the aristocracy and set themselves up as a council, were in no hurry to adopt the provisions about a police force: by 1839, when the first Chartist petition was presented, about one-third of the towns to which the Act applied initially had not done so. Others took only token steps to enrol 'police', simply calling the old watchman by a new name. Even so, some of the larger towns (including Bristol) established police forces on the Metropolitan model, and enlisted the help of experienced officers from London to build them up. London's experience in the new methods of crowd control was thus disseminated.

In all this activity to strengthen the civil power there is an element of good timing or, more probably, good luck. The formation of the Metropolitan Police anticipated the Reform Bill Riots by less than two years, and the new force unquestionably saved London from severe destruction. The formation of the first of the borough forces in 1835–36 anticipated by only three years the most prolonged, and at times the most threatening, of all the early quasi-revolutionary movements, when for nine years violence was never far below the surface of public life.

In May 1838 William Lovett, Francis Place, and other moderate radicals, disappointed by the very modest extension of the franchise which the Reform Bill had granted, drew up a 'People's Charter'. Soon it had provided the spark which set ablaze the smouldering hopes and fears of two despairing generations, fused suddenly into something not far removed from a religious campaign – as well it might be, for its roots lay deep in the methodist chapels of the industrial north. Yet the demands of the Charter were neither extravagant nor new: universal suffrage, voting by ballot, payment of Members of Parliament, equal electoral districts, and the abolition of a property qualification for membership of Parliament (all of which, so clearly right, have long been taken for granted) and annual Parliaments (which never was a sensible idea). This sober political programme, although it remained the core of Chartist policy for nine years, was overlaid by a diversity of more clamorous demands. Multitudes seized on the Charter as the direct road to the millenium. The demand, as one Chartist publication put it, was simply that 'all shall have a good house to live in with a garden back and front, just as the occupier likes, good clothing to keep him warm and to make him look respectable, and plenty of good food and drink to make him look and feel happy'. Many streams and tributaries flowed into the great tide of Chartism. Anger at the working of the Poor Law (1834) contributed to it, together with the inhumanity of the new workhouses, where a man was parted from his wife and children in order to be treated in conditions 'as disagreeable as were consistent with health'. Tens of thousands of ready converts were found from the men thrown out of work because the old hand-industries of the North and Midlands were dying. The work of Paine and Cobbett fed it. It echoed the ancient cry of the peasants of medieval England, who had demanded 'justice' as long ago as 1381. Carlyle recognised Chartism at its birth: 'The bitter discontent grown fierce and mad, the wrong condition therefore or the wrong disposition, of the working classes of England. It is a new name for a thing which has had many names, which will yet have many.'

During the Summer and Autumn months of 1838 the bitterness and frustration welled up, as recollections of the fate of the Luddites, the Blanketeers, the Pentridge 'revolutionaries', above all Peterloo, combined to inspire the movement with a grim resolve that this time 'success' must come. But what did 'success' mean? It meant, of course, different things to different groups, and arguments developed among the faithful about whether moral force was sufficient, as the middle classes and artisans maintained throughout, or whether the time had come to resort to physical force, which had an insistent appeal to the despairing millions in the North. In July 1839, as Chartists marched in Manchester bearing banners salvaged from the fields of Peterloo, their comrades in London presented the first great petition, bearing a quarter of a million signatures, to Parliament. It was rejected, and already the early idealism was tarnished. Militant leaders emerged, such as Oastler and O'Connor, and once again, as in the time of the Luddites, rumours circulated that men were drilling on the northern moors by night and preparing for armed insurrection. This time there was evidence that bands of grim-faced northerners, calling their comrades out on token strikes, were arming themselves with pikes and muskets. 'Peaceably if we may, forcibly if we must,' was O'Connor's motto; and the foolscap pages of that most telling of all indices of social tension, the Home Office papers entitled 'Disturbances', filled up with reports of strikes and riots from all parts of the country.

We may now, however, note a significant change in the manner of the Chartists' conduct in comparison with that of the working class movements only a generation earlier. The advocates of physical force lost ground to the advocates of moral force. The mood was conciliatory. As in 1831, there seems to have been a deliberate intention to intimidate by the threat of violence rather than to secure concessions by its direct use. Occasionally resort was made to the traditional methods of arson and destruction of particular houses or factories, but this was rare. More commonly the Chartists employed no more violence (or its threat) than they judged to be necessary for their purposes. The outstanding example came after the rejection of the second petition (which this time carried over three million signatures) when Chartists throughout much of the North-West and Midlands resolved to strike for higher wages as, in effect, the Luddites had done. But the Plug-Plot Riots involved no destruction of machinery. Great parties of men, some armed with muskets and pikes, surged from town to town in order to draw plugs out of factory boilers, so stopping the engines from working and preventing other workers from black-legging. The menace was implied rather than overt – although actual violence broke out, involving loss of life, wherever the men met resistance. F. C. Mather, in his book *Public Order in the Age of the Chartists*, has pointed out that for a while the Plug-Plot Rioters were virtually in command of Stockport and Bolton, yet they behaved with restraint. Even so Melbourne was sufficiently concerned (as no doubt it was intended that he should be) to describe the situation to the Queen as 'certainly very near, if not actually, a rebellion'. Yet, for all the inflammatory slogans, the marching and counter-marching through the affected districts and the vast meetings with all their brave, seditious talk, the abiding impression is one of moderation. 'Viewed in their entirety,' writes Mather, 'the disturbances of the Chartist period were far less destructive than those of a previous generation. If unrest was more widespread than in the comparatively stable, silver age of the eighteenth century, it was also more restrained in character, more restrained also than in the early years of the nineteenth century.'[18] And the author quotes with approval the contention of J. L. and Barbara Hammond that 'violence, the most important fact in the Gordon Riots, was the least important fact in the Chartist demonstrations; that unlike the mob, drawn by a strong passion, which spent its inarticulate fury in burning Newgate prison to the ground, the men and women who kept the Chartist movement alive had a steady and responsible quarrel with the conditions of their lives'.

This steadiness and responsibility were matched, and hence encouraged to grow, by a similar moderation on the part of the authorities, whose wisdom stands out in refreshing contrast to that of the ruling oligarchies of the 1790s and 1816–19. Russell set the tone in 1839 and Peel's Tory government in 1841 assumed an outlook only a fraction less liberal. No Home Secretary earlier than Russell, surely, would have dared to declare that 'the people had a right to free discussion that elicited truth. They had a right to meet.' 'This gentleman's exhortation to arm', Russell replied to an anxious enquiry for advice from Lord Harewood, the Lord Lieutenant of the West Riding, 'is not likely to induce them to lay out their money on muskets or pistols. So long as mere violence of language is employed without effect, it is better, I believe, not to add to the importance of these mob leaders by prosecutions. I should for the same reason wish the great meetings for universal suffrage and the like to be uninterrupted, care being taken to guard against a breach of the peace by civil force – or if necessary by military aid.'[19] This startling view gained ground. Some magistrates in the disturbed districts raised subscriptions for the poor (as Wilberforce and others had done in 1812) and some town councils allowed the Chartists to use the town hall or court room for their meetings.

How providentially well-timed had been the Municipal Corporations Act; and what a remarkable change of outlook by the rulers since Peterloo, only twenty years earlier. It was as though a legacy of eight centuries of violence was being swept away in the single generation that reared William Morris and Hardy, sent Darwin sailing round the world in *The Beagle* and brought Dickens to the maturity of his genius. The Government deliberately abstained from repression, believing that it would be counter-productive. There was no arbitrary interference with civil liberties, no such extension of capital punishment as had been directed at the Luddites. There was no suspension of *habeas corpus*, no panic legislation, no public declaration, so to speak, of hostilities. No use was made of Pitt's Unlawful Societies Act of 1899, no use of the Seditious Meetings Act of 1817; and the sanction of the law of libel, Professor Radzinowicz has pointed out, was invoked only with the greatest restraint, even though it could have been used to incriminate many Chartist publications. Here 'was a reflection of changed times and changed attitudes as well as of Russell's own liberalism. . . . The policy of the Government may have been in some degree dictated by minor expediencies, but it also took wise note of the temper of public opinion.'[20] Radzinowicz has also drawn attention to a similarly striking shift in the attitude of the Government and of the courts towards the ringleaders of violence: 'The extent of Government leniency has been sadly under-estimated. . . . There is no justification for the contention, freely repeated by most historians of the movement, that arrests were indiscriminate and prosecutions ruthless.' Of 400 persons convicted for 'political' offences during the period from the beginning of 1839 to the middle of 1840, twenty-two were tried for high treason and sedition; only half were convicted, and none was executed. A mere eight were sentenced to transportation. Nothing occurred which remotely resembled the mass executions of the Luddites. The upper crust of English society trembled, and a dismayed Queen complained to Peel that 'she is surprised at the little (or no) opposition to the dreadful riots in the Potteries. . . . It is all very well to send troops down in numbers and to publish Proclamations forbidding these meetings, but then

K

they ought to act, and these meetings should be prevented.' Yet as General Napier, the enlightened officer who commanded the troops in the Northern District, observed, 'Half the land has been openly in arms and not a drop of blood spilt on the scaffold.'[21]

Why, then, the mutual restraint? Part of the answer no doubt lies in the fact that the self-education so honourably undertaken by the labouring classes had taught them that good ends do not have to be sought by violent means. The mellowing influence of some radical leaders, too, a number of whom now had seats in Parliament, had its effect on the rank and file. The Chartists were forward-looking, seeking a share in the political power the masses had never enjoyed, not reactionary, yearning hopelessly for a past they could no longer recapture. Consequently they were not driven to violence by the bitterness of frustration, as the Luddites had been. Trade Unions had been legalised since 1824, and the democratic processes were slowly reaching out towards the labouring classes. Despite the rejection by Parliament of successive petitions a glimmer of hope now lay on the horizon. The authorities, for their part, were influenced by a combination of expediency and humanity. They were also able to rely increasingly, as the new police grew in number, on the more effective and intelligent, and hence more moderate, exercise of the civil power.

In London the Chartist disturbances gave the police plenty of chances to perfect their early methods of maintaining public order, but even here they were tightly stretched. The outstanding lesson they learned was that the wisest use of police was always to prevent violence from breaking out, rather than to suppress it after it had done so. They kept well in the background at major Chartist meetings, holding adequate reserves out of sight of the crowd and making no attempt to interfere. However, one or two men in plain clothes would be sent to mingle with the audience with instructions to report to a senior officer at once if there were evidence that disorder might develop, possibly because a speaker was using inflammatory language. In this way the police were able to time any intervention with nice precision. A troublemaker could be arrested with the minimum use of force, and the remainder of the crowd restrained from excess by the sudden appearance of a large number of policemen. By such tactics the police were generally successful in preventing outbreaks of disorder, while at the same time interfering only exceptionally with freedom of assembly and freedom of speech. In 1842 the Home Secretary could write to Peel, then Prime Minister: 'We have had a quiet night in London, and the suppression of the tumults here [by the new police] has had a magical effect ... in allaying the excitement in distant quarters which waited for a signal from the Metropolis.'[22]

In a number of important areas outside London Chartism led directly to the creation of new police forces fashioned on the London model. At first many towns applied to the Home Secretary for the loan of Metropolitan officers, but most of these requests had to be refused. Men could not be spared from London for any length of time, and experience showed, in any case, that small detachments operating in a strange area among hostile crowds could not hope for the success they enjoyed in London, for they could not carry with them to the provinces the essential key to it – the goodwill and approval of the public. At the beginning of the Chartist period, therefore, by far the greater part of England and Wales was still policed by the old, discredited system of parish constables scattered thinly over the area, most of whom were Chartist sympathisers. These areas included not only the incorporated towns that had made no more than a nominal attempt (or none at all) to comply with the requirement to set up a police force, but also the unincorporated towns and, especially, the crowded, sprawling areas which made up the bulk of the new manufacturing districts in the North and Midlands, where to have called out the *posse comitatus* would now have been equivalent to calling out a Chartist army. Legislation was accordingly rushed through Parliament in August 1839 permitting counties to set up their own constabularies, and most of those in the troubled districts did so.

Yet much the greater part of the country was still, even at the end of the Chartist period in 1848, policed by the haphazard methods that had been employed against the Luddites. An epoch, however, was nearing its end. Within the next decade a pattern of the new police was to be developed everywhere, and the old methods were scrapped for good. We may now, in the context of Chartism, view them for the last time in their final stage of dissolution.

Much of the picture is familiar. The magistrates, under the authority of the lords lieutenant, were again the pivot round which all local arrangements turned. As preventive measures they could bind over offenders to keep the peace under the Act of 1361, issue warrants for the seizure of arms or papers, and ban meetings. The parish constables, as their agents, could now be written off. When disorder threatened the first act of the magistrates was to enrol special constables. Often, however, these proved to be of little more value than the parish constables, since they were untrained, undisciplined, and frequently extremely unwilling to face an armed mob composed of men who might recognise them and mark them out for reprisal. Moreover, the only stratum of society from which magistrates could safely recruit special constables was the middle class, and in the manufacturing districts this was small. Some magistrates turned, therefore, to that other well-tried device of earlier times, the formation of armed voluntary associations of the wealthier people, particularly property owners. But now this weapon, too, was falling into disfavour. Early on in the disturbances, in May 1839, the Home Secretary issued a circular to the magistrates which undertook that the Home Office would supply arms to any 'principal inhabitants of a disturbed district' who wished to form an association to protect life and property. The response, luckily, was slight, and after 1839 the arrangement lapsed. The Chartists were not slow to point out the danger of starting an arms race that was likely to lead to class warfare.

Where else, then, were the magistrates to obtain the force they needed (or thought they needed) to strengthen their authority? By this time the militia, too, had lapsed into disuse, for it could no longer be trusted, and the Home Secretary rarely consented to the loan of Metropolitan policemen. There remained the yeomanry, reduced in strength from 18,000 in 1817 to 14,000 in 1838. Ten years earlier, in 1828, it had been re-modelled at Wellington's insistence. 'It is much more desirable', he said, 'to employ cavalry for the purposes of police than infantry; for this reason, cavalry inspires *more terror* at the same time that it *does much less mischief*. A body of twenty or thirty horse will disperse a mob with the utmost facility, whereas 400 or 500 infantry will not effect the same object without the use of their firearms, and a great deal of mischief may be done.'[23] But in 1838 there came reports that even the yeomanry were not always reliable, and the lessons of Peterloo had sunk in. The appearance of the yeomanry infuriated a crowd, and farmers were in any case reluctant to spend the summer months on military duty.

In these trying circumstances the barrel was finally scraped. Someone in Manchester hit on yet another way of propping up the tottering structure of the civil power. Why not mobilise the Chelsea Pensioners, many of whom lived in the disturbed districts? They constituted a force, admittedly elderly and dissolute, whose reliability could be taken for granted. The Home Secretary fell in with the idea, and for a while encouraged the magistrates to swear the pensioners in as special constables, holding out the threat that their pensions would be stopped if they refused to enrol. There were, however, difficulties. Many pensioners had no enthusiasm for their new role; the intimacy with which they had been living with the local population split their loyalties; and, when acting in small parties, their discipline was weak. These considerations prompted Wellington to press for their more systematic employment. A start was made during the Plug-Plot Riots of 1842, when several hundred men were put under military command in Lancashire. Then, in the following year, an Enrolled Pensioners Act provided for their compulsory enrolment under military discipline to aid the civil power. They were issued with muskets and bayonets, drilled, and required to report for eight days' training every year. An Act of 1846 extended the arrangement to Greenwich Pensioners also, and by 1848 a total of nearly 9,000 pensioners had been enrolled. Power to call them out was vested in the Home Secretary, who was authorised to delegate it to lords lieutenant. Thus in the final collapse of the old system of maintaining order, when parish constables, special constables, militia, yeomanry and armed voluntary associations had all been found wanting, the state threw in its last boozy reserves. The grotesque expedient served, if for nothing else, to underline the extent to which, in the un-policed districts, the authorities were now almost wholly dependent on the combination that had finally put an end to the Luddite outbreak – spies and soldiers.

Espionage, during the Chartist period, was more elaborately

developed than at earlier times, and more carefully controlled. The Home Office kept their hands comparatively clean, warning magistrates from time to time of the dangers of employing spies and giving little encouragement to their use. Nevertheless, the Home Secretary placed stipendiary magistrates in Manchester and the Potteries who acted as his confidential agents, and senior army officers called for reports from their subordinates on the state of public opinion in the disturbed areas. The Postmaster-General acted on warrants to intercept mail, and directed local postmasters to report any unusual activity. Press reporters were similarly employed to send reports to Whitehall on Chartist meetings. The Home Office also contrived – until they were found out – to turn the advance of welfare legislation against the Chartists. The first Factory Act was passed in 1833, and a Parliamentary storm blew up when it leaked out that the Department had given directions to the newly appointed inspectors of factories to send in confidential reports about 'the state of tranquillity or excitement' in their districts. The new police, wherever they were available, played an important part in gathering information; and in London, while the Metropolitan Police themselves seem to have behaved with probity, they were authorised to employ their own spies to ferret out secrets. Some of the provincial forces, however, under local direction, had no scruples about infiltrating the Chartist organisation, and there is evidence that some of them may have employed *agents provocateurs*.

During the years of 'peace, retrenchment and reform' since Peterloo the strength of the regular army had been run down, and during the Chartist period it numbered some 30,000. By the end of 1839 about 10,500 soldiers were concentrated in the areas affected by disorder – rather fewer than had been used against the Luddites in 1812, but even so a formidable force. Magistrates, aware of their weakness, frequently sought to requisition troops as a first resort; the Government insisted that the proper use of the military was to hold it in reserve, and that soldiers should be brought in only as a last resort. In this gingerly attitude towards the use of superior force can be seen an important reason why the Chartists, in turn, favoured the tactics of moral rather than physical force. The army was too small, in any case, to provide a police force that was any match for the extensive disturbances during the peak periods of Chartist activity in 1839 and 1842; although the latter year was the first in which railways became available on any scale for moving troops. What this implied for the machinery of law and order was described by a delighted Quartermaster-General two years later in evidence to a select committee of Parliament – 'This mode of railway conveyance has enabled the army . . . to do the work of a very large one; you send a battalion of 1,000 men from London to Manchester in nine hours; that same battalion marching would take 17 days; and they arrive at the end of nine hours just as fresh, or nearly so, as when they started.'[24]

The manner in which troops were employed seems generally to have been sane. The usual method of dispersing dangerous rioters was by means of a cavalry charge; the soldiers only opened fire if they were themselves attacked, but musketry fire was then invariably effective. The loyalty of the troops, in these circumstances, does not seem to have been at risk. The nation was lucky in having, in the outstanding officer who commanded the Northern District from 1839–41, a man who, following the traditions of Generals Maitland and Grey in dealing with the Luddites, possessed compassion, a sense of proportion and good humour. Major-General Sir Charles Napier, a cousin of Charles James Fox, must have been an immensely stabilising influence. He expressed himself in forthright and picturesque language. His opinion on the dilemma in which a soldier could find himself in dealing with rioters has already been quoted (page 75). Magistrates he held in low esteem. 'The Tory magistrates are bold, violent, irritating and uncompromising; the Whig magistrates sneaking and base, always ready to call for troops, and yet truckling to the mob.' And what did the requisition of troops mean?

> Came a call for troops to disperse a mob in the country. I rode out, ordering dragoons to follow me. Mr. N—— and I found the mob, which would not notice us and marched on. Old N—— put on his spectacles, pulled out the riot act, and read it in an inaudible voice – to whom? Myself and about a dozen old women, looking out of their doors to see what we were at! We came back, found another mob, and ordered it to disperse. No. N—— told *me* to disperse it. I laughed, the dragoons laughed, the young women of the mob laughed and then old N—— laughed.[25]

The years of Chartism mark the great turning-point in the

struggle against violence in Britain. Moderation, restraint, common sense, good humour: these, outstandingly, were the characteristics, shown by all classes involved in the struggle, that distinguish the upheaval from all the disorders of earlier times. The nation was fast maturing and English life becoming more civilised: not merely, as during the eighteenth century, for the upper and middle classes, but for the top crust of the lower classes as well. Not everywhere yet, but in nearly all the areas where public order had for generations posed a problem, the new, relatively mild forces of Metropolitan-style police were taking over from the ineffective parish constables, the discarded militia and yeomanry, and the inappropriate force of the military. A relatively enlightened Government showed sympathy towards distress and displayed a readiness to understand the causes of under-privilege. There was genuine talk of redressing grievances. The courts were dealing with 'political' offenders more leniently than at any former period in our history. The total combination of these things goes far towards explaining why in 1848, when the Chartists presented their third and final petition to Parliament, Britain witnessed the most impressive popular demonstration that had ever up to that time been staged.

In February 1848 a revolution broke out in France, when after two days' fighting the King was deposed and a Republic declared, founded on universal suffrage, and semi-socialist in character. Thus 'Chartism had triumphed,' Halévy observes, 'but in France, not in England.'[26] In the following month rebellion broke out in Hungary and Austria; Metternich fell; and within days revolution spread even to 'solid Germany itself', as Carlyle lamented. Europe's aristocratic foundations trembled, and in England the Chartists pulled themselves together. The hour had struck, but what to do? How seriously were British revolutionaries to take themselves? Some were for a *coup d'état*, some for a conference. Endlessly the arguments swayed to and fro among the leaders in their little headquarters in John Street, off the Tottenham Court Road, and the Government's spies faithfully reported each day's outcome to the Home Secretary. Riots broke out in Glasgow, Manchester and the Potteries, and during March mass meetings were held in London which, however, passed off quietly, for the London mob could now be dismissed even by *The Times*: 'A

London mob, though neither heroic, nor poetical, nor patriotic, nor enlightened, nor clean, is a comparatively good-natured and harmless body' – 9th March.

How marked the difference from Paris, Berlin, Vienna! Yet the Government took precautions. The Chartists announced that a mammoth demonstration was to be held on Kennington Common on 10th April. An Aliens Removal Bill was introduced into Parliament to authorise the deportation of foreign revolutionaries, and Wellington, at the age of 80, was appointed to his final command. He brought in 7,000 troops from the provinces together with 1,300 Chelsea Pensioners, but concealed them in the Tower, the Bank and other buildings, while requisitioning steamers on the river to provide them with mobility should the need arise. The Queen and the Royal Family left for Osborne, and many middle-class families took the hint and went too. Meanwhile the Government issued a proclamation appealing for volunteers to be enrolled as special constables. The response was immense, and came from every class of society and from people in all parts of the country. Peel enrolled, together with some 200,000 others. Many people living in the vicinity of Kennington Common offered their homes for the police to rest in, and undertook to provide them with refreshments during what promised to be a trying day. Then, on 9th April, final plans were laid at a conference at the Home Office between the Home Secretary, Wellington, the Commissioners of Police and the Lord Mayor. 'On the continent,' says Halévy, 'the Government, without any support except the army, was impotent in face of a popular rising and the discontent of the middle classes. In England the Government kept its troops hidden and encouraged the people to defend itself against revolution.'[27] This, in the best traditions of Saxon and medieval England, they did.

On the morning of 10th April columns of demonstrators, with superb organisation, converged on Kennington Common. As always on such occasions the number has been disputed, but an estimate of 30,000 seems reasonable. In attendance on them were six times as many special constables, several thousand Metropolitan policemen and some Chelsea Pensioners. The chief actors were the Chartist leader Feargus O'Connor and Richard Mayne, one of the Commissioners of Police. All England and half Europe were tense for news of what might come of the encounter. It lasted for only a few minutes. Four small, pale-blue pages of a message that Mayne at once scribbled to the Home Secretary, now lying in a bundle of old Home Office papers comprising offers of help from the public, tattered posters, letters from Wellington, all the usual flotsam of a great day, tell the whole story –

$\frac{1}{4}$ to 12
Kennington

I have seen Mr. O'Connor and communicated to him that the petition would be allowed to pass and every facility given for that, and its reaching the House of Commons, but no procession or assemblage of people would be permitted to pass the bridges.

Mr. O'Connor gave me his word that the procession would not attempt to cross the bridges, but he added that the petition should be sent in cabs. I had sent Mr. Mallalieu to ask Mr. O'Connor and two or three of the rioters to come to see me to accept such a communication.

There was considerable excitement among the people as Mr. O'Connor came to me. It was evidently supposed he was taken into custody. I never saw a man more frightened than he was, and he would I am sure have promised me anything. He had some difficulty in keeping people about us on the road quiet, and got on top of a cab to tell them he had accepted a friendly communication on which he was resolved to act.[28]

The cabs trundled across Westminster Bridge bearing a petition which Parliament again rejected. The crowd dispersed, and that night the middle classes thronged the streets singing 'God Save the Queen' (but ' "God Save our Shops" is what they ought to be singing', muttered the disappointed Chartists). The soldiers and special constables went home and the Queen returned to London. So, 120 years before 27th October 1968, England had given Europe a notable lesson. 'The continental rulers', says Halévy, 'could not fail to perceive the humiliating contrast between the weakness of their own Governments and the solid strength of the social and political fabric of England.' Palmerston summed up the implications for Britain in a sentence. It was, he said, 'a glorious day, the Waterloo of peace and order'.[29]

A renewed struggle against public violence in Britain spanned the next sixty years, from the 1850s until the First World War. The period started in peace and ended in storm; saw liberty growing and order declining. But the pressures of radicalism that fomented its unrest forced open their own safety valves: after bitter clashes Hyde Park and Trafalgar Square became the nation's accepted rallying places. The national character, meanwhile, underwent contortions. At first it assumed a solemnity unknown before or since, as Parliament climbed up to the pinnacle of its prestige. Then, at about the turn of the century, as the old Queen was near to dying, the nation relaxed. It grinned at itself, sunned itself in the late Edwardian afternoon, and watched impassively as impatient workers and women tried to topple Parliament off its pedestal, but succeeded only in helping the Kaiser to put an end to an age. By this time that ancient bastion of local order, the magistracy, had long been eclipsed by the growing competence of a police force that was not yet, however, always able to dispense with the aid of soldiers during the worst times. The violent encounters between *them* and *us* or (as you will) *us* and *them* were concentrated mainly in the 1880s and in the years 1910–14. By the standards of the Great Struggle the threat they posed was inconsiderable; but the episodes were sharp enough to carve out the channels of a lesser struggle against violence by a bewildered society that was still far from understanding how violence was to be curbed.

The end of the Hungry Forties marked the beginning of an era of comparative tranquillity in public life. Britain grew increasingly prosperous. The repeal of the Corn Laws (following the potato famine in Ireland) brought cheaper bread. Cheap and fast travel by rail widened men's horizons. England opened her shop windows to the world in Albert's Great Exhibition of 1851. The last Chartist meeting took place four years later, in 1855, at Kensal Green cemetery; but this time it was a great gathering of relieved mourners who came to preside over the burial of poor, mad Feargus O'Connor and all he represented. Already the spreading mantle of Victorian respectability had smothered the life out of working-class assertiveness. A fresh generation of sober-headed unionists was setting out to refashion the trade union movement to their own lofty standards in a revolt, as G. D. H. Cole and Raymond Postgate put it, 'in favour of prudence, respectability, financial stability and reasonableness, and against pugnacity, imagination and any personal indulgence'.

To this new generation of sobersides the idea of collective violence was abhorrent. Strikes, machine-wrecking and rioting were seen as evils, impeding society on its march to better times. Happiness was to be sought through self-knowledge, self-education and self-help. It might be true that the working man had nothing to lose but his chains; it was certainly true that he had nothing to sell but his labour. His duty was therefore clear: to improve his skill, be industrious and temperate, live frugally and save for a rainy day. By these means he would put up the price of his labour and contribute to society's contentment as well as his own. How remote was this attitude from that of the bewildered Luddites, haunted by memories of the vanishing rural England of the eighteenth century, and the pitiable Chartists, sullenly coming to terms with the nineteenth! It is the voice of Wesley again, not the voices of Paine and Cobbett, that we hear in that most typical of *Songs for English Workmen to Sing* (1867) –

> Work boys, work and be contented
> So long as you've enough to buy a meal;
> The man, you may rely,
> Will be wealthy by and by
> If he'll only put his shoulder to the wheel.

It was during these placid, middle years of the great Victorian Age, when the influence of Arnold was building one set of

Spartan virtues into a public school system whose products were to rule an Empire, and the working classes were building another set into the social fabric at home, that the revolution in policing was quietly completed. By the early 1850s England and Wales still had only 7,400 policemen. Rather fewer than half the counties had set up police forces, and most of those in the boroughs were still too small to be effective. In many areas the long-discredited system of parish constables continued to exist side by side with the new police. Lacking the spur of public disorder, local enthusiasm for professional policing waned; if a uniform, nation-wide system was wanted the Government would have to impose one.

This point was taken by Palmerston, who became Home Secretary early in 1853. He caused a Select Committee on Police to be set up, and on its report was founded the most important general police statute ever enacted in this country – the County and Borough Police Act, 1856. Henceforward it became obligatory, and no longer optional, for all counties to establish police. The Act empowered the Crown to appoint inspectors of constabulary to report on the efficiency of all forces, and it authorised an Exchequer grant to be paid in support of every force (other than those for populations of less than 5,000) certified to be efficient. This pattern of public administration had much in common with the arrangements being made for other social services at the time – education is perhaps the nearest parallel; and so successful was it in reconciling central supervision with local management that it has survived with little alteration to our own time. In 1856, however, when Sir George Grey (he had succeeded Palmerston as Home Secretary early in the previous year) introduced the Bill it was assailed by that familiar display of outraged liberalism with which British Parliaments had always pounced on any attempt to strengthen the police. The Bill was a threat to the liberties of a country which depended on local institutions that had been in existence since the time of King Alfred. It was the most un-English measure ever introduced, it was an insult to the nation, and soon the Home Secretary would have 'spies all over the Kingdom'.

The outbursts over, common sense prevailed. The Bill became law, and by 1857 the number of policemen had nearly doubled, to about 13,000. During the remainder of the century, guided by the new inspectors of constabulary and coaxed, or occasionally coerced, by the Home Office, the local forces were generally (though not invariably) strong enough to deal with any outbreak of local disorder without calling for help from the military. And as the police grew in professional competence they drew away from the tutelage of the magistracy, particularly in the towns, where the watch committee, not the magistrates, controlled them; after 1888, when county councils were formed, a similar change can be seen in the counties.

From the start these new forces were crippled by the inadequacy of their detective departments. An earlier generation of magistrates had learned from the Luddites and Chartists that successful policing depends on a flow of accurate information from spies and informers; but soon after their formation the Metropolitan Police were in trouble because a Sergeant named Popay was discovered to have insinuated himself in the guise of a poor artist into a subversive movement, where he acted as a double agent. This conduct was condemned by a Parliamentary Committee as 'most abhorrent to the feeling of the people and most alien to the spirit of the Constitution', and the Home Office and the Police Commissioners took the lesson to heart. They did not dare to set up a detective department until 1842, and even then it was only eight strong. (These pioneers, however, were extolled by Dickens in *Household Words*.) As late as 1869 the Commissioner still considered that a detective system was 'viewed with the greatest suspicion and jealousy by the majority of Englishmen and is, in fact, entirely foreign to the habits and feelings of the nation'.

The Fenians, as much as anyone, were responsible for breaking this attitude down. In December 1867 two Fenians were in Clerkenwell Prison, awaiting trial. The police, warned that an attempt would be made to rescue them, took no notice; and on 12th December a constable looked on idly as a party of men attempted to blow down the prison wall. They failed, for the fuse was damp; so they took their equipment away to improve it. Next day they trundled along a keg of gunpowder on a wheelbarrow, and this time succeeded in blowing down a section of the wall, killing four people and injuring forty others. The prisoners were in an inner yard, and so were unable to escape, but the man who lit the fuse, Barrett, outstripped them to fame as the last man to be publicly hanged in England. Meanwhile 50,000 special constables were hastily enrolled, and *Punch* denounced the C.I.D. as the Defective Department. Several years later the Department was discovered to be not only defective, but wicked: in 1877 three of its total complement of four chief inspectors were convicted at the Old Bailey on charges of corruption. As a result a re-modelled C.I.D. was set up, some 200 strong, which six years later had grown to a force of 800.

The Irish were also responsible for the formation, within the C.I.D., of the Special Branch. This started in 1884 as a 'Special Irish Branch', and became known by its present title when its activities broadened. The Branch comprises a body of regular police which, since its inception, has been intimately concerned with public order and with any who threaten to disturb the peace. Thus the C.I.D., and particularly that part of it which forms the Special Branch, can be regarded as the respectable descendant of a not always very creditable succession of the famous and infamous, including Elizabeth I and her Ministers, Charles II, Pitt and Oliver the Spy.

While all these logical steps were being taken to strengthen the police they were pitchforked into a series of struggles in London that swayed, and then decisively settled, a fresh balance between order and liberty. The climax of these struggles came on 13th November 1887, a day that has gone down to history as 'Bloody Sunday'. The struggles this time concerned the right to demonstrate; more precisely, the right to demonstrate in the two politically significant areas of Hyde Park and Trafalgar Square.

Under a Metropolitan Police Act the Commissioner had authority to make regulations to prevent the obstruction of streets and to give directions to the police to maintain order, and it was a criminal offence to disregard these. (Prosecutions under the Act were made as recently as 1962 against members of the Committee of 100 after a sit-down in Parliament Square.) These powers, however, did not restrain nineteenth-century agitators from seeking out national rallying places. By the 1850s freedom of speech (and a free press) had been very largely won as a result of the great struggles earlier in the century, but without national forums in which the right could be exercised its value was limited: there were no cheap newspapers or national broadcasting organisations to propagate minority views. Yet the open spaces of London were being built up. St. George's Fields had gone; so, too, had much of Kennington Common.

A demonstration was called for Sunday, 1st July 1855, against a Bill then before Parliament which would have prevented Sunday trading in London. Of the two founding fathers of the Metropolitan Police only Mayne was now left; and with doubtful legality he purported to ban the meeting. Nevertheless, a large crowd flocked into Hyde Park, which a subsequent enquiry (it had the high status of a Royal Commission) showed to have been unarmed and to have contemplated no violence, though it was attended by the usual riff-raff of thieves and pickpockets. In the main the demonstrators contented themselves with shouting slogans, yelling and whistling, but at about half-past three the superintendent on duty, a man named Hughes, expressed anxiety about danger to vehicles in the carriageway through the Park; and with Mayne's authority he ordered the police to draw their truncheons to clear the crowd. A number of people, including well-dressed women, were forced ankle-deep into the Serpentine. The crowd began to shout back at the police, and scuffles broke out. Some young soldiers joined in, and the crowd turned on them. Meanwhile an angry section had marched down Park Lane to attack the house of the Member of Parliament who had promoted the Sunday Trading Bill, and again the police drew their truncheons. In the upshot seventy-two people were arrested and many were charged with riotous conduct and assaults on the police. Forty-nine policemen were injured, most of whom were struck by stones or sticks. The subsequent enquiry put much of the blame on Superintendent Hughes, who seems to have been free with his language, and also with the use of a horse whip. The enquiry held that he was not justified in ordering the police to resort to violence, particularly as no attack had been made by the crowd.

This Royal Commission refused to recognise any right to public assembly in Hyde Park. Meetings should be 'interdicted or suppressed', for 'to make Hyde Park an arena for the discussion of popular and exciting topics would be inconsistent with the chief purpose for which it is thrown open to and used by the public'. Londoners, however, took a different view. Eleven years later, in 1866, the Reform League, demanding the vote for the working man (but not, as some earnest Members of Parliament were urging, only after he had passed an examination run by the Civil Service Commission), called a 'monster meeting' in Hyde Park. It was to be held on 23rd July; and, says the historian of the women's suffrage movement, Roger Fulford, 'the programme of that exciting day was to stimulate the minds of women to a realisation of the triumphs of scuffling with policemen and of the tempting glories of violence'.

Mayne, again with the Home Secretary's authority, prohibited any assembly in Hyde Park. The reformers protested angrily. John Bright, a leading member of the League, insisted on the right of 'millions of intelligent and honest men' to meet in the Park or anywhere else; yet to the police, 'to meet in the streets is inconvenient, to meet in the parks is unlawful'. The Home Secretary refused to yield, and Mayne took up his post on horseback within the Park, near Marble Arch, with 1,600 policemen. He ordered the gates to be locked and when the marchers arrived he sent them back. Some obeyed and made for Trafalgar Square. Others decided to take the police on. They tore up the Park railings and broke in. The railings were handy as weapons against the police, and soon stones were flying too. Mayne was seen with blood streaming down his face, and many policemen were seriously hurt. Eventually, towards evening, the Guards were called out to clear the Park – the first time that soldiers had been summoned to the aid of the Metropolitan Police since the force was created. For his action in purporting to ban the meeting the Home Secretary was severely criticised by Parliament. The demonstration rallied support for a new Reform Bill, and hastened the measure which became the Reform Act of 1867 – extending the vote to a further one million men. In that year a wiser Government actually allowed a Reform meeting to take place in Hyde Park, and the Home Secretary, Spencer Walpole, resigned as a result of this change of front. Five years later, in 1872, an Act of Parliament recognised Hyde Park as a legitimate place for public meetings; and it is this Act which still governs the Park's use today, and its now traditional forum for soap-box orators.

The struggle to secure Trafalgar Square for public meetings

goes back to 1817, the dark year of Pentridge, the Blanketeers and the last suspension of *habeas corpus*. A Seditious Meetings Act of that year declared illegal any meeting for the purposes of petitioning Parliament of more than fifty persons within one mile of Westminster Hall during a sitting of Parliament. This ban probably accounts for the fact that in 1833, when members of a body styled the National Union of the Working Classes resolved to hold a mass meeting, they selected a site at Coldbath Fields, Clerkenwell. The Commissioners, with the Home Secretary's authority (though with the usual doubtful legality), banned the meeting, and during the resulting affray between policemen and demonstrators a policeman was stabbed to death.

Fifteen years later the ban on meetings within a mile of Westminster was deliberately ignored. In March 1848, a few weeks before the final great Chartist demonstration on Kennington Common, the finishing touches were being put to the newly constructed Trafalgar Square. A meeting to protest against income tax was called in the Square on 6th March. The police declared it to be illegal, but about 1,500 people nevertheless assembled. Only twenty or thirty police were on hand. Their presence, and evident weakness, provoked the crowd. Hooligans tore down the hoardings from the unfinished Nelson's Column and chased the police with sticks and stones to Charing Cross. A running battle continued for upwards of an hour until strong police reinforcements arrived and forced their way into the Square, in turn driving the crowd out, and making several arrests.

For years afterwards the right to assemble in Trafalgar Square does not seem to have been challenged, and the police contented themselves with trying to maintain order. In 1887, however, the issue became one of the first importance, involving the Metropolitan Police in what was probably the most severe struggle with demonstrators that they have ever been asked to undertake. As an overture came the comedy, bordering on farce, of 'Bloody Monday', 8th February 1886. The event is worth recalling in some detail as it provides a rare illustration of the consequences of any lapse in police efficiency.

Early in that year the Metropolitan Police Commissioner was Sir Edmund Henderson, who had succeeded Mayne. Two years before, in 1884, the first socialist body in Britain was founded,

Hyndman's Social Democratic Federation. (It was the birth-year also of the Fabian Society.) The Federation, whose leading members in addition to Hyndman included John Burns and William Morris, preached revolutionary socialism, though in Britain the going was hard: any attempt to found a Labour Party was hopeless, Hyndman had warned Marx in 1881, since English working men were given over to 'beer, tobacco and general *laissez faire*'. Nevertheless by 1886 Hyndman had recovered his optimism about the Federation's prospects. Equally optimistic was a body called the United Workmen's Committee, which announced its intention to hold a meeting in Trafalgar Square on Monday, 8th February. Seeking police protection the Committee claimed to be 'a body of hardworking peaceable men, who intend to conduct their meeting with moderation and with temperate language'. Immediately afterwards the Social Democratic Federation declared their intention of holding a rival demonstration in the Square, and the newspapers reported that they had threatened to seize the platform from the United Workmen's Committee. The Committee replied by offering to provide their own 'well regulated staff' to prevent anything unseemly happening.

During the weekend the Commissioner framed his orders. Out of a total force of 14,000 he allocated only sixty-six to Trafalgar Square, with 563 in reserve. Of the latter, twenty-three were to be at Vine Street (near Piccadilly Circus) and 100 at St. George's Barracks (which stood on the site now occupied by the National Gallery). The remainder were to be in the immediate neighbourhood of the Square. At midday on the Monday of the meeting the Commissioner discussed these arrangements with the Home Secretary, who pointed out the danger of two opposing factions confronting each other; but the Commissioner was satisfied that he had enough men available. He said that long experience had taught him that demonstrators invariably returned home along the routes by which they had come. These were to the east and south of Trafalgar Square; and it was there that the reserve of police needed to be concentrated. This proved to be a fatal mistake.

The Superintendent in charge of police arrangements in the Square was named Walker. He was 74 years old, and had forty-eight years' service in the force. His method of controlling the situation was to wear civilian clothes and stroll about among the crowd; consequently it was virtually impossible for anyone to find him. The Commissioner also wore civilian clothes. Walker arranged for about half the sixty-six policemen on duty to be distributed on the outskirts of the crowd to prevent the streets from being blocked. The other thirty were concentrated around Nelson's Column. At about 2.30 p.m., as the demonstration was about to start, the twenty-three men posted in Vine Street were despatched to Arlington Street. The orders from Scotland Yard were that they were to be on hand outside Lord Salisbury's house because the working men wanted to give him an ovation. It was symptomatic of the misunderstandings of the afternoon that the inspector in charge understood that he was put there to protect Lord Salisbury's house against hostilities. Nobody in fact told Lord Salisbury what they were for, and he was no doubt astonished to see them.

By 3 o'clock the meeting was growing disorderly. The original sixty-six policemen in Trafalgar Square were reinforced, and the police made several charges on the east side of the Square to break the mob up into detachments and keep a traffic lane open. Then, by about twenty to four, the Commissioner and Superintendent Walker thought the demonstrations had been successfully broken up. As he had predicted, men were beginning to go down Northumberland Avenue and the Strand. Unfortunately neither of them happened to notice what was going on on the far side of the Square. Other policemen, however, were more observant. They noticed a large contingent breaking away towards Pall Mall. Five or ten minutes later the Commissioner himself began to suspect that part of the crowd might be going in that direction. He told Superintendent Dunlap, who was standing next to him in the Square, to order the 100 men in reserve in St. George's Barracks to move to Pall Mall. Dunlap passed on the order to 'a constable of considerable standing and, as he considered, of intelligence', named Hulls; but when Hulls delivered the message at St. George's Barracks it had got distorted. He told the Superintendent there to take his men, not to Pall Mall, but to the Mall – to guard Buckingham Palace. The 100 men went off in two parties, but by the time they crossed Pall Mall to go down the Duke of York Steps the mob, estimated at 3,000–5,000, was already well away to the west, smashing windows in Pall Mall, surging into St. James's Street and along Piccadilly. The 100 reserves duly reached the Palace at about 4.30 and remained quietly there for the rest of the afternoon, doing nothing.

In the meantime, at about 4 o'clock, when Hulls was delivering the wrong message to St. George's Barracks, a chief inspector ran from the Square to tell Colonel Pearson, an Assistant Commissioner at Scotland Yard, that the mob had broken out to the west. Pearson sent the chief inspector back to find Superintendent Walker. He failed to do so, and returned to Scotland Yard with news that there was rioting in Pall Mall. He was again sent back to the Square to find Walker, but he was still unable to do so; consequently he, too, was sent off to St. George's Barracks to tell the men there to go to Pall Mall. By the time he reached the Barracks at about 4.20 p.m. the reserves were, of course, standing patiently outside Buckingham Palace.

The chief inspector returned to Scotland Yard *via* Pall Mall and reported that the police had already left St. George's Barracks. He also said that there was no mob in Pall Mall although buildings had been damaged. This was true, since the mob was now smashing Piccadilly. Then it split. Some went to Hyde Park by way of Hyde Park Corner; others made their way up South and North Audley Street to Oxford Street, smashing windows and looting. On the way they passed the end of Arlington Street. The twenty-three men on duty there to guard Lord Salisbury's house watched the mob passing about 200 yards away, but decided that they had no authority to leave their post. Then at about 4.55 p.m. an officer named Inspector Cuthbert with a detachment of sixteen police at the top of Marylebone Lane saw the mob, at once charged it, and successfully broke it up. He telegraphed to Scotland Yard, so giving them their first news of the rioting since 4 o'clock, when the chief inspector had been sent on vain missions to find Superintendent Walker.

The Home Secretary was furious. On the following day he instructed the Commissioner to have troops 'kept in their barracks to be in readiness to assist the civil power if required'; then he set up an enquiry with himself as chairman, and shortly afterwards handed himself back the report. It described the police arrangements as 'most unsatisfactory, and very defective in their conception'. Scathing remarks were made about the Commissioner and Superintendent Walker. To add insult to injury Walker had had his pocket picked while in Trafalgar Square. The report strongly criticised the lack of initiative shown by the 100 reserves who were waiting at Buckingham Palace and the twenty on duty in Arlington Street who watched the mob go by, and it complained of the absence of reserves to the north and west of Trafalgar Square, leaving the whole of the West End open to mob violence. The enquiry also insisted that regular messages ought to have been sent to the Home Secretary, so that he could if necessary have authorised the use of soldiers. Some leaders of the socialists, including Hyndman, were prosecuted at the Old Bailey on charges of sedition, but they were acquitted.

West End shopkeepers were dismayed when they discovered that no-one was prepared to compensate them for their losses, and their dismay this time bore fruit. It resulted in the embodiment, in a modern statute (the Riot (Damages) Act, 1886), of the ancient Saxon principle (applied, it will be recalled, after the Gordon Riots, among other occasions) that every hundred was liable for damage resulting from disorder. For the Saxon hundred was now substituted the modern police district, and the liability for compensation was placed on the police authority – not, it seems, on the principle that the police are necessarily to blame when they fail to prevent disorder, but on the more ancient principle that the individual who suffers should have his loss made good at the expense of the community as a whole, conveniently defined, in modern terms, as a police district.

Sir Edmund Henderson was obliged to retire, mourned by the *Pall Mall Gazette* as 'an excellent man, amiable, kind-hearted to a fault, but the times demand a chief constable with more iron in his blood and more executive energy in his head'. The newspaper delighted in the appointment of an ex-soldier as Commissioner, Sir Charles Warren, whom it described as 'a stern, just, incorruptible, religious man, a kind of belated Ironside, born in a century which has but scant sympathy with his puritan ideals'. It was soon writing very different things about him. Warren was no doubt brought into the force to reorganise it on more military lines to deal with mob violence in the streets of London.

The summer of 1887 passed off as quietly as Queen Victoria's Golden Jubilee. The next trouble started at the beginning of October. Then, day after day, huge gatherings of unemployed collected in Trafalgar Square. Complaints poured into Scotland Yard from local tradesmen and from the general public. A typical letter, from the Royal College of Physicians, spoke of 'the chronic revolution which has its scene just outside our Building in Trafalgar Square . . . in no other town in the civilised world would such scenes be permitted for a single hour'. It was an outrage that the Red Flag should be set up at the foot of 'our great naval hero's monument'. Another correspondent pointedly reminded the Commissioner that in 1780 the Lord Mayor of London had been convicted at the Old Bailey for criminal negligence in not suppressing riots.

The Commissioner, under this sort of pressure, wrote agitated letters to the Home Secretary. On Saturday, 22nd October he complained, 'We have during the last month in my opinion been in greater danger from the disorganised attacks on property by the rough and criminal elements than we have been in London for many years past. . . . The language used by the speakers at the various meetings has been more frank and open in recommending the poorer classes to help themselves from the wealth of the affluent.' On the following day, Sunday 23rd, the mob demonstrated in Westminster Abbey. A couple of days afterwards the Commissioner was again imploring the Home Secretary for advice and direction how to handle the situation – 'I am only keeping the peace in London at the present time by escorting these mobs on all occasions with a large number of men, amounting to about 2,000 a day, who are either taken from their beats which they ought to be patrolling or from night duty. This has now been going on for 18 days, and it is quite impossible that it can continue much longer without the men becoming quite worn out and so harassed that there will be danger of them losing their tempers.' Could he not, the Commissioner asked ominously, in view of his personal responsibility, be authorised 'to take such measures as I may consider to be necessary?'

This request that the Commissioner might be allowed to take the law into his own hands greatly alarmed the Home Office. Referring to the demonstrations, the Permanent Under-Secretary of State observed that 'no-one could make illegal what by law is legal and any attempts to do so, however well intended, would be disastrous'. The Commissioner, for his part, had no patience with Home Office nerves. Warren's letters daily took on a more determined tone, and on 31st October he was reporting, 'the position becomes every day more and more difficult to deal with; the mob which at first was disorganised is now beginning to obtain a certain cohesion. From constant practice the roughs are beginning to find exactly what they can do with impunity . . . by some private signal they appear to be able to get together now to the number of 2 or 3,000 in two or three minutes about the region of Charing Cross.' The Home Office asked the Law Officers whether these roaming bands were illegal, but were told that they were not; and the Commissioner had to be reminded, 'The police, at all events, must keep within the law.'

But Warren either could not or would not understand the Law Officers. Relations between him and the Home Secretary grew increasingly strained; and early in November the Commissioner must have accused the Home Secretary of something rather like bad faith. 'What is important is the disrespectful tone of his letter', minuted an angry Permanent Under-Secretary of State. 'Not a word of regret at his having attributed to the Secretary of State an opinion the opposite of which he had expressed, or of regret at the language the Commissioner had used, the impropriety of which had been pointed out to him, nothing but justification of himself and a blunt denial that he made any mistake. In my opinion the letter ought by no means to be passed over without a rebuke. I think it very probable that the entire correspondence will be called for by Parliament.' Evidently, however, the Commissioner realised that he had gone too far, for he asked for his offending letter to be withdrawn. No trace of it now exists among the records either at the Home Office or at Scotland Yard. Meanwhile Gladstone was stirring the muddy waters by recalling memories of the unfortunate Superintendent Walker, who could not be found during the earlier disorders in Trafalgar Square. He made a famous speech on 4th November advising anyone who was interrogated by the police to give their name as 'Walker'.

Eventually the Commissioner prevailed on a reluctant Home

Secretary to let him make an order closing Trafalgar Square against political meetings. The order was made on Tuesday, 8th November, and was much applauded by the local tradesmen and *The Times*; but it was at once seen as a challenge by the radicals, and the next day the *Pall Mall Gazette* thundered:

> Sir Charles Warren . . . has taken upon himself to deny to the citizens of London the right to hold public meetings in Trafalgar Square. It is a usurpation of the most insolent kind. It ought not be tolerated. Sir Charles Warren has no more right in law to forbid the holding of public meetings in Trafalgar Square than he has to close St. Paul's Cathedral or to break into the office of the *Pall Mall Gazette*. He, the Chief Commissioner of the Police, who are constituted and paid for the enforcement of respect for the law, is now the first law breaker in London. He is guilty by his proclamation of an outrage on the rights and liberties enjoyed from time immemorial by every inhabitant of the Metropolis, and those rights and liberties the people of London are by no means inclined to sacrifice at the bidding of a soldier in jackboots, even though he surrounds the Square with his police cavalry, and has troops with ball cartridge ready to massacre an unarmed populace.

In this deteriorating atmosphere, on the eve of 'Bloody Sunday', Warren spoke confidently of his policemen – he did not believe 'there is any body of men in this country or any other, equal to the Metropolitan police force for honesty, bravery, truth or any other good quality'. On the Saturday the Law Officers, asked again for their opinion about the legality of meetings in Trafalgar Square, advised robustly that the police should 'occupy the Square in force to prevent any persons entering the space vested in the Crown'. It was on this advice that the police acted. Warren's hastily scribbled messages to the Home Secretary, now in the Public Record Office, give one version of what happened next.

> *13 Nov. noon.* The Police are in possession of Trafalgar Square and all is quiet.
>
> 1 p.m. All quiet . . . I have requested the G.O. Commanding troops to move four squadrons with two magistrates from Regent's and Hyde Park to Horse Guards Parade.
>
> 2.45. Meetings have commenced at a few places and bands are marching on Clerkenwell Green.
>
> 3.45 p.m. Large crowds are now approaching Trafalgar Square and there are signs of considerable disorder amongst them – many

of them are armed with sticks and they have stated their determination to take Trafalgar Square. At present the strength of Police appears quite sufficient to quell disturbance but darkness will soon come on.

4.5 p.m. There are riotous proceedings in Waterloo Place and near Bow Street and I have called for two squadrons to go to Trafalgar Square from Horse Guards to relieve the Police of the great pressure on them.

4.30. Two squadrons of Life Guards are now in Trafalgar Square and another has gone to Waterloo Place where I am told there was serious riot occurring. I have called for more mounted troops to be in readiness at Horse Guards in case of need and have called on the 400 foot Guards in St. George's Barracks to line north side of Trafalgar Square to liberate the Police there – we hold the Square [indecipherable] but there are disorderly mobs in all directions and I cannot send the aid asked for to several places. . . . Burns and Graham have been arrested, the latter is injured.

5.0 p.m. Matters are quietening in Trafalgar Square. . . . Some police officers have been seriously injured and it is said that one has been stabbed.

5.15 p.m. A second attack was made on Police at lower end of Parliament Street armed with sticks. One P.C. stabbed in the back. . . . Some of the lowest class of roughs have been about this afternoon.

6.0 p.m. Everything appears to be quietening down. . . .

Many arrests were made and charges were brought of assault and disorderly conduct. Seventy-seven policemen were injured. Next day, 14th November, Graham (a Member of Parliament) and John Burns were charged at Bow Street, and Oscar Wilde was in the public gallery to watch the proceedings. Both were later convicted at the Old Bailey of unlawful assembly and sentenced to short terms of imprisonment. Asquith defended Graham and afterwards had Burns as a member of his Cabinet. William Morris went away to include his own version of the battle in *News from Nowhere*. Meanwhile letters of thanks poured into Scotland Yard from people all over London.

Not everyone, however, was pleased with the upshot of the battle. *Reynolds News* declared – 'The brutal police proceedings of last Sunday in Trafalgar Square will never fade, while life lasts, from the memory of any actual beholder. Already the day has by tacit consent been designated Bloody Sunday.' Referring to 'the flower of the working men of the Metropolis', the newspaper went on, 'peaceable citizens, men, women, and even urchins barely entering their teens, were in many hundreds of cases ruthlessly ridden down by mounted blaggards and bludgeoned by police infantry, as if they had been a gang of mutineers or daring burglars. To crown all, when the cowards saw that the citizens were getting exasperated and preparing to deal with them, according to their deserts, the shameless order was given to bring out the military, to shoot down the unarmed bread earners of London in cold blood.'

On 18th November Warren announced an indefinite ban on meetings in Trafalgar Square, and the Home Office issued orders to the Metropolitan magistrates to swear in 20,000 special constables for two months. A second demonstration was called for the following Sunday, November 20th, but this time the demonstrators found the Square packed with special constables. Again Warren sent back hour-by-hour reports of the situation to the Home Secretary in his room at the Home Office; but this time things passed off quietly. Only one policeman was hurt.

The radicals, however, were determined to find their martyr. It took them rather more than a fortnight to do so, but on 5th December the *Pall Mall Gazette* carried the triumphant headline –

KILLED BY THE POLICE!
A MARTYR OF TRAFALGAR SQUARE

The popular cause has now received the consecration of martyrdom. Among the hundreds of victims whom the police have bludgeoned, ridden over, and crippled, one at last has died from the effect of injuries received. The police smashed his thigh on Sunday fortnight. It was an ugly compound fracture of the thigh bone – so serious that the bone protruded through the flesh, but as he was only a poor man, a law writer so reduced in circumstances as to have a child in the union workhouse, little or no notice was taken of his fate. Besides, had not *The Times* told us that he had been guilty of the heinous crime of hooting the police? So poor Linnell was carried to Charing Cross Hospital and left there, to get better or, as the result proved, to die as the case might be. He had no friends – no relatives save the little one in the workhouse. His very name was unknown; so he lingered with his horribly fractured thigh for nearly a fortnight, no one knew that he was gradually growing worse, until on Friday last he gave up the struggle, and yesterday the Sunday newspapers announced his death. Poor Linnell! He was only thirty-five, and the world had gone hardly with him. . . .

Dickens could have done no better. Next day the newspaper announced that there was to be a public funeral for Linnell with bands, funeral marches and a procession starting from Trafalgar Square. William Morris himself had composed a funeral hymn, and was to make a speech at the graveside. Nasty rumours then reached the police, which Warren reported to the Home Secretary. Linnell had died on Friday, 2nd December and Warren pointed out that the process of decomposition would have begun by the time of the funeral procession on Sunday, 18th December. There were rumours that the promoters had arranged for the body to be placed in a very light wooden shell, so that if the police refused admission to Trafalgar Square the coffin could be dropped during the tumult and the body thrown out on to the pavement, so as to cause a revulsion of feeling against the police. The Law Officers were again consulted; could the law insist that the body should be buried earlier for sanitary reasons? Alternatively, could the police insist that it would have to be put in a solid coffin? The Law Officers advised that neither of these courses was feasible, and the unhappy Commissioner complained to the Home Secretary – 'This exhibition of a corpse for the purpose of a demonstration will severely shock the feelings of the great bulk of the population, while interference with the procession would be equally repugnant to them.' This time he was inclined not to interfere in any way, but to keep the police in reserve to prevent disorder. In the event the procession passed off quietly and Alfred Linnell, whatever his deserts, has achieved immortality in the eyes of G. D. H. Cole and Raymond Postgate (*The Common People*) as 'the first English Socialist Martyr'.

Gradually, after this, violence in London diminished. In the following year, 1888, Jack the Ripper distracted the attention of both police and public. Warren finally lost all patience with the Home Secretary. Again he sought authority to take any action 'however illegal' to detect the culprit, and was again refused; so, a year after 'Bloody Sunday', he resigned. Matthews, the Home Secretary, survived him in office for three years. Asquith succeeded him in the Liberal Government which came into power in 1892. He was at once pressed to allow a fifth anniversary meeting of 'Bloody Sunday' to be held in Trafalgar Square. Warren's ban was still in force. As the former defending Counsel for Graham, Asquith felt obliged to side with the radicals; and the arrangements he introduced – allowing meetings on Saturday afternoons, Sundays and Bank Holidays – have satisfied nearly everyone since.*

These events abound with lessons for any study of public order. They show that, as Peel put it when he introduced his Police Bill into Parliament in 1829, the Metropolitan Police were still, sixty years after their formation, experimenting with 'a cautious feeling of the way'. They bring out yet again the strong revulsion of the British against any attempt to impose a quasi-military system of policing, or to invest the police with military qualities. They show, on the other hand, how unscrupulous even 'respectable' demonstrators can be, if they care enough about a cause to give up a week-end for it, in propagating stories of alleged police brutality; these perhaps offer some compensation for their trouble. They remind us how important it is to isolate the police from political controversy. They teach us, or ought to, that when conflicting systems of virtue clash, involving violence between earnest demonstrators and conscientious policemen, it is irresponsible to talk of victory for either. They show, in the compromise arrangement for vesting authority in a Minister whether to permit a meeting, a recognition that any attempt to censor the expression of political opinion would have to be justified to Parliament. Above all, perhaps, they illuminate the manner in which the balance between order and liberty was struck in the streets of London; out of scuffles rather than text books, but accompanied by a resolve not to use force immoderately. Had there not been an overwhelming majority of restrained demonstrators on the one hand and an overwhelming

* The present use of Trafalgar Square for meetings is governed by Regulations made by the Minister of Public Buildings and Works under the Trafalgar Square Act 1842 and the Parks Regulation Acts, 1872 and 1926. The Minister's written permission is required by anyone who wishes to organise a meeting or procession in the Square, or to make a speech. It is of interest that, while the bulk of Sidmouth's Seditious Meetings Act of 1817 was repealed in 1967, the section which bans meetings of more than fifty people in Westminster while Parliament is sitting was retained on the Statute Book.

majority of tolerant policemen on the other, it is beyond doubt that rioting would have been very much more severe. As it was a quality of British toleration saved the day, and it is possible that police and radicals emerged from the encounters with a rather precarious respect for one another.

From politics to religion: the activities of the Salvation Army, in the meantime, had been influencing the balance between order and liberty, and its contribution, as things fell out, was to tilt the scales slightly towards the latter.

The Army was founded by William Booth in 1878, and during its early years it attracted much hostility. People poked fun at the military bearing of the marchers and the brassy noise with which, in the early days, they stampeded mean streets. They offered a sitting target for hooliganism, and soon a rival 'Skeleton Army' was set up, its banner the skull-and-crossbones. Conflicts between the two were severe, and meetings of Salvationists commonly degenerated into disorder; in Worthing in 1884, for example, the Riot Act had to be read, and troops were summoned. Our concern, however, is with a meeting called by Salvationists two years earlier in Weston-super-Mare. Several clashes had already occurred in the town between the Salvation Army and the 'Skeleton Army', and the magistrates feared further disorder. They therefore issued a proclamation which purported to 'require, order and direct all persons to abstain from assembling to the disturbance of the public peace'.

By what authority could magistrates ban a meeting? It was an issue as old as the magistracy itself, and still at this time an open one. In 1881 the Home Secretary, Sir William Harcourt, had advised the Stamford magistrates (who had their own troubles with the Salvation Army) that while processions as such were not illegal, it was open to the magistrates to ban them if the police thought they might lead to 'riotous collisions'. At all events the Weston Salvationists ignored the ban. The march took place, and subsequently the magistrates had the leaders arrested, held that they had committed the offence of unlawful assembly, and bound them over to keep the peace. They refused and were sentenced to three months' imprisonment in default, but appealed successfully to the High Court. This judgment (*Beatty v Gillbanks*) marked an important milestone in the law dealing with public order, for the judges held that there was no authority that a man may be convicted for doing a lawful act (e.g. marching in procession) if he knows that by doing it he may cause another to do an unlawful act (viz., create disorder). The case therefore helped to expose the fallacy that magistrates had any authority to ban a meeting on the mere grounds that it *might* provoke disorder. Subsequent Home Secretaries withdrew Harcourt's advice and ventured no further than to maintain that, by purporting to ban a meeting, magistrates would do no more than serve warning that it might degenerate into an unlawful assembly. Defiance of the ban, however, would be no crime unless in fact an unlawful assembly resulted. The important principle of law that emerged, therefore, recognised a significant extension of the freedom of public procession and public meeting in this country. Part of this freedom, however, as we shall see in the next chapter, was retracted by the Public Order Act, 1936, the Government's reponse to the activities of the British Union of Fascists.

To understand the causes of the next major outbreaks of violence in Britain, after the turn of the century, we must now attempt to bring into focus some of the broad trends of national life from the high noon of the great Victorian Age, in the 1870s. It was a period, above all, of earnestness, piety, optimism and national self-confidence. Gladstone transformed the Whigs into a Liberal Party, and a massive Empire fostered growing prosperity at home. J. S. Mill refashioned Bentham's cheery utilitarianism and gave the Liberals a serious, empirical, questioning philosophy that broke sufficiently with *laissez faire* to express itself in social reforms. It was a great age of humanitarianism. Factory and Mines Acts, intelligent trade unionism and the co-operative movement were doing far more than the Luddites or Chartists had done to remedy the evil consequences of the Industrial Revolution, and life was sweetened by a growing concern for the poor and for children. Moreover 'Victorian society', in the judgment of G. D. H. Cole and Raymond Postgate, 'was one of a very high degree of political liberty. Speech and political thought were freer than they had ever been before, or are today.'[1]

The age also saw the flowering of the English public schools, to which Trevelyan could attribute 'much of the success and much of the failure of modern England. . . . They were one of the great institutions unconsciously developed by English instinct and character.' In two generations Thomas Arnold's reforms at Rugby had influenced every public school in the country, and a cult of muscular Christianity was founded on fagging, corporal punishment, the classics, petty tyranny and cold baths. The new race of clean-living athletes carried the white man's agreeable burden far afield. They also set uncompromisingly high standards of behaviour (at least in public) at home, setting the seal on the lofty spirit of the age, and influencing by their example those less favourably (though perhaps more happily) born. Anti-intellectual, afraid of any show of emotion or private feeling, their imperturbable caste displayed to half the world the quintessence of the *flegme britannique*.

During the hey-day of the English public school the nation's self-confidence was boundless. In 1876 Queen Victoria was created Empress of India. Two years later Disraeli brought back 'Peace with Honour' from the Congress of Berlin; and in the music halls the vulgar let rip –

> We don't want to fight, but by Jingo if we do,
> We've got the ships, we've got the men,
> And got the money too.

Joseph Chamberlain summed up the whole romantic imperialist dream with words Hitler might have plagiarised for his own –

> I believe in this race, the greatest governing race the world has ever seen; in this Anglo-Saxon race, so proud, so tenacious, self-confident and determined, this race which neither climate nor change can degenerate, which will infallibly be the predominant force of future history and universal civilization.[2]

For several generations the voices of protest in this paternalistic society were, outside London, muted or dumb. Yet beneath the superficial orderliness of affairs the influence of the early evangelical socialists was paving the way for fresh explosions of collective violence on a scale unknown since Chartist times. Concern for what Charles Booth called the 'submerged nine-tenths' of the population was expressed in the voluntary social work undertaken by such bodies as Toynbee Hall (1884), the Salvation Army and the teetotal movement. The members of the old craft unions were prospering, but the great London Dock Strike of 1889

Soldiers escorting police after severe rioting in Liverpool.
17th August 1911

The General Strike, 1926. A unique event. Police v. Strikers at football. The two teams before the match at which the wife of the Chief Constable of Plymouth kicked off showed up, to quote G. D. H. Cole and Raymond Postgate again, 'enormous stagnant pools of misery and degradation which society and the Trade Union leaders had forgotten'.[3] John Burns, the dockers' leader, like Francis Place in 1831, was wise enough, after his experience during the Trafalgar Square riots two years earlier, to come to terms with the Metropolitan Police, and he organised the dockers' processions obediently to their advice. Consequently 'Superintendent Forster's helmet next to Burns' white straw at the head of the marchers was an infuriating spectacle to the company directors', who were eventually forced to concede the 'dockers' tanner' without any serious outbreak of violence. A fillip was thus given to the formation of great trade unions for unskilled workers.

Was a revolutionary situation building up in the 1890s? Hyndman seems to have believed that even in apathetic Britain a revolution might succeed, but he deluded himself. He failed to reckon with the public school ethos, and like Marx he failed, as Sir Arthur Bryant puts it, 'to see that in an ancient country like England with its strong social character and representative institutions, revolution would be deflected into smoother channels'. By the end of the century his influence had been eclipsed by that of the prophets of the new Left: Keir Hardie, MacDonald and Snowden, supported by the Fabian intelligentsia, cut Britain off from the main current of continental communism. Instead they steered the newly formed Independent Labour Party (1893) towards evolutionary, not revolutionary, socialism; and in 1906 John Burns found himself a member of Campbell-Bannerman's Government.

Yet in a broad sense the situation was undoubtedly a revolutionary one, for the old Victorian way of life, so cultured and civilised at the top, so raw beneath, was as surely doomed as had been the seemingly stable medieval life of the late fourteenth century. Once again personal and social disciplines, as well as political attitudes, were under attack. In letters written to her father in 1886 while she was staying with a working-class family in the north of England, Beatrice Webb could praise the 'charm of direct thinking, honest work and warm feeling' of the poor, and recognise how they taught her 'the real part played by religion in making the English people, and of dissent teaching them the

M

art of self-government, or rather serving as a means to develop their capacity for it'. But it saddened her to think that religious faith was destined to pass away. 'One wonders what will happen when the religious feeling of the people is undermined by advancing scientific culture; for though the "Co-op" and the chapel at present work together, the secularism of the "Co-op" is half unconsciously recognised by earnest chapel-goers as a rival attraction to the prayer meeting and the Bible class.'[4] The early harbingers of the permissive society were on the wing. Huxley and Bradlaugh were tilting at simple religious faith, and the cynical glitter of the *fin de siècle* writers and artists was working away to transform the nation's manners, just as certainly as society's foundations were being undermined by the new social-ism. We lurch out of the nineteenth century and into our own attended not only by the inspired gloom of Hardy and Hous-man, but also by the midwives of aestheticism and decadence, Wilde, Beardsley, Whistler, Arthur Symonds, *Les Fleurs du Mal, The Yellow Book, Salomé* and *Dorian Gray*.

The old era scarcely survived the death of the old Queen. 'A tendency to violence and excitement had already invaded the new century', writes Trevelyan.[5] A new type of newspaper, 'living on sensation', the *Daily Mail*, had been started in 1896. A new type of statesman with a 'shrill demagogic note' entered politics from his native Wales. A new, militant type of woman was demanding the vote. And a new revolutionary movement, syndicalism, came to Britain from France and America. Its philosopher, George Sorel, in his *Réflexions sur la Violence* (1908), preached class warfare and offered a programme to the British worker of revolution by 'social general strike'. So, once again, after a period of many years, the appeal was for direct action, the tocsin sounded for violence. In America, under this disruptive influence, the 'Industrial Workers of the World' embarked on violent clashes with their employers. In France Sorel was debated excitedly in cafés on the Left Bank. In Britain he raised a yawn. Tom Mann struggled to overcome the apathy of the workers, but with little success: conspicuously less than Paine had won, that other Englishman who more than a century earlier had imported into this country the seeds of revolutionary thought from France and America.

Here then, in the early years of our century, is a society suffering from strains and tensions of which it is largely unaware: not so much a sick society unconscious of disease, as a swiftly maturing society suffering the growing pains of a civilisation in which the *folies de grandeur* of devouring a quarter of the world for an Empire warred with a flippant reaction against its self-righteous founders. The genius of Kipling, perhaps, more than any other, caught the spirit of this time, with all its excess of pride, gusto, nostalgia, decaying self-confidence:

> God of our fathers, known of old,
> Lord of our far-flung battle line,
> Beneath whose awful Hand we hold
> Dominion over palm and pine –
> Lord God of Hosts, be with us yet,
> Lest we forget – lest we forget!

For a decade, 1900–09, the spate of social reform was incessant: Children Acts, Health Acts, Housing and Town Planning Acts, Coal Mines Acts, the Old Age Pension, tumbled over one another onto the statute-book. The Liberal landslide of 1906 brought talent, even genius, into the Cabinet, and the liberal spirit of Victorian England lived on into the new age. But during these same first years of the century real wages had been going down – a reversal of the trend of the nineteenth century. Miners, railwaymen and transport workers hankered after a great Triple Alliance of unions to show their power. Tom Mann promised the earth today; MacDonald and Snowden promised nothing. Many in the working classes lost faith in Parliament; so did the militant suffragettes, rebelling against security and incited to violence by the restless spirit of the new century. By 1910 the output of social legislation was slackening. The demand for fresh leaders was strident. Within four years the Liberals found that the immense goodwill that returned them to power in 1906 had vanished, and disorder and violence had returned to Britain on a scale that had not been experienced for generations. 'What happened in the years immediately before 1914,' to quote Cole and Postgate, 'was that not one powerful group, but several at the same time, found Parliament standing with apparent immobility in the way of things which they wanted much too strongly to be prepared to give up without a struggle. They felt too seriously about these claims to be limited by the traditional rules of the game. Before the impact of these forces Liberal parliamentarianism found itself helpless and afraid.'[6]

The years of strife were heralded by Winston Churchill's arrival at the Home Office in February 1910, and they were characterised by the most massive use of soldiers to repress violence since Chartist times.

Since 1869 soldiers had been called out on twenty-four occasions, and in only two cases had the order to fire been given. One of these incidents, however, was ugly. It occurred in September 1893 in the mining village of Featherstone, in Yorkshire. There had been strikes in several villages, and on the morning of 7th September a menacing crowd armed with cudgels complained of blacklegging at Ackton Hall colliery. It was Doncaster Race week, and the bulk of the police force was on duty at the races. The colliery manager appealed to the Chief Constable for troops, and late that afternoon a small contingent of twenty-eight soldiers arrived; but no magistrate could be found to give them orders. All day the crowd had been swelling as men poured into Featherstone from distant areas, sensing an opportunity for a showdown. The sight of the troops infuriated the mob, and fearing to provoke violence the commanding officer, Captain Barker, led his detachment into an engine shed on the colliery premises. As dusk fell the crowd bombarded the shed with stones and lumps of old iron, smashed the windows and beat down the doors. Rioters armed with bludgeons surged in, demanding the withdrawal of the soldiers. Someone tried to start a fire in an attempt to burn the troops out, and Barker followed the unhappy example of Colonel Brereton in Bristol in 1831: he undertook to remove the troops if the strikers went home. The bargain was struck, and at about 7 o'clock the soldiers forced their way through a dense mob and took up a position several hundred yards away. Thus encouraged, the rioters began systematically to burn down the colliery buildings. The manager renewed his efforts to find a magistrate, and shortly before 8 o'clock a justice named Hartley arrived. The troops closed in again and the crowd, now estimated to number 2,000, attacked them with showers of stones and bricks. Barker and Hartley were both injured. Hartley appealed several times to the crowd, and then read the Riot Act by the light of a lantern.

The troops advanced with fixed bayonets, and another hail of missiles greeted them. By now huge flames were lighting up the scene and the tiny detachment of soldiers was in a desperate situation. At about 9.15 Hartley ordered them to fire on the crowd. A stunned silence followed the report of the rifles, and then came renewed stone throwing and cries of, 'Go on, it's only blank.' But the ammunition was live, and on the second volley about a dozen people were hit and two men, both spectators, were killed, one of whom was a local Sunday School teacher.

So rare was such an event in 1893 that the Government promptly set up an enquiry. It vindicated the actions of both the magistrates and the soldiers and rehearsed yet again, for a generation happily unfamiliar with such matters, the law and practice relating to the use of soldiers in aid of the civil power. Asquith, who was then Home Secretary, next ordered a further thorough review of the whole subject, and the subsequent report (1894) contains a convenient statement of the well-established principles, with its insistence that 'the first duty of responsible local authorities where there is danger of serious disorder is to prevent it breaking out; the second is, if such disorder arises, to suppress it promptly and effectually, with the exercise of no more force than is necessary'. Magistrates and commanding officers were given the uncomfortable reminder that they would 'each be responsible respectively for anything done or ordered by them which is not justified by the circumstances of the case'. These same principles were reviewed yet again by a Select Committee of Parliament in 1908, so when Churchill arrived at the Home Office two years later they were freshly in mind.

The persistent legend that Churchill 'ordered' troops to Tonypandy is, however, untrue; and the Home Office papers conclusively refute the allegation, so long held against him, that 'his' use of troops exacerbated a dangerous situation. The facts are as follows.

At the beginning of November 1910 rioting broke out among miners in the Rhondda Valley, and the local magistrates asked the War Office to send troops to Tonypandy. Churchill asked the Chief Constable of Glamorgan for a report, and on 8th November the Chief Constable announced a serious clash: 'Many casualties on both sides. Am expecting two companies of infantry and 200 cavalry today. . . . Position grave.' After consulting Haldane, the Secretary of State for War, Churchill replied as follows:

> Your request for military. Infantry should not be used till all other means have failed. Following arrangements have therefore been made. Seventy mounted constables [in fact, 100 were sent] and two hundred foot constables of Metropolitan Police will come to Pontypridd by special train leaving Paddington 4.55 p.m., arriving about 8.0 p.m. They will carry out your directions under their own officers. The County will bear the cost. Expect these forces will be sufficient, but as further precautionary measure 200 cavalry will be moved into the district tonight and remain there pending cessation of trouble. Infantry meanwhile will be at Swindon. General Macready will command the military and will act in conjunction with the civil authorities as circumstances may require. The military will not, however, be available unless it is clear that the police reinforcements are unable to cope with the situation. Telegraph news Home Office and say whether these arrangements are sufficient. – CHURCHILL.

This telegram was followed by a message to the strikers undertaking that, 'confiding in the good sense of the Cambrian Combine workmen', the soldiers would be held back for the present, and only the police employed. The situation, however, deteriorated, and that evening, after speaking to the Chief Constable, Churchill authorised the cavalry to move in. A second contingent of 200 Metropolitan Police was despatched during the night and a third, consisting of a further 300 men, the following afternoon, in all providing the Chief Constable with a force of 1,400 men, of whom 120 were mounted, together with 500 soldiers under the command of General Macready, son of the famous Victorian actor William Macready. Churchill's attitude towards the use of troops, however, remained consistent. Macready was told to 'act as you think best for the preservation of order and the prevention of bloodshed . . . vigorous baton charges may be the best means of preventing recourse to fire-arms'. These tactics paid off; soon Macready reported, 'A football match between the strikers and the soldiers was played at Tonypandy in which the soldiers were victorious.' The Metropolitan Police remained in the area until the situation was quiet, and on 18th November the Chief Constable reported: 'I have again reminded the police of your instructions to me to act with firmness in dealing with a hostile crowd, especially now, when the police are in such force.'

Churchill's reply was characteristic: 'You are quite right to act vigorously with your police force against serious riot. A certain amount of minor friction is, however, inseparable from present situation. Both sides are unreasonable in many ways and I should recommend you to go gently in small matters.'

The year 1911 was probably the most violent that Britain had experienced since 1842, when Chartist activity reached its zenith. In August the London dockers came out on strike, and in the same month Liverpool suffered almost total paralysis from widespread strikes. The city long remembered its own 'Bloody Sunday', 15th August. Tom Mann organised a great march of strikers for that day, culminating in a demonstration outside St. George's Hall. The scene was reminiscent of Peterloo; the processions marched with discipline carrying brightly coloured banners, and attended by bands. Mann persuaded the Chief Constable to keep the police out of sight so far as possible, and the Chief Constable agreed; but he kept a large body of men in reserve, including a contingent from Birmingham. He also called for 100 soldiers from the Royal Warwickshire Regiment, and arranged for two gun-boats to be anchored in the Mersey. Little was left to chance.

As so often happens on such occasions people came away with different accounts of how the rioting started. All agreed, however, that it began with a scuffle between police and youths. The most likely explanation is that given afterwards by one of the strikers, who contended that the riot was 'in no way due to the police or to the strikers, but to the hooligan element which was present in strong force'. Disorder spread with lightning speed. Mann appealed to the crowd to go home, but the appeal came too late. Police reinforcements were rushed out and repeated baton charges followed. Showers of missiles were flung at the police, and a fierce battle broke out in Lime Street. The Superintendent from Birmingham was knocked down and had a leg broken. A policeman who took part in the battle recalled to the author fifty years afterwards that tempers were none too sweet – 'My lot was 12 hours daily, no time off and no extra pay, lasting some six weeks. . . . Coming up St. John's Lane at full gallop with drawn staffs came about thirty mounted men; they charged into the crowd in proper Cavalry style (I had to run myself) dozens were

169

laying around, and then things did warm up especially at the N.E. of St. George's Hall. They even tore up the large chains and used them on us. The soldiers came out facing Islington and our Chief Superintendent appealed to the Commanding Officer to open fire, which he absolutely refused.' The Chief Constable, from a first-floor window, 'kept on shouting like a sergeant-major "stop using your batons", but no-one took any notice'. Later the writer was involved in 'the most violent fight I have ever seen'. A policeman was kicked to death, and after that 'officers and all joined in, no quarter given and none expected'. Eventually the Riot Act was read and the mob dispersed, leaving several hundred wounded and two dead.

The stoppage of work in Liverpool had national consequences. A railway strike spread throughout the country, and now Churchill took a decision of greater moment than any of which he has been accused over Tonypandy. It was, however, a balanced decision. On 18th August, three days after the Liverpool riot, he sent a telegram to the Lord Mayor assuring him of adequate troops and urging him to enlist special constables: 'It is important that rioters should feel that the maintenance of order does not rest in the hands only of uniformed authority.' Then next day he sent out a telegram to all police authorities in 'disturbed areas' conveying the startling news that 'The Army Regulation which requires a requisition for troops from a Civil Authority is suspended', and General Officers Commanding the military areas were instructed to use their own discretion where to send troops.* Detachments were assigned to the more important trains, others guarded signal boxes and level crossings. The military faced difficult decisions: in Manchester, for example, the local tradesmen requested troops and the Lord Mayor begged that on no account should they be sent in; as a compromise a few men were eventually posted to guard the railway stations. In scores of towns rioting was severe. Strikers attacked trains, crossings and signal-boxes and engaged police and soldiers in fierce battles. Readings of the Riot Act were frequent. In Chesterfield the troops charged rioters with fixed bayonets, and in Llanelly, after the Riot Act

---

* There is an interesting (though inexact) parallel between Churchill's order and that issued to the troops by King George III at the height of the Gordon Riots (page 85).

had been read and a short warning given, a detachment of the Worcester Regiment opened fire and killed two rioters. Yet the conduct of the strikers seems, on the whole, to have been characteristically moderate. Police reports attributed much of the damage to drunken hooliganism, and the Chief Constable of Nottingham was emphatic that 'the behaviour of the strikers in this County has been creditable to them in every way'.

For his action in allowing troops to be used without any requisition from the magistrates Churchill was, of course, widely criticised; but the Law Officers (Rufus Isaacs and John Simon) defended it on the well-established ground that the soldier possessed all the rights and duties of the ordinary citizen in dealing with crime, and that he was bound in some circumstances to act on his own responsibility – a doctrine, it will be recalled, that had been expressed *ad nauseam* after the Gordon Riots. Nor was Churchill lacking in outside support for the strong action he had taken. The Chief Constable of Nottingham thanked the Home Office 'most sincerely' for their help, adding, 'In my experience over many years' standing, if I may venture to say so, in no previous case has the Home Office inspired more confidence in those under their command.' The military, too, were far from displeased. 'During the weeks the strike was in progress,' General Macready told the Home Office in October, 'recruiting generally went up.' The figures were better than at any time during the previous two years: 'Evidently the action of the Government and of the Army did not disgust the recruiting market!'

The year 1912 was scarcely less violent than 1911. Upwards of one million workers were on strike, and the newly founded *Daily Herald* advised its readers: 'We say, "Prepare your organisation and then Strike". Strike and Strike Hard.' But were the militants justified in putting their fellow workers literally in the firing line? Tom Mann and his fellow agitators, remembering the strikers who had been killed the year before, published a leaflet appealing to soldiers – 'You are Workingmen's Sons. . . . *You* are called upon by your Officers to *Murder Us*. . . . Boys, Don't Do It. . . . Think things out and refuse any longer to Murder Your Kindred. Help Us to win back Britain for the British and the World for the Workers.'

Mann's was the first serious attempt to suborn the loyalty of the

Armed Forces since Thelwall had stirred up the Naval mutinies in 1797; and Asquith's Government now turned to Pitt's almost forgotten Incitement to Mutiny Act of that year. Proceedings under it were launched against Mann and four others. 'Soldiers were the last resort of the State to preserve the property and persons of the peaceable citizens', declared the prosecution, referring to 'this mischievous and pernicious paper'. All five defendants were sentenced to short terms of imprisonment, but in the face of a public outcry the Home Secretary recommended the exercise of the Prerogative of Mercy, and the sentences were reduced.

Faithful to the traditions established by Russell during the Chartist disturbances, the Government acted moderately in dealing with the great strikes of 1911 and 1912. Considering the magnitude of the threat, police and soldiers seem on the whole to have behaved with restraint. Even so the Government of 1914 were at their wits' end to solve the problem of public order. They were distracted by the rebellion of the workers, the Irish problem, and the menace of war. And as though these were not cares enough for any Government the years 1911–14 saw the new phenomenon of the militant suffragettes.

'Votes for Women!' ran the slogan, and more reasonably, 'I am a law-breaker because I desire to be a law-maker.' The suffragette movement was the climax of more than a century of protest. In 1791 the formidable Mary Wollstonecraft (she was the wife of Godwin, the minor radical philosopher, and Shelley's mother-in-law) took a hint from Tom Paine and published *A Vindication of the Rights of Women*. Her tract shocked the conventional by its frankness and its demand for education for women to put them on a par with men. The first Chartist programme offered women the vote, but most 'respectable' early Victorian society swept the problem of female emancipation under its arch mat. Then, while the cause of adult suffrage was uppermost in everyone's minds after the Reform League Riots in Hyde Park in 1866 (page 147), Mill moved an amendment to the Bill which was introduced into Parliament in the following year. This would have extended to women the same franchise that the Bill proposed for men; but the amendment was defeated, and in Manchester the first of numerous Women's Suffrage Societies was founded. Elizabeth Fry, Florence

Nightingale, George Eliot, the Brontës and others, meanwhile, had established their reputations. In 1869 Mill published his book, *The Subjection of Women*; and in the same year a public meeting in favour of women's suffrage was held in London with a distinguished body of speakers which included Mill, Charles Kingsley, John Morley and Sir Charles Dilke. It also included a 22-year-old girl, Mrs. Fawcett, who was to remain at the heart of the movement until final success was attained – she lived until 1929. These unlady-like activities, however, outraged Queen Victoria, who complained of the 'mad, wicked folly of women's rights, with all its attendant horrors, on which her poor feeble sex is bent'. But the Queen worried unnecessarily. The calm, high-principled talk of women's suffrage got nowhere during her life-time. The cause only began to gather momentum after Richard Pankhurst, a Manchester lawyer, Fabian, and member of the Independent Labour Party, died in 1898, leaving a frail widow and four children.

Mrs. Pankhurst and her daughters Christabel (a law student) and Sylvia (an art student) formed the Women's Social and Political Union in 1903. Its militancy was soon evident: in 1905 Christabel was arrested following an election meeting at which Winston Churchill was the candidate. She was fined, refused to pay, and went to prison. Churchill, refusing 'to be henpecked on a subject of such grave importance', magnanimously called at Strangeways Prison to pay the fine, but the offer was declined. After that the militancy of the movement increased. The Pank-hursts, joined by Mrs. Pethick Lawrence, having knocked at the doors of each of the political parties in vain, resolved on the programme of direct, extra-Parliamentary action for which Christabel's imprisonment had provided a fitting overture. Soon their movement had eclipsed Mrs. Fawcett's moderate National Union of Women's Suffrage Societies, and in contrast to her milder suffragists their supporters were being known as suffra-gettes. From that time the nation was offered the spectacle of rival pressure groups pursuing identical ends, the one contemptuous of the State and resolved to break the law to draw attention to its demands, the other committed to constitutional remedies. The suffragettes were claiming, in effect, that because the ordinary democratic processes were denied to them since no Party would take up their case, they had no alternative to direct action; the suffragists replied that direct action would so outrage public opinion as to jeopardise even further the prospect of ultimate success. In the clamour of these contending voices we hear the shrill notes of the restless new century drowning, for a time, the more sober counsels of the old.

Our concern here is not with the manner in which Mrs. Fawcett and her colleagues (they included such distinguished women as Elizabeth Garrett Anderson, Maude Royden and Eleanor Rathbone) patiently cultivated public opinion, but with the Pankhursts' resort to illegality. Certainly they were provoked. They were constantly teased by glimpses of success, as Parliament time and again trifled with, and then hastily dropped, proposals for women's suffrage. (But they did not, or would not, understand that no Liberal Government would risk its political life by supporting a measure that – unless it was accompanied by *universal* adult suffrage, which would have involved the abolition of any property qualification – was likely to work in favour of the Tories.) They demonstrated outside Parliament, clashed with the police, and gloried in hysterical loyalty to one another in the gloom of the Black Maria and the miseries of Holloway Prison. They chained themselves to railings in Downing Street and harried leading politicians. Churchill was pursued by a woman with a muffin bell who sought to drown his speeches, and Asquith was hailed as the Murderer of Featherstone. One of the last prosecutions for the old common law offence of unlawful assembly took place in 1908, when a suffragette was jailed for six weeks. By 1909 the prisoners in Holloway were copying from Tsarist labour camps the weapon of the hunger strike, and the prison authorities replied with forcible feeding.

The suffragettes' campaign was now, however, beginning to make an impression on Parliament; and in 1910 the Government introduced a Women's Suffrage Bill. But a cruel disappointment was in store. In the Autumn Parliament was dissolved, following the quarrel with the House of Lords, and the suffragettes, loved by few politicians, felt cheated by all. Their 'Black Friday' came on 18th November, in a severe clash with the police in Parliament Square. Innumerable complaints followed, alleging that women had had their hair pulled and their clothes half torn off, and that policemen had punched, kicked and pinched the demonstrators in tender places. Churchill robustly defended the police in Parliament against this 'copious fountain of mendacity'.

The situation continued to deteriorate. In 1911 the women stepped-up the scale of organised violence, and when arrested treated the courts with the same contempt with which they viewed any organ of state, merely exploiting them as public platforms. They did not, however, follow the *Daily Herald*'s advice to carry non-co-operation to the point of forming a Guild of Honour of women who undertook to bear no children till the vote was won. On the contrary, they kept as close a hold on reality as had the Luddites. 'The argument of the stone', declared Mrs. Pankhurst, was 'the time-honoured, official, political argument'. Obedient bands of women systematically smashed shop windows in the West End of London and in Downing Street. The Pankhursts were again imprisoned, but by their fresh violence they had forfeited much public sympathy. 'They led their little army with brilliance,' writes Roger Fulford in his book *Votes for Women*, 'but they led it to disaster'; for (in Ensor's words) had militancy 'not been persisted in, some kind of Women's Suffrage Bill would probably have passed the Commons between 1909 and 1914'.[7] The prospects of this, however, were now bleak.

Shedding all restraining influence the Pankhursts moved on from the stone-throwing of 1912 to a campaign of personal violence and carefully planned arson in 1913. The contents of pillar boxes were fired with rags soaked in paraffin, and houses and churches were burned. When the prospect of another Suffrage Bill was lost early in 1913 the violence reached its peak in a final outburst of neo-Luddism. Plant houses at Kew were smashed, railway stations and hotels were burned down, and a house under construction for Lloyd George was damaged by bombs; for this last offence Mrs. Pankhurst was sentenced to three years' imprisonment. For a speech inciting the women to violence Lansbury was bound over in the sum of £1,000, with two sureties of £500, and in default to be imprisoned for three months; he refused to enter into the order, and was jailed. The technique of the hunger strike was now commonplace, and Parliament replied by passing the so-called Cat and Mouse Act, which enabled the Home Secretary to release a prisoner whose health was suffering from starvation and to have her re-arrested when she had recovered. Sylvia Pankhurst hit back by having herself paraded in public on a stretcher, so stirring up fresh hatred among the faithful. Emily Davison flung herself under a horse on Derby Day and gave the movement its martyr. In the following March (1914) Mary Richardson slashed Velasquez's *Rokeby Venus* in the National Gallery, with the startling claim that she had 'tried to destroy the picture of the most beautiful woman in mythological history because the Government are destroying Mrs. Pankhurst, the most beautiful character in modern history'. Soon afterwards hoards of women attacked Buckingham Palace, but the time for domestic squabbles was fast running out. A few weeks later the Germans attacked Belgium and sex war, class war, Irish troubles, even Mrs. Fawcett's quiet game of patience, were rudely interrupted. All domestic violence was dwarfed by the fresh danger that menaced and unified the whole nation. The Pankhursts, set free from prison for the last time, devoted themselves to addressing recruiting meetings, and when the war was over the vote was theirs

6: The Conquest

The soldiers who streamed home to a land fit for heroes to live in from a war to end war commemorated their victory with fresh violence.

The first year of peace, 1919, saw a revival of the industrial strife that had threatened to engulf the Government in 1914. Returning soldiers rioted, impatient for demobilisation. Railwaymen came out on strike. In Glasgow William Gallacher, afterwards a leading communist, fought in savage battles against the police during a strike of engineers; so did a later Minister of Defence, Emanuel Shinwell. An impoverished nation, its economy disrupted, was suffering the strains that had afflicted Britain after the final defeat of Napoleon. And if a grand finale to collective violence in Britain is sought, riots in Liverpool in August 1919 conveniently provide one. An orgy of violence in the classic style swept over the city. For the last time soldiers were called out. The Riot Act was read for the last time. The last rioter was killed by a soldier's bullet. It was all of a piece with that climacteric year, the last great fling of violence in this country: 1919.

It would, of course, be absurd to point to a single year when collective violence was eliminated from our society, or even reduced to acceptable limits. The fact is, however, that the half century after 1919 has been a relatively tranquil period (like that which followed 1850); and it is in this half century that we have to seek out events, or attitudes, that mark the transition from a turbulent society to a peaceable one. Pre-eminent among these events is the General Strike of 1926, to which we come later. Our first concern, however, must be with a police strike in 1918 which directly helped to create the only conditions on which a General Strike could have been undertaken, and handled, without violence: a contented police force, in harmony with the strikers, yet respected as a neutral body within the state.

The loyalty of the police had generally been taken for granted, although a couple of minor strikes in the Metropolitan Police (in 1872 and 1890) had put the authorities on warning that all was not well. To men who complained of long hours, poor pay, harsh discipline and no weekly rest-day the language of militant trade unionism had had an insidious appeal. The strike of 1872 had been principally over the demand for 'the right to confer' about their grievances. This was prominent again in the strike of 1890, but now more general conditions of service were also in issue. To restore order in Bow Street on that occasion the authorities had to call in the Life Guards. In the years immediately before the First World War the demand for 'the right to confer' (which meant the right to combine in a trade union) was still being refused by a Government which, as we recalled in the previous chapter, was embroiled in troubles enough with insurrectionary strikes incited by the syndicalist teaching of Sorel and Mann. It was the worst possible time, in the Government's view, to run risks with the loyalty of the police.

To policemen this attitude seemed unfair. They could not accept that they should be excluded from the benefits of collective bargaining; and in 1913 an ex-chief inspector named Syme (a man soured by injustice and already set on a successful career of martyrdom) started a clandestine Police Union, which men joined at the risk of dismissal. During the war their discontent grew. Rising prices soared beyond the reach of police pay, and by 1918 the Police Union was attracting wide support. Late in August of that year a policeman was dismissed for taking part in union activities. The Union replied with an ultimatum demanding the man's reinstatement, a pay rise, and its own recognition. These demands were backed by the threat of strike action if they were not conceded within forty-eight hours. The Government made no response; and by noon on Friday, 30th August, some 6,000 Metropolitan policemen came out on strike. By the evening the strike was virtually total.

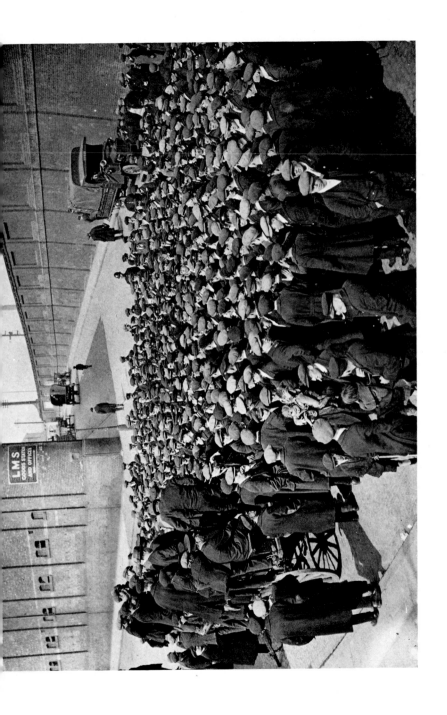

The General Strike, 1926. A mass meeting of strikers in progress

The General Strike, 1926. Police escort buses as a soldier looks on.
(The military were generally kept in the background during the strike)

The war was at a critical stage, and the Government's eyes were focused on events in France. Lloyd George quickly turned his attention to the new danger at home. With most of the army abroad the nation could not tolerate a strike of police; yet to permit them to form a trade union would compromise their impartiality in industrial disputes. Freshly in mind, the writing on the wall still wet with the blood of the slaughtered ruling classes, were the lessons of the Russian Revolution: a police trade union, perhaps followed by an army trade union, could pave the way to Bolshevism in Britain. The Prime Minister, pondering the situation, had riflemen posted to guard buildings in Whitehall, and a machine gun was placed in the Foreign Office quadrangle. These instinctive steps, however, solved nothing. Lloyd George instructed General Smuts, in the Home Secretary's absence from London on holiday, to find a formula for peace. But Smuts failed, as he was bound to have done, since the men's representatives refused to talk to him except as a union, and he refused to talk to them except as policemen.

That night London was almost as defenceless as during the Gordon Riots, but there were no reports of looting. The absence of many young Londoners away fighting in France probably had something to do with this. The morning newspapers brought a chorus of sympathy for the strikers, and Lloyd George agreed to meet the men's representatives at Downing Street at midday. People stared in astonishment as orderly columns of marching policemen converged on Westminster from all parts of London, all in the greatest good humour. Downing Street was packed while the parley went on. Eventually the strike leaders emerged triumphant. The Prime Minister had offered them a substantial pay rise, and the dismissed man was to be reinstated; but he insisted that no union could be recognised in war-time. He undertook, however, to set up representative machinery for the Metropolitan Police.

The men were jubilant and the strike was called off. But soon jubilation gave way to anger. The Commissioner was made the scapegoat for the strike, and was obliged to follow some of his nineteenth-century predecessors into hasty and undignified retirement. In his place the Government brought in General Sir Charles Macready, Churchill's right-hand man at Tonypandy.

Macready, like Warren before him, set out to give the Force a taste of military leadership. He clashed with the leaders of the banned Police Union, and they in turn fell out with the Home Secretary, claiming that Lloyd George had tricked them: in refusing to allow a union in war-time, the men argued, the Prime Minister had implied that one would be recognised when the war was over. The Government, however, stood firm, believing, probably correctly, that a manœuvre was on foot by organised labour to secure control of the police in a way that would encourage their sympathy in industrial disputes.

The quarrel came to a head in the Summer of 1919; and now it is instructive to compare the course of events in Britain with those in Boston, Massachusetts, where an identical situation was developing at the same time, and for the same reasons. The pay of the American police had also failed to preserve for them a pre-war standard of living, their hours were long, and discipline was ill-administered; so they, too, created a clandestine union to represent their interests. Like the British Police Union it was banned.

In Britain the explosion came at the beginning of August, in America in September; but in Britain it came as no surprise. The Government had forestalled major trouble. In March they had set up an enquiry (the Desborough Committee) to carry out an urgent review of the conditions of service of the police. The enquiry reported in May, and the Home Secretary announced his acceptance of its principal recommendations: police pay was to be greatly increased, and the police were to be given special machinery for making collective representations. They were, however, forbidden to belong to a trade union or to come out on strike. A Bill to give effect to these changes was brought into Parliament early in July, and the militants in the Police Union whipped up support for a second strike in the hope of preventing the Bill from becoming law. They appealed again to Lloyd George, but, preoccupied with the peace negotiations, he declined to intervene; so did the Labour leaders. Encouraged, however, by half-hearted promises of support from other unions, the Police Union called its second strike on 31st July. It was a tragic error, and most policemen knew it. Out of a force of 70,000 only 2,300 responded to the call – rather more than 1,000 in London, 950 in Liverpool, and small contingents in four other towns. Within twenty-four hours the strike was virtually over in London. Liverpool, however, suffered two days and nights of rioting on a scale that recalls, at times, the horrors of the Gordon Riots.

Memories of 'Bloody Sunday' in August 1911 still lived on in Liverpool eight years later. The population in the dock areas hated the police, they were prone to violence, and they remained under the spell of the heady, revolutionary talk of Tom Mann. No union man was going to show solidarity with the enemy when rumours circulated that the police were coming out. This antagonism was mutual. The morale of the police was low and their leadership weak. By the evening of Friday, 31st July half the Force was out on strike. That night rowdyism broke out on a small scale, for as yet the extent of the police withdrawal had not been realised; but it soon was. On the following morning, Saturday, the Lord Mayor appealed for special constables to come forward and he begged the Home Secretary for troops. But were even soldiers adequate to protect a city with a reputation for violence so notorious as Liverpool's? The Lord Mayor was an imaginative man. Perhaps, also, he remembered what had happened to the Lord Mayor of Bristol in 1831. At all events, he persuaded the Home Office to call on the Navy, and that night the battleship *Valiant*, mounting fifteen-inch guns, sailed from Scapa Flow to Merseyside, accompanied by two destroyers.

The Lord Mayor had not under-estimated the capacity of his fellow citizens for violence, once they realised the extent of the police strike. When darkness fell Liverpool was guarded by only half its police force, some special constables and about 900 soldiers. The soldiers, however, were kept out of sight in order not to provoke trouble. This, of course, was the normal practice; but a policy of parading the minimum show of force, effective in dealing with responsible demonstrators, had the opposite effect in dealing with the half-starved crowds who now swarmed into the streets to loot Liverpool. The mob, like the London mob during the final stage of the Gordon Riots, were out to get their own back after years of squalor and misery. 'Gangs of twenty and thirty men rushed out of the pubs, sweeping the police out of their path', write Mr. G. W. Reynolds and Mr. Anthony Judge in their book *The Night the police went on strike*. 'Men who had already smashed their way into the shops tossed out goods to others waiting outside. Soon they were joined by the women and children, many pushing handcarts to wheel away their plunder. . . . By midnight, London Road was a seething mass of drunken, rampaging humanity. Women fought frenzied battles with each other over every scrap of clothing they could lay hands on.'[1] The soldiers swept in with fixed bayonets, an armoured car arrived, and, for what seems to have been the last time in Britain, a magistrate read the Riot Act.

Terrible scenes of havoc greeted Liverpool's shopkeepers on the Sunday morning, but worse lay ahead. Fortified by sessions of lunch-time drinking, after the pubs had opened, the mob resumed their business in the afternoon. Faithful to the pattern of the Gordon Rioters, they smashed their way into liquor stores (drinking whisky this time though, not gin); and it was during a drunken brawl that a rioter was shot dead – evidently by a stray bullet, since the soldiers were shooting in the air to drive the mob back. So grave was the outlook that Tom Mann himself appealed for people to help the thin force of police who still remained loyal. He failed, however, and more troops were rushed into the city. Four tanks took up threatening positions in front of St. George's Hall. But Sunday night saw a repetition of Saturday's orgy. Battles between rioters and soldiers, police and specials raged throughout the night. The mob flung stones, the police repeatedly charged with batons, and the soldiers used their rifle butts, firing warning volleys into the air. Casualties were heavy, and the damage to looted property severe. But then, on the Monday, it rained, and the rioters had had enough. When the *Valiant* arrived with her escorting destroyers Liverpool was settling down to count the cost. It fell most heavily on the striking policemen, none of whom was ever reinstated.

Events in Boston followed a similar course a few weeks later, but on a grander scale. In August the Police Commissioner told the leaders of the banned Boston Police Union that they were to be charged with insubordination. The Mayor set up a committee, hoping to mediate, and early in September it proposed a compromise so like the British arrangements that the Mayor must surely have studied them. The Police Union was to be disbanded, but no action was to be taken against its leaders; a 'private' union was to be permitted; and an enquiry was to be set up into the conditions of service of the police. But the Police Commissioner was subject to state, not local, control. He refused to entertain the Mayor's proposals; and on 8th September he dismissed nineteen men for joining the Union. The reply was a threat of strike action unless the Commissioner was himself dismissed. In the upshot more than 1,000 out of the city's force of 1,500 policemen came out on strike on Wednesday, 9th September; and that night, *The Times* reported, 'a gang of hooligans roamed through the streets of the city, smashing shop windows and looting their contents'. The Mayor, like the Mayor of Liverpool, appealed to the population, and a force of some 600 emergency police, mostly Harvard undergraduates, was formed the same day. They were, however, powerless against the violence that now swept the city, and on the following day the State Governor, Calvin Coolidge, sent in 5,000 soldiers with words that sped him on his way to the White House not long afterwards: there was 'no right to strike against the public safety by anyone, anywhere, any time'.

To describe the riots that followed during the next three days would be tedious. The soldiers brought machine guns and light artillery, and the cavalry charged with drawn swords. The mob broke into the city's liquor stores. The casualties totalled seven killed and fifty injured. It was the battle of Liverpool again, but larger than English life. It was also different in another way: to Americans the riots represented something more sinister than a mere outbreak of mob violence. They were a threat to the American way of life. 'The attempt to overthrow Americanism here is doomed to failure', declared the *Boston Transcript* on 9th September. 'Behind Boston in this skirmish with Bolshevism stands Massachusetts and behind Massachusetts stands America.' The national newspapers were soon writing of Boston's gallant stand against 'Red Dictatorship', and President Wilson interrupted a whistle-stop tour selling the Versailles Treaty by pronouncing the riots to be a 'crime against civilisation'.

The important point to note about the American and British experiences at this time is not the similarity of events, which is interesting rather than surprising, but their different consequences. President Wilson issued a message from the White House declaring that 'any organisation of the police forces of the country for the purposes of bringing pressure to bear on the public should not be countenanced or permitted'. This view was widely shared; but the police were left with a legacy of bitterness and frustration, and for three months Boston was patrolled by soldiers. Some Americans today are critical of the failure ever since that time to advance significantly beyond President Wilson's attitude towards collective machinery for the police to represent their grievances, and would regard its continued absence as a serious weakness in the arrangements for maintaining order. In Britain, meanwhile, the Police Bill against which the strike of 1919 was directed became law. It set up a Police Federation to which all policemen up to the rank of chief inspector automatically belong, and this has for many years been a nationally respected body which enjoys all the advantages of a trade union except the right to call its members out on strike or to affiliate with other unions. These arrangements have fostered the contentment and goodwill of our police for half a century. They paid immense dividends at the time of the General Strike seven years later; and they must be seen as marking an important step in the conquest of violence in Britain. It was part of the way in which the nation has come to terms with its police, an expression of confidence in their maturity.

A Government which had publicly expressed its confidence in the police was able to face the remaining two years of post-war industrial unrest with resolution. It could also afford to adopt unprovocative attitudes, for much of the militancy of the pre-war period had been drained away in the Flanders' mud. What was left of Mann's syndicalism had been caught up in the more strident call of communism, but few in England heeded Marx's materialist utopia. The spirit of the new age was one of characteristic moderation, with a reversion to something like that apathy which we observed among the working classes in the England of the seventeenth and early eighteenth centuries, and again after the collapse of Chartism. The fact that three-quarters of a million young men had been killed in the war may also have affected the situation.

This moderation was once more matched by a corresponding restraint by the Government. When the railwaymen called a strike in September 1919 they won little sympathy from other trade unions, but neither were they greeted with the militant response that Churchill had offered in 1911. This time the authorities calmly assumed that the strikers would behave peaceably, and they did. This time the soldiers were not given general marching orders, as in 1911; and this time there was virtually no disorder. The Government insisted that the greatest possible use should be made of special constables, and that chief constables were not to apply for military aid except in cases of real need. There were scarcely any applications.

This second railway strike, in 1919, led to important changes in the means of preserving order. Both it and the strike of 1911 served to remind the nation how dependent it now was on swift transport to carry perishable foodstuffs from one area to another. A railway strike could imperil the basic means of civilised life. Awareness of this, coupled with the not unsuccessful experience, during the war, of confiding in the Government the powers provided by the Defence of the Realm Act, explain why fresh legislation came before Parliament in 1920. The object was to make available permanently the flexible powers that a modern state needs to deal with an 'emergency' – the current euphemism for widespread strikes, disorders or (in the nineteenth-century jargon) disturbances. This object was achieved by the Emergency Powers Act, 1920. It enables the Home Secretary, once a Royal Proclamation has been made declaring a state of emergency to exist, to make regulations to secure the essentials of life for the community. These deal with the supply of food, transport, and other necessaries of modern life, as well as with the preservation of public order. The regulations have to be laid before Parliament, and after one month both they and the Proclamation lapse, unless renewed.

'By the Emergency Powers Act', claims Mr. A. J. P. Taylor, Lloyd George 'made permanent the dictatorial powers which the Government had possessed in war-time under the Defence of the Realm Acts – as big a blow against the traditional constitution as any ever levelled.' This seems an extreme view. The Act has repeatedly proved its value since 1920, and is employed in modern times. It has rarely been criticised. It enables the minimum powers to be granted to the authorities for a minimum time, and the grant of these powers is subject to Parliamentary approval. The passing of the Act marks a clear step in the centralisation of the means of dealing with disorder – should an 'emergency' lead to it. This step was logical. When Churchill took the requisitioning of troops out of the hands of magistrates in 1911 he was restoring the situation to what it had been before about 1740. Until then as we have seen the Privy Council, still influenced by the libertarian spirit of 1688, reserved all troop movements to themselves. Subsequently, for a period of about 170 years, the local magistrates were free to call upon troops within their own jurisdiction, although the Home Secretary authorised troop movements on a wider scale. In theory the magistrates still possess this power to call on military aid, just as they may call on any citizen to help to suppress disorder. In practice, nowadays, a call from a magistrate for soldiers would be considered by the Government under arrangements embodied in the Queen's Regulations for the Army. Thus while the primary means of dealing with disorder, the police, remain local, the arrangements for co-ordinating action to deal with widespread emergencies are central. We need not look for sinister designs behind the Emergency Powers Act.

The new arrangements were tested within twelve months. During the war the mines had been controlled by the Government, and on their return to private ownership the owners imposed severe wage cuts. Early in 1921 the miners threatened to come out on strike against the cuts. Coal was then the nation's principal fuel, and a prolonged strike could rapidly bring industry to a halt. The miners', moreover, was the strongest trade union. There is no need here to enter into the complex negotiations that followed the threat, but when the Triple Alliance of pre-war days began to talk of sympathetic strikes by railwaymen and transport workers also, the Government put the Emergency Powers Act into operation. The regulations included a temporary power to prohibit meetings or processions. The threat to public order, however, failed to materialise. The other unions backed out, an act whose shameful nature in the eyes of loyal trade unionists has caused 15th April 1921 to be dubbed 'Black Friday'. Subsequent distress during the three months of the strike (when apart from the strikers one-sixth of the insured population were unemployed) was acute, but disorder was virtually unknown. The miners were eventually compelled to return to work on the owners' terms.

Three years after the last Chartist petition Albert the Good staged his Great Exhibition to a nation on the threshold of a long period of public tranquillity. Three years after the industrial upheavals of 1921 his grandson opened an even grander Empire Exhibition at Wembley that flaunted Britain's imperial majesty for the last time before the curtain fell. Each, in its way, demonstrated the nation's stability and powers of quick recovery from strife. That stability was put to its greatest test two years later.

When the French reoccupied the Ruhr in 1923, exports of coal from Britain boomed, prices rose, and in 1924 the miners' wages went up too. But the conditions were freak. A year later the boom was over; exports of coal dropped, prices fell, and the miners were being asked to accept wage cuts. Interminable negotiations dragged on between the leaders of the miners' union and the owners, with the Government trying to see fair play. The miners, disappointed by the inability of the first Labour Government to help them, were in a mood for direct action; but they were sorely tried by their leaders. Their chairman, A. J. Cook, was an ardent communist, given to haranguing his captive audiences with messianic zeal. Their secretary, Herbert Smith, his ensign the cloth cap stuffed in the jacket pocket, rarely opened his mouth except to mutter 'Nowt doin'. However, Lord Birkenhead (F. E. Smith) said of the miners' leaders, 'I should call them the stupidest men in England if I had not previously had to do with the owners.'

In the Summer of 1925 the Prime Minister, Baldwin, had to deal with both. Faced by a difficult economic situation he declared that 'all the workers of this country have got to take reductions in wages in order to help put industry on its feet'. The colliery owners responded with zest; the miners, predictably, threatened to strike. The Government bought nine months' time by granting a temporary subsidy to the industry and setting up a Royal Commission. The delay also enabled emergency measures to be prepared, and when the Commission reported, in March 1926, contingency planning was well advanced; the Government was thus more favourably placed to deal with a General Strike than were the trade unions to co-ordinate one. For several weeks the report of the Commission (it offered cuts today in return for jam tomorrow) was debated endlessly – though whether the intransigence of the owners, coupled with Smith's 'Nowt doin' and Cook's militant 'Not a penny off the pay, not a minute on the day', can be called debate is open to question. Deadlock persisted; and amid muddle and misunderstanding a national strike was called for 3rd May. The Triple Alliance lumbered into reluctant action. The railwaymen and transport workers joined the miners, and other unions undertook to call their men out as a second reserve.

There is no need here to review the day to day progress of the strike. We must, however, examine the attitudes of both sides involved in it if we are to understand why, in the event, fears of a national catastrophe proved to be unfounded.

Possibly the outstanding feature of the General Strike was its display of national self-discipline. Among the strikers the response was almost total. To a man they were loyal to a cause, and scarcely any returned to work until the strike was over. Mr. A. J. P. Taylor has well described their action as follows –

> These were the very men who had rallied to the defence of Belgium in 1914. The voluntary recruitment of the First World War and the strike of 1926 were acts of spontaneous generosity, without parallel in any other country. The first was whipped on by almost every organ of public opinion; the second was undertaken despite their disapproval. Such nobility deserves more than a passing tribute. The strikers asked nothing for themselves. They did not seek to challenge the Government, still less to overthrow the constitution. They merely wanted the miners to have a living wage. Perhaps not even that. They were loyal to their unions and to their leaders, as they had been loyal during the war to their country and to their generals. They went once more into the trenches, without enthusiasm, and with little hope.[2]

The response to the Government's call for volunteers was equally remarkable. They flocked to recruiting centres in their tens of thousands. Employers urged their young men to help. Undergraduates, like the Harvard men who had lent a hand at the time of the Boston police strike, dropped their studies with relief and enrolled as special constables, tram drivers, lorry drivers, and in countless other jobs. Even old people and the middle-aged signed on for emergency work. Everywhere there was great good humour, and to those who struggled to get to their ordinary work in the chaos of a transport strike, the whole thing, as Mr. Julian Symons puts it in his book *The General Strike*, 'was undeniably a lark'.

The extraordinary solidarity with which both strikers and other citizens responded to their respective calls can only be explained by the fact that each side believed deeply in the issues at stake. The light-hearted mood induced by a break from routine ought not to blind us to this. For the strikers, the struggle was a desperate gamble: a demand for justice and a fair wage, a resumption, almost, of the struggle of the Luddites and the Chartists, but without their violence. It could have been the great revolutionary strike of which the syndicalists had dreamed, but the workers seem never to have regarded it as more than a bread and butter job. Yet it was not wholly reactionary, for it looked forward to a time when workers would participate in their own affairs in a more just democracy. The Government saw it very differently. To them, the strike posed a threat to the constitution itself. For the closest precedent the ruling classes had to look back to the seventeenth century. Duff Cooper (later Lord Norwich) has told us in his book *Old Men Forget* that in articles written at the time he 'insisted that the dispute in the coal industry was no more the real issue during the General Strike than was the levy of ship-money the real issue during the Civil War. On each occasion the issue had been whether the country was to be governed by Parliament or not.'[3] Baldwin, possibly for devious reasons, took the same line. The strike put the country 'nearer to civil war than we have been for centuries past'. An attempt by Sir John Simon, the Attorney General, to declare it illegal, however, got nowhere; and Simon's opinion has subsequently been authoritatively disputed by the distinguished academic lawyer, Professor A. L. Goodhart.

With this lofty conception on both sides of the seriousness of the issues at stake there went a determination to avoid violence. The Strike Committee insisted that, to keep them out of mischief, the strikers should occupy their time in that most typically British manner, playing organised games. An announcement in the strikers' newspaper, the *British Worker*, went –

> The General Council suggests that in all districts where large numbers of workers are idle, sports should be organised and entertainments arranged.
> This will both keep a number of people busy and provide amusement for many more.

What would a Luddite have made of it? Or of the Cardiff Strike Committee's advice: 'Keep smiling. Refuse to be provoked. Get into your garden. Look after the wife and kiddies. If you have not got a garden, get into the country, the parks and playgrounds.'

The good humour was general. Mr. Symons tells us that there was a group in the Cabinet, led by Churchill, who favoured the use of troops to break the strike, with a parade of armoured cars in the big cities. The Government did no such thing, and the army played a negligible part in the strike. From the first the Government relied on the firm discipline of the nation to provide volunteers to keep going the essential services on which the necessaries of life depend. The volunteer workers, sometimes perhaps too high-spirited, shared the prevailing good humour. What if all the windows in trams and buses were smashed? Notices appeared instead – 'I have no pane, dear mother, now'; 'Try our fresh air cure'; 'Keep your bricks please, all windows broken'. It was all a lark, outrageous, comical, and British; and the police were in their element, friends of all, showing astonishing forbearance under provocation. American newspaper correspondents, says Mr. Symons, 'who had come over to report on a revolutionary situation, found strikers playing football matches against the police'. In Plymouth the Chief Constable's wife kicked off in a match which the strikers won by two goals to one. The prudence of the Government in 1919, in insulating the police from trade union activity, is one of the outstanding lessons of the General Strike.

There was a darker side to the picture. Mild as the national leaders of the strike were, they were unable always to control their more militant followers (let alone the hooligans who sometimes joined in) and reports came of disorder in some towns; but these, to quote Mr. Symons again, were merely 'rumblings before a storm that never broke, damped as it was continually by the insistence of trade union leaders that the strikers must offer no provocation, in the form of stone- and brick-throwing. There was a good deal of provocation, but it remained, almost without exception throughout the country, sporadic and unorganised.'[4] Much of this disorder, in fact, seems to have been due not to any intention on the part of the strikers to turn to violence, but to the provocation sometimes offered by special constables.

The specials, it will be recalled, had under an Act of 1831 been available only when sworn in by a magistrate whenever a riot broke out or threatened. This limitation was removed at the beginning of the war in 1914, and sanction was given for special constables to be appointed regardless of the threat of riot. During the industrial disputes after the war the Home Secretary urged chief constables to make full use of specials, as one means of avoiding the need to bring in the military to supplement the regular police, and the idea of constituting them as a permanent reserve gained favour. This became legally permissible as a result of a law passed in 1923, so that at the time of the General Strike a reserve of the special constabulary was immediately available. More were urgently required; and the Home Secretary broadcast an appeal for 'a strong and indeed enormous force' to come forward. A total of some 140,000 were sworn in – more, probably, than at any time since 1848. So great was the demand for truncheons that Scotland Yard had to send to High Wycombe for a lorry load of chair legs. These were fitted with lengths of rope for the use of those not lucky enough to have conventional truncheons.

The newly enrolled special constables, thus equipped with bludgeons, received little training. There was no time for it. Many were young men, with a high proportion of undergraduates, high-spirited, and out for fun. Some seem to have thought that they were there to fight a class war, and behaved accordingly. The strikers are hardly to be blamed for seeing them as representatives of the 'enemy' class – a situation that recalls the charge of the yeomanry at Peterloo, with its sharp lesson of the danger of employing a citizen army against working people. After the shock of Peterloo, the practice had grown up of using the yeomanry away from their home areas; in 1926 contingents of special constables, similarly, were often employed away from their homes so as to reduce the danger of friction. The parallel is not without interest.

It is tempting, too, to press another analogy from much earlier times. The Home Office papers relating to the General Strike are not yet available for study, and it is not known to what extent the Special Branch of police may have contributed to its peaceful outcome by supplying information about the strikers' plans and attitudes. Mr. Symons, however, asserts that some soldiers were sent to the strike areas in plain clothes with instructions to report on 'what these chaps are saying and thinking'. This, if true, provides an intriguing if tenuous link with the great days of English spying, when Generals Maitland and Grey defeated Luddism, and Major-General Sir Charles Napier contributed to the defeat of Chartism, by the wholesale employment of spies and informers. But it must be stressed that in the Britain of 1926 the only significant employment of soldiers was the humdrum one of providing protection for food convoys moving perishable goods from the docks.

From the Government's point of view the strike amply vindicated the Emergency Powers Act of 1920. A Proclamation was declared before ever the first of the strikers came out. England and Wales were divided into ten divisions (there was a separate one for Scotland) under a civil commissioner; most of these were junior ministers. The commissioners had reserve powers in the event of a breakdown of essential supplies, but there was no breakdown. As during many of the earlier 'disturbances' we have already examined, the hub of Government activity during the General Strike was the Home Office: but now a fresh consideration must be taken into account. There was a second national hub of activity, at Eccleston Square, where the opposition set up camp; and in the quality of national leadership exercised from these two centres is to be found yet another reason why the nation survived the General Strike unscathed. The Permanent Under-Secretary of State at the Home Office was Sir John Anderson (afterwards Lord Waverley) who in due course was to be a member of Churchill's war cabinet, and whom the Prime Minister nominated as his successor had he been obliged to step down during the war. A principal leader of the Strike Committee was Ernest Bevin, afterwards to be a colleague of Anderson's in the war cabinet, and a great Foreign Secretary. The contribution made by two such outstanding men towards the peaceable outcome of the General Strike would need a separate study, but there can be no doubt about the value of the qualities of wisdom, common sense and moderation which each brought to bear in calming the situation.

The strike only lasted until 12th May, when the other unions withdrew their support, leaving the coal dispute to drag on until the Autumn. The Emergency Regulations were renewed until December, and then withdrawn. It is arguable that, had so flexible an instrument been invented at the onset of the Industrial Revolution, the nation would have been spared much violence. This, however, is an untenable view, for it overlooks the organic nature of the Government's response in 1926 and the way in which this response, and the conduct of the strikers, was intimately bound with up the structure of society as a whole. The Emergency Regulations must be seen as only a fragment of a total response that drew on centuries of experience and stretched the nation's capacity for self-defence to the limit.

To many of those immediately affected by it, the strike, seen at first as a not altogether unwelcome break from routine or at worst as a tiresome inconvenience, was afterwards generally considered to have brought the country close to the edge of disaster (although whether it really did so is open to doubt, given the strength of the British social fabric). A thankful nation voted the police heroes of the year, and subscribed about a quarter of a million pounds for a National Police Fund which is used for welfare, compassionate and recreational purposes among the police and their families. The instinct was a very proper one. It does not need a cynic to suggest that it was partly motivated by the relief of the propertied classes at finding themselves still alive, their property intact. ('Diana asked me this morning how soon we could with honour leave the country', Duff Cooper noted in his diary on the second day of the strike. 'I said not till the massacres begin.') Nor, on the other hand, does it need a romantic to observe how, in making this gesture of goodwill towards the police, a mature society was publicly recognising the primacy of order in communal life. Neither the centuries of turmoil, the Civil War, the Industrial Revolution, nor even the sick writers and artists of the nineties had succeeded in eroding the native self-discipline of Anglo-Saxon England.* In what had been

* It has had many assaults on it since 1926 and is under attack at the present time. We may, however, take pride as a nation from the fact that after three policemen were murdered in Shepherd's Bush in 1966 the public once again showed a remarkable and spontaneous sympathy for their police by raising a further great subscription, known as the National Police Dependents Fund.

potentially the most menacing confrontation since the Civil War the nation gave the world an outstanding display of civilised behaviour. Not all the world, however, understood this. Why were not more policemen killed? Raymond Postgate was asked when addressing an audience in Paris soon after the strike was over. Was it not proof of treachery when the General Council issued orders to strikers to play games and cultivate their gardens rather than to go into the streets and fight the police?

These questions, it seems, were still being asked behind the barricades in Paris forty-two years afterwards.

The General Strike did not, of course, mark the end of collective violence in Britain. Renewed unrest came with the economic depression of the thirties, bringing disorder in Manchester, Birkenhead and other towns. It also brought the hunger march into prominence as an instrument of working-class protest. The marchers, behaving with decorum, awakened echoes of the year 1817, with its pitiful, pioneering march of the Blanketeers from Manchester. That dark year was also recalled in another way in 1932, when Tom Mann and others were bound over for inciting hunger marchers to take part in a demonstration near Parliament before presenting a petition: the binding-over order was made under the Seditious Meetings Act of 1817. New wine could be poured into old statutes, but new laws to deal with public order were also needed to contain two wilder political currents of the time and prevent them from spilling over into violence. These currents, for the most part running counter to one another in their aims and methods, each led to a change in the law relating to the public peace; and in each case the effect was to shift the balance a little towards order, and away from liberty.

The first change in the law concerned Pitt's elderly Incitement to Mutiny Act of 1797, and this must be seen as a reaction to the activities of communists in this country. (A Communist Party had been founded in 1920, but its appeal had never been popular.) Pitt's Act, it will be recalled, had been resurrected after one hundred years in order to prosecute Tom Mann and his co-authors of the pamphlet published in 1912 which admonished soldiers not to shoot against workers. Early post-war Governments had been impressed by the Act's usefulness as a weapon against communists. It proved, however, a more deadly weapon against Ramsay

MacDonald. The decision of his Attorney General, alleged to have been dictated by political expediency, to withdraw proceedings under the Act against a man named Campbell caused the first Labour Government's downfall. In the following year Baldwin did better, when twelve leading communists (they included Campbell) were convicted under the Act and sentenced to imprisonment. Two further prosecutions occurred in 1931 and 1933, but by this time the Government were preparing a more flexible Bill to deal with sedition.

This measure, which became the Incitement to Disaffection Act, 1934, outraged many. Mr. David Williams, in his recent book, *Keeping the Peace*, recalls that the *New Statesman* greeted it as 'the most insidious attack on the freedom of printing and speech that any British Government has planned since the days of Pitt and Dundas'. This view proved to be exaggerated. Only one prosecution seems to have been undertaken under the Act; and now, to quote Mr. Williams again, it 'lies a little forlorn on the statute-book', and was probably, after all, not much more than 'a convenient focusing point for all the doubts and suspicions of a bitter and frustrated period'.[5] Pitt's Act, meanwhile, has never been repealed.

However, if the Sedition Act of 1934 is regarded as no more than a minimal encroachment on liberty, the same cannot be said of the Public Order Act that joined it on the statute-book two years later. This was the Government's response to the activities of Sir Oswald Mosley and his followers, who saw fit to revive the medieval practice of parading through the streets of London in quasi-military array. So bizarre a situation was not to be tolerated, especially when it appeared that the fascists were employing the tactics of intimidation and violence against their opponents. The Government felt obliged to seek additional powers to strengthen the law. Livery statutes had been enacted during the Wars of the Roses to stop the growth of private armies, the Home Secretary reminded the House of Commons. Now, five hundred years afterwards, the lessons of contemporary Germany were plain for all to see: Britain was not prepared to licence armies of disciplined thugs who flaunted an open threat to a system of parliamentary democracy that had been so painfully won after so long a struggle. The Public Order Act, 1936, declared it illegal to wear a political

o

uniform of any sort in public, and it banned quasi-military organisations. These measures went a long way towards stamping out fascism in this country.

A nation aghast at events in Germany could accept such restrictions on private liberty at home without fuss. More controversial, however, was a provision in the Public Order Act which takes us back, in some ways, to the legal jungle that had tripped up so many during the years of the great and lesser struggles against violence a century earlier. A thorny point then, it will be recalled, concerned the right of a magistrate to ban a meeting or procession altogether, and not a few riots had occurred over the purported exercise of this right, and its subsequent defiance. Nevertheless, the right of public procession had reached its apogee in 1882 after the test case involving the Salvation Army (page 160); and to working-class movements it had been a valuable instrument of protest – for the hunger marchers, their chief weapon of publicity. In this respect the Act of 1936 put the clock back. It enabled the police, when they had reasonable ground for thinking that a procession might lead to disorder, to impose conditions on the organisers, for example as to the route which the procession should follow. But the Act went further than this. It allowed the police to apply to the local council for an order banning a public procession altogether in a designated area, and the ban could last up to three months. The order, however, was not valid unless it was also approved by the Home Secretary – an interesting balance of local and central responsibilities that, written out in statutory form, can be seen to be much the same as it was *de facto* at the time of Peterloo. (In London the order is made by the Commissioner of Police with the Home Secretary's approval; the exclusion of the magistracy from the arrangements is significant.)

This Act, as has been said, stole from liberty what it gave to order. It is right to be apprehensive about measures of this kind but it is easy to be over-critical. Viewed as a whole, in its historical context, the Act can be seen to have been faithful to a very ancient principle of law in this country. Sir Frank Newsam, a former Permanent Under-Secretary of State at the Home Office, cites it in illustration of a problem with which we have been concerned throughout this book. 'Legitimate agitation must not be allowed to degenerate into violence', he writes in his book *The Home*

Office; 'but if the law has to be strengthened it must be strengthened no more than circumstances require.' The Public Order Act, the author points out, 'made it possible to curb those activities that were most likely to cause disturbance, without depriving anyone of the right to express his opinion in public'.[6]

There has been violence in our public life in recent times, but by the standards of the past its scale has been inconsiderable. Protest movements have learned to exploit the techniques of non-violence – the march, the mass demonstration, the sit-down, sit-in, civil disobedience, and to some extent the organs of mass propaganda. A study of these forms of protest would carry us far beyond the bounds of an exploration of violence in our society. For the present it may, perhaps, be accepted that half a century after the last conspicuously violent year in Britain, 1919, collective violence has been as nearly eliminated from our society as our native ingenuity could contrive. And the price paid in curtailing individual liberty has been infinitesimal.

7: Luck or Judgment?

There is, no doubt, both luck and judgment in our experience in dealing with collective violence, and in gathering the threads together we may try to strike a balance between them, reviewing briefly the main elements that have influenced the pattern of violence in our society: the national character, the attitudes of Governments and protesters, the nature of our police, and the working of the law and the processes of justice. Pre-eminent among them, and thoroughly diffused through all, is that most elusive element, the national character.

For a portrait of ourselves we have to look to others; and in his book *The Character of Peoples*, Mr. André Siegfried, a Frenchman, has obligingly provided one. He observes generously that the English 'have exercised a decisive effect on the world and contributed as much as, if not more than, anyone else to the development of Western civilisation'. We are ungregarious, but possess a highly developed sense of civic duty: 'You can get the most out of an Englishman by appealing to his sense of duty; where a Latin is concerned you must appeal to his self-respect.' Our outstanding achievement is in applying this sense of duty in political organisation. 'England has solved problems that have puzzled all other countries. She has taught us – and proved her lesson by practical example – that one can obey the laws of the land without sacrificing one's dignity; that liberty does not necessarily mean licence or authority tyranny.'[1]*

* We also have a passion for playing with balls, we are deeply influenced by our climate and by nature, we are liberals, love animals more than our fellow men, and have produced in the concepts of fair play and the English Gentle-

This streak of national self-discipline has been constantly observed throughout this book. We first saw it at work in the Saxon tythings and noted how the principle of self-policing survived, in the institutions of the parish constabulary and militia, until the last century. In the magistracy, that great bulwark of law and order for six centuries, we retain this link with early times; the majority of offenders against public order are still dealt with by lay magistrates' courts. The Special Constabulary represents another link with earlier times, and the law of the land still requires every citizen to respond to the call of a magistrate or constable to aid in suppressing disorder. For upwards of one thousand years the whole nation has been involved more or less closely in the arrangements for maintaining the peace. It is only relatively recently, with the growth of professional police forces, that this involvement has been weakened. The attempt to strengthen it during the General Strike by the enrolment of large numbers of special constables was not altogether successful.

We have been lucky, in developing this responsible attitude towards the obligations of citizenship as well as its rights, in being spared the upheaval of foreign invasion. Our evolving society has often benefited from the influences of waves of immigrants; but it has not, for nine hundred years, been subordinated to them. The nation has grown up harmoniously in its exquisite English countryside, and even when the industrial blight came its fabric was strong enough to resist strains that sent continental governments tottering. In England the art-form of the demand for *liberté, egalité, fraternité* was the carefully weighed-out sermon in the Methodist chapel and the grim-faced group muttering away in the pub and ordering, for comradeship and relief, another round. It was all quiet, not strident, and there was nothing particularly noble about it. The Luddites and the Chartists did not want to overthrow society any more than had the peasants of 1381, Cade's men, or Cromwell's soldiers. Their violence was almost always discreet in its methods and objects,

man qualities that are uniquely noble. But: 'One Frenchman, an intelligent man; two Frenchmen, a great deal of talk; three Frenchmen, utter disorder. Should we perhaps envy our neighbours on the other side of the Channel? One Englishman, an idiot; two Englishmen, a great deal of sport; three Englishmen, the British Empire.'

and their behaviour restrained. English rebels have mostly been homespun folk. The true English revolution owed little to Marx – we took virtually nothing in return for providing him with a country to breathe freedom in, the facilities of the Reading Room of the British Museum and a few cubic feet in Highgate Cemetery. Our own revolution was achieved by some enlightened working-class leaders aided by the compassion of a few generations of mid and late Victorian gentlemen – reformers who helped the underdogs to come to terms with industrialisation; and the underdogs, in turn, helped each other in the English brand of socialism and trade union activity. 'In their dreams for the future', writes Sir Arthur Bryant, 'the early English socialists sought a gentle Christian paradise after their own kindly middle-class hearts. Morris's *News from Nowhere* published in 1890 is as far removed from Marx's *Capital* as the Gospel of St. John from the Book of Judges.'[2]

If national self-discipline and a late-flowering humanitarianism are allowed as elements in our national character so, too, might be the native love of debate, with its readiness for compromise manifest in the conduct of all the Anglo-Saxon races, and given full rein in the courts leet of medieval England, when the art of local self-government first took root. Is this, perhaps, an ignoble streak that runs through the English character, this refusal to press logic to its limits, the readiness to compromise (even occasionally to compromise principles) in order to meet the other's point of view, reserving violence only for a last resort? In two great Englishmen of our own century, the brothers Chamberlain, we see this trait carried to its limits: Neville, who insisted on flying out for a final parley with Hitler at Bad Godesburg when everything had already been said; and Austen, denouncing logic as a guide to political life with what, to an Englishman, is superior reason –

> I profoundly distrust logic when applied to politics, and all English history justifies me. Why is it that, as contrasted with other nations, ours has been a peaceful and not a violent development? Why is it that, great as have been the changes that have taken place in this country, we have had none of those sudden revolutions and reactions for the last 300 years that have so frequently affected more logically minded nations than ourselves? It is because instinct and experience alike teach us that human

nature is not logical, that it is unwise to treat political institutions as instruments of logic, and that it is in wisely refraining from pressing conclusions to their logical end that the path of peaceful development and true reform is really found. (House of Commons, 24th March 1925.)

The voice of statesmanship of this order was not heard much before Chartist times. Earlier governments were largely indifferent to disorder, and readier to suppress it than to enquire into its causes. From the third decade of the nineteenth century, however, political skill takes on increasing prominence as a means of dealing with protest, with a new readiness to understand the causes of grievance and to remedy them. After trade unions had been made legal in 1824, for example, there was a decline in working-class violence; and in the next decade the Reform Bill agitators and Chartists were neither suppressed nor to any great extent appeased. They were tolerated, and managed (manipulated, some might say) by Governments careful to ensure the loyalty of their soldiers and police.

It is significant that after Peterloo there was no panic and surprisingly little error in the violent confrontations between rulers and ruled during the nineteenth century; but this result is due as much to the moderate character of the protest movements as to the restraint shown by successive Governments. Agitators, too, were refusing to press logic to its limits. Political assassination, not uncommon in America and France, has been unknown in this country since Perceval was shot dead in the lobby of the House of Commons by a madman in 1812. For much of the nineteenth century violence was usually an accident, not a policy. When it was deliberate it was either blind and ignorant (as it had been in the case of the Luddites) or else the restrained outcome of a conflict of deeply cherished principles, as in the case of the riots in Trafalgar Square in 1887, which divided the contenders, in their way, as deeply as society had been divided during the Civil War, for fundamental liberties were again at stake: time and again an order purporting to ban a protest meeting has led to violence, when the Englishmen's passion for free speech has overcome his instinctive regard for order.

The decision not to forbid the protest march on 27th October 1968 has only to be seen against the background of the banned meetings in Coldbath Fields in 1833, the riots in Hyde Park in 1855 and 1866 and those in Trafalgar Square in 1887, for its wisdom to be apparent. It has also to be seen against the background of that most valuable of all lessons for a study of collective violence in Britain, the non-violent General Strike, when the maturing sense of public responsibility of the strikers had matched that of the authorities. Plenty of force was available, with a great deal of law to back it up, but little was used. Intimidation of the strikers was feasible, but it was rejected. Both sides in the encounter 'played the game' according to unwritten rules, as though the standards of Arnold's public schoolboys had permeated all classes. Logical positions, during the General Strike, would undoubtedly have led to violence, just as mutual tolerance was its solvent. The Frenchman who asked Raymond Postgate why the strikers had not gone out into the streets to kill policemen instead of going into the parks to play football with them was, in his way, logical; but it was a logic that few Englishmen could accept. Duff Cooper's summing up needs no comment: 'Happily no grave errors of judgment were made by either side, and the remarkable result was achieved of complete victory without vindictiveness on the one side or rancour on the other. The air was cleared, and from that day to this relations between capital and labour have been happier in Great Britain.'[3]

A police force which from its inception was conceived as an organic part of the nation, not as an instrument of state oppression, must mirror the people from whom it is recruited. Its character is their character. It is restrained to the extent that they are restrained, moderate as they are moderate, kindly as they are kindly, stupid as they are stupid. We have already stressed the good fortune that delayed the introduction of an army or police force into this country until the nation was sufficiently advanced to be able to live with fresh hazards to liberty on acceptable terms; and noted how the character of our police, when they were eventually set up, was shaped by a mellowing, and not a primitive, national character: in this way we avoided what would almost certainly have been the irrevocable step of arming our police.*

* In contrast to the Americans, for example, whose nation was born out of a rebellion that was 'illegal', though widely regarded as 'legal', and who needed an armed police force to control an armed population and centuries

Fox's declaration that he would rather be governed by the mob than a standing army expressed as sound an instinct in 1780 as that which had influenced the Tudor disputants in the sixteenth century. It was only by a slow and gradual process, as fresh principles of law were evolved, teaching the nation that it was possible to live with a standing army without submitting to tyranny, that a safe way was charted for the establishment of the New Police in 1829. Like the soldiers, the law allowed them to use no more force than necessary, and like the soldiers they were subject to the ordinary laws of the land and not – as in some continental countries – to a special code of law such as the French *droit administratif*.

From the start, when they were first practising non-violent methods of crowd control against the Reform Bill demonstrators and the Chartists, the police have been wholly dependent for their success on the continuing approval and goodwill of the public, and they are now as mild as it is possible for them to be while yet remaining a force capable of protecting people against criminals and governments against minority groups. They rely on a controlled application of force, scrupulously careful to offer no provocation. The *bona fides* of protestors are taken for granted, unless there is proof to the contrary. When Rowan parleyed with Francis Place in 1831 and Mayne with Feargus O'Connor in 1848, and when Superintendent Forster rode with John Burns at the head of the marching dockers in 1889, they set precedents that have been followed ever since. Nowadays it is common for the police to work out an agreed route with demonstrators, so that there need be no uncertainty except on the part of any who refuse to co-operate. No special permission is required to march: the right of demonstration is restricted only by the ordinary laws dealing with public order, save in the exceptional case where a ban is imposed under the Public Order Act, 1936; and no such ban has been imposed on any major demonstration since the war. The police are in attendance to help people to have liberty to express their views. When in earlier times violence has broken out it was often due to misunderstanding, intransigence, or over-reaction by the police or the military. Misunderstanding has

of frontier violence. A police force can hardly be disarmed until the populace which it serves has been disarmed.

sometimes been due to the uncertainty of the law: doubt about the right of the Salvation Army to march, for example, and about the status of Hyde Park and Trafalgar Square as places for public meeting. Examples of over-reaction are scattered throughout the pages of this book; but we need not look beyond our own century to note the contrast between 1911, when soldiers were sent in to aid the police to deal with a railway strike, and 1919, when a wiser Government kept the military in reserve, using only the police.

The police – it cannot be stated too often – have never been, and are not today, a *corps d'élite* arrogantly lording it over the population. They regard themselves, and rightly, as citizens in uniform. Foreigners remarked on the conduct of the policeman who, in Grosvenor Square on 27th October 1968, on seeing a demonstrator with an unlit cigarette between his lips and unable in the crush to get his hands free to light it, politely offered his own lighter; and they marvelled when, later on, police and demonstrators joined together in singing *Auld Lang Syne* and then called it a night. To the British this was a very proper culmination of a great sporting event, but one is bound to ask whether we can continue to carry on in this manner at a time when our police service is becoming increasingly professionalised. The rapport established for years between a predominantly working-class police, organised for the most part in small local units, and the mass of the population, will not necessarily survive the present changes in police organisation (the grouping of forces into larger units, changes in recruitment policies, and growing professional skills) and the accompanying changes in the class structure in Britain. The place of the police in the community demands continuing study, and the recent interest shown in the subject by the Church of England's Board for Social Responsibility is to be welcomed.

An adequate treatment of the effect of the criminal law on collective violence would require a separate book. Here we can do little more than note its variety, abundance and adaptability. In earlier chapters we have dealt with only a small part of the common and statute law concerning public order, and many of the laws on which the police commonly rely today have scarcely been mentioned. They make up a varied assortment: the offences of obstructing the highway, assaulting the police or obstructing them in the course of their duty, committing malicious damage or carrying offensive weapons, creating a threat to the peace by using 'threatening abusive or insulting words or behaviour', the common law offences of committing a public nuisance, and the making of an affray – 'the fighting of two or more persons to the terror of the Queen's subjects'.

Clearly there is no lack of law, though much of this formidable battery is rarely invoked. The difficulty for the police (and, since the creation of the office, of the Director of Public Prosecutions) is to exercise a reasonable discretion in enforcing it, and sometimes in adapting old laws to new situations remote from their original purposes. The incongruity of prosecuting twentieth-century communists under Pitt's Incitement to Mutiny Act of 1797, and the leaders of the Hunger Marchers of the Thirties under Sidmouth's Seditious Meetings Act of 1817, has already been noticed. The much earlier Justices of the Peace Act 1361, on the other hand, originally passed to deal with the marauding soldiers of the fourteenth century, has been of enduring importance, and the use of preventive justice has actually increased in modern times in spite of sustained assaults on the ancient statute. The underlying principle that (as a modern Judge has put it) 'individual liberty may be sacrificed or abridged for the public good' has been extensively applied by magistrates' courts in binding over would-be demonstrators 'to keep the peace and be of good behaviour' – with the alternative of a prison sentence if they fail to enter into the order. In principle this seems an objectionable power. It is unnecessary to commit an offence to be bound over; it is merely sufficient to do something which in the opinion of a magistrate is socially undesirable. If the protestor of conscience refuses to change his mind and behave differently in future (refusing, for example, not to stage a sit-down protest) he may be sent to prison for six months. A 'free' country cannot be proud of a law which enables people to become prisoners of conscience.

The general effect of this whole body of law, clearly, has been to curtail liberty; and every generation has a duty to ask, How far has this curtailment gone? A modern scholar who has specialised in this field is apprehensive. 'The total impression is that there has been a general increase in legal restraints on liberty since 1870',

205

writes Mr. I. Brownlie in his recent book, *The Law Relating to Public Order*. Political action which is 'spontaneous and of a grass roots character', he suggests, is distrusted by authority. Activity tends to be channelled into large party organisations, and minority groups find it hard to get a public hearing without protest marches or civil disobedience. Rights of free speech 'once lost are not reinstated by statute and, when threatened, are not preserved by legislative action: they have proved to be much more vulnerable than our ancient monuments and historic buildings, our countryside and green belts . . . those responsible for administrative action, and especially police action, have the great responsibility for self-control and judicious application of the law.'[4] (So also, it might be added, have demonstrators a great responsibility for self-control: the actions of the British Union of Fascists, it will be recalled, led to some curtailment of liberty by the Public Order Act, 1936.)

A moderate nation with a mild police force to enforce the laws has been well served, on the whole, by the moderate attitude of the courts in administering justice to rioters or other disorderly people brought before them. We have noted exceptions, as when deterrent justice has been exercised as an instrument of state policy, for example in medieval and Tudor times (the punishment of Cade and of Aske and his followers are outstanding examples), or when suppressing the Luddites and the 'Swing' rioters. More characteristically the courts have tempered justice with leniency. It is refreshing to remind ourselves of the amnesties granted once the deterrent mass punishments had been executed in 1381 and 1813. It is also good to remember how the common sense of an English jury saved Hardy and his comrades from the gallows (and worse) in 1794. We also noted how a change of state policy and of judicial temper occurred at the time of the Chartists, when the police used no more force than was necessary, the Chartists no more violence, the judges no more punishment. During the twentieth century the courts seem to have followed no consistent policy in punishing offenders who have provoked disorder for political purposes. The prosecution of Tom Mann was something of an event in 1912, but as we have seen the Home Secretary intervened to reduce the punishment awarded by the court.

What has it all achieved in England, the protest that ends in violence? No two opinions would be likely to concur. Most people would probably regard the circumstances of the Civil War as justifying resort to illegal violence, and it seems likely that the violence of 1831 and 1866 spurred two Reform Bills on their way to the statute-book. The riots in Hyde Park in 1855 and 'Bloody Sunday' in November 1887 helped to establish national rallying places in London where, within limits, speech is free. All these may be counted as gains. It is arguable, too, that 'Wilkes and Liberty' rioters struck more than a rhetorical blow for freedom, and helped to launch a tide of radicalism in England that was able to absorb without revolution the shock wave that was soon to come from France. Peterloo was not wholly in vain; and the agitation of the Chartists, though it achieved little in their time, prevented England from falling behind other nations in the advance towards social justice: years afterwards, when the middle classes supported a 'Chartist' programme, five of the original six points were conceded.

The record of what violence has failed to achieve runs, alas, through the pages of this book, and forms the detritus of a whole history of lost causes and disappointed hopes. The primitive and reactionary violence of the centuries of turmoil, when England was being hammered into a nation state, achieved Magna Carta, but little else. The Peasants' Rising, Jack Cade's Rising, Kett's Rising, Aske's insurrection, were all grand, tragic and hopeless. The Gordon Riots failed to secure the repeal of the Catholic Relief Act. The Luddites failed to stop the spread of steam looms and stocking frames. The food rioters and rick burners achieved temporary and local successes, often at the cost of human life, that barely influenced national affairs; it was only when they were allowed to join trade unions that the working classes gathered the corporate strength with which to bargain successfully with their employers, and violence declined. The violence of the insurrectionary strikers of 1911–12 achieved nothing. The violence of the suffragettes actually set their case back – a striking example of the way in which demonstrative protest can be counter-productive in a hostile climate of public opinion. 'You see in it only the folly and the wickedness,' said Lord Lytton addressing the House of Lords with words that might apply to many situations described in this book, 'but I also see in it the pity and the tragedy.... I have

207

seen the exhibition of human qualities which I consider to be as rare and as precious as anything which a nation can possess. I have seen these qualities given to a cause which in itself is as great and as noble a cause as you could well find, but given in such a way as to defeat the very objects that they sought to obtain. . . . And that to my mind is tragedy.'

Such a catalogue of human disappointments is not merely sad, it is (for the present purpose at all events) valueless; for the national balance sheet of the gains and losses of collective violence cannot be struck in the materialistic terms of achievement only. Certainly it is tempting to write history off and rest on the laurels awarded us by André Siegfried – 'Discipline in liberty: that is beyond question, one of the finest English achievements.' Does it read like an epitaph, and is it one? That other Frenchman, Albert Camus, goes uncomfortably near to making out a case to show that a nation which for years has virtually rejected violence as the logical end of collective protest is politically effete. The words we have already quoted in Chapter 1 bear repetition: 'Human insurrection, in its exalted and tragic forms, is only, and can only be, a violent accusation against the universal death penalty. . . . The rebel does not ask for life, but for reasons for living.' Where, in the supreme balance of human values, does Britain stand? If we take modest pride in what our predecessors have achieved it must only be to provide a base from which to look to our future. That base, at all events, is firm enough; and in establishing it we may now try to answer the question posed at the beginning of this book: How have the British transformed a turbulent nation into (to return again to the words used by the chief London correspondent of the *Washington Post*) 'a non-violent, relatively gentle society'?

In Britain the balance between order and liberty is not based on any written constitution, guarantee of liberty, or social contract. It is an organic thing, a natural growth on a society that feels secure, and whose police, prosecutors, protestors and judiciary act responsibly (for most of the time) within this framework of security. Part of the answer to our question lies in the fact that since about 1820 British Governments have grown increasingly responsive to public opinion and more ready to alleviate conditions leading to discontent; as a result, Governments have been

accepted by most people as 'legitimate', and only a few have
wanted to overturn them by physical force. A very important
part lies in the deployment, since 1829, of an unarmed police force
whose deliberate policy is to show restraint and to offer no
provocation to violence. Experience shows that such a force (in
contrast to a brutal or oppressive force) is likely to prevent the
recurrence of outbreaks of violence rather than to encourage their
repetition. Part of the answer, again, lies in the humanising, since
the 1830s, of the judiciary, and in the political wisdom shown in
the reluctance of authority to ban meetings and demonstrations
or to prosecute agitators for seditious speech. We must note, too,
the firm control exercised by the leaders of modern protest
movements in contrast, say, to that of Lord George Gordon, the
elusive Ludd or the clever Francis Place, giving a better chance
for a show of force to be paraded without bloodshed. Another
most important part is to be found in the character of the radical
and trade union movements in Britain, with their willingness to
seek social justice by constitutional means and not by violence.
Revulsion from the excesses of the French Revolution convinced
the intelligentsia and middle classes that revolution in Britain
would not be in their interests, and after 1850 the trade unionists
were confident enough of their place in society to pursue their
ends by orderly change rather than social conflict – an attitude
encouraged by the Reform Act of 1867. So, from as early as the
1880s, the radical movement became an integral part of the
political structure of the state and not (as in some countries) a
rival to it. This stability, in turn, owed much to the moral
strength of the poorer classes, and the cohesion of social groups
whose members were able to share increasingly in growing
national prosperity.

There are, clearly, a number of answers to our question, and it
is difficult to assess what weight should be given to each; but it
may well be that the whole of the answer, virtually, is compre-
hended in the good luck we have enjoyed in living for so long on
an island free from foreign invasion while our nation has slowly
learned self-discipline and tolerance, and grown confident enough
of its internal security to be able to police itself, and to live, in a
relaxed manner. For a final impression of our society today we
may, perhaps, turn to another foreigner, this time a young

American who wrote to the author while this book was in preparation; she was taking a post-graduate degree at Oxford, having graduated at Stanford University. After praising the 'flexible and temperate efficiency' of our police she goes on, 'Americans in England are instantly infected by the comfortable security on which your society seems to rest: they describe a new sense of freedom from fear they never really knew they had. I never knew what safety felt like till I came here.'

What agreeable talk this is, and how beguiling! 'Anything which makes the British more complacent than they are already,' observed the *New Statesman* after the events of October 1968, 'is a minor national disaster.' For reasons which are not understood the world today is full of violence, and Britain is not isolated from it. Here the boredom of a smug and secure society may be (must be?) maddening to those who feel excluded from its benefits and from any effective part in shaping its future. A few hold the political theory that the state is itself a form of organised violence which it is legitimate to fight; they would reject the present system totally, and somehow start afresh. There is nothing new in that. A recent leading article in *The Times* pointed out a truism: 'the tactics of mass violence are not the tactics of democracy, but of those who want to destroy democracy.' Of course, runs the dialogue, but there is also that other virtue, antagonistic to authority, the ageless, classless voice of the most generous spirits of each fresh generation, spending their salad days in challenging accepted ideas and systems in the only ways in which they feel that they can make their protest heard. Salad days, especially such as are devoted to the Grand Delusion that sent More after his *Utopia*, Coleridge hankering after the banks of the Susquehanna and William Morris to *Nowhere* are not to be lightly squandered. There are more agreeable ways of passing them than sitting down on dirty pavements and marching in a protest that may end up, at best, with a bad cold and blisters, at worst at Bow Street with a criminal record. 'Intensely discontented men are not will-less pawns in a social game of chess', comments the American Commission on the Causes and Prevention of Violence. 'They also have alternatives, of which violence is usually the last, the most desperate, and the least likely of success. Peaceful protest, conducted publicly and through conventional political channels, is a traditional American option.' It is also a traditional British option, but this is more apparent to the old and contented than the young and discontented.

Serious-minded people who care enough to march and demonstrate have something to care about. Democracy merely imperils itself by being insensitive. When frustrated protest degenerates into violence and violence into counter-violence it is liberty that suffers in the long run, because authority usually feels obliged to intensify its measures of law enforcement. This, unhappily, does not seem to be as widely understood as it ought to be. The real danger today comes from people who, through ignorance, may destroy the values they seek to preserve. A National Opinion Poll taken shortly before the demonstration in October 1968 showed a majority (though a small one) to be in favour of banning political demonstrations altogether, and a two-thirds majority in favour of allowing our police to use tear gas. This, as a *Guardian* editorial observed, is not a healthy state for public opinion to be in. Professor Ted Gurr, of the Center of International Studies at Princeton University, who made a comparative study of civil strife for the American Commission, concludes: 'Police tactics [in America] have in many cases been inconsistent and repressive, intensifying rather than minimising discontent. These conditions can be corrected by strengthening local organisations and improving the quality and training of police. Such policies may reduce levels of violence; if the experience of other nations is a guide, only the resolution of the underlying discontents that give rise to strife will eliminate it.' Whether by luck or judgment we in Britain have succeeded to a precious inheritance. We are only likely to be able to hand it on to future generations if we take the trouble to understand how we have so far contrived to strike a good balance between order and liberty. That is all that this book is concerned with, but in itself it is not enough. We have also a duty to look ahead and try to understand the fresh causes of discontent that in a virile nation will always spring up to threaten that balance.

A case has been made out for suggesting that during the past fifty years we have gone a long way towards conquering collective violence in Britain, but there could be no greater delusion than to suppose that violence can ever be conquered finally. To assert such a thing now, of all times, would be ludicrous, when millions of people are feeling de-humanised by the terrifying growth of the modern state, the remote and impersonal authority of vast corporations, the eclipse of God, and the pace of techno-logical advance. To protest today against violence in Biafra or Vietnam, or against apartheid or an over-material civilisation, or anything else inhuman is to recover a bit of the common stock of humanity. It is a search for worthwhile reasons for living. Protest is timeless, and the question for our generation is not whether it will go on but whether it need destroy order or interfere with liberty or end in violence. Miss Mary Macarthy, reporting for the *Sunday Times*, has suggested that what happened on 27th October 1968 was 'a unique, improbable event, something to cherish in our memory book, for, short of Utopia, we shall not see it again'. We have the political capacity and experience to show this view to be mistaken. It is to be hoped that we also have the will.

Bibliography and References to Quotations

The more important of the sources from which this book has been compiled are as follows –

Allen, Sir C. K., *The Queen's Peace* (1953)
Annual Register
Beloff, Max, *Public Order and Popular Disturbances 1660–1714* (1938)
Boynton, L. O. J., *The Elizabethan Militia 1558–1638* (1967)
Brownlie, I., *The Law relating to Public Order* (1968)
Bryant, Sir Arthur, *Makers of the Realm* (1955 edn.), *Protestant Island* (1967)
Camus, Albert, *The Rebel* (Peregrine Books edn. 1962)
Clode, C. M., *The Military Forces of the Crown* (2 vols, 1869)
Cole, G. D. H., and Postgate, Raymond, *The Common People 1746–1946* (4th edn. 1949)
Critchley, T. A., *A History of Police in England and Wales 900–1966* (1967)
Dangerfield, G., *The Strange Death of Liberal England* (1966 edn.)
Darvall, F. O., *Popular Disturbances and Public Order in Regency England* (1934)
Ensor, R. C. K., *England 1870–1914* (1936)
Fulford, Roger, *Votes for Women* (1957)
Halévy, Élie, *The Age of Peel and Cobden* (1947), *The Rule of Democracy* (1952 edn.)
Hamburger, Joseph, *James Mill and the Art of Revolution* (1963)
Hammond, J. L. and Barbara, *The Town Labourer 1760–1832* (1917), *The Skilled Labourer 1760–1832* (1919 edn.), *The Village Labourer* (1966 edn.)
Hewitt, H. J., *The Organization of War under Edward III, 1338–62* (1966)
Hibbert, Christopher, *King Mob* (*The Story of Lord George Gordon and the Riots 1780*) (1959)
Hobsbawm, E. J., *Primitive Rebels* (1959)
Hobsbawm, E. J., and Rudé, George, *Captain Swing* (1969)

Holdsworth, W. S., *A History of English Law*, Vol. 1 (7th edn. 1956) and Vols 2–13 (1909–52)

Hollister, C. W., *Anglo-Saxon Military Institutions* (1962), *The Military Organization of Norman England* (1965)

Jenkins, Roy, *Asquith* (1964)

Keen, Maurice, *The Outlaws of Medieval England* (1961)

Kendall, P. M., *The Yorkist Age* (1962)

Laver, James, *The Age of Optimism* (1966)

Mather, F. C., *Public Order in the Age of the Chartists* (1959)

Moylan, Sir John, *Scotland Yard* (1934)

Newsam, Sir Frank, *The Home Office* (1954)

Oman, C., *The Great Revolt of 1381* (1906)

Osborne, Bertram, *Justices of the Peace 1361–1848* (1960)

Political State of Great Britain

Priestley, Harold, *Voice of Protest* (1968)

Radzinowicz, L., *A History of English Criminal Law*, Vols 1–4 (1948–68)

Read, D., *Peterloo, The 'Massacre' and its Background* (1958)

Reith, Charles, *British Police and the Democratic Ideal* (1943)

Reynolds, G. W., and Judge, A., *The Night the Police went on Strike* (1968)

Rudé, George, *Wilkes and Liberty* (1962), *The Crowd in History, 1730–1848* (1964)

Russell, Claire and W. M. S., *Violence, Monkeys and Man* (1968)

Seth, Ronald, *The Specials* (1961)

Sheppard, E. W. S., *A Short History of the British Army* (1950 edn.)

Siegfried, André, *The Character of Peoples* (Trs. Edward Fitzgerald, 1952)

Storr, Anthony, *Human Aggression* (1968)

Symons, Julian, *The General Strike* (1959 edn.)

Taylor, A. J. P., *English History 1914–1945* (1965)

Thompson, E. P., *The Making of the English Working Class* (Pelican edn. 1968)

Trevelyan, G. M., *English Social History* (1944), *History of England* (Illust. edn. 1956)

Webb, Sidney and Beatrice, *English Local Government* (Vols. 1–4, 1906–22)

Williams, David, *Keeping the Peace* (1967)

Home Office Papers and Official Reports

(a) *Home Office Papers*. These have been drawn upon for the following –

Chartist activities in 1848 (pages 138–40), H.O./O.S.2410

Trafalgar Square riots in 1887 (pages 153–8), H.O. A/47976

Colliery Disturbance in South Wales and Railway Strike in August 1911 (pages 167–71) – *Miscellaneous Home Office Reports and Memoranda (Strikes etc.) 1886–1912*

(b) *Official Reports*. The more important of these are as follows –

Report on the Alleged Disturbance of the Public Peace in Hyde Park on Sunday, 1st July 1855, P.P. Vol. XXIII (1856)

Report of Committee on the Disturbances in the Metropolis on Monday, 8th February 1886, C. 4665 (1886)

Report of the Committee on Disturbances at Featherstone on 7th September 1893, C. 7234 (1893)

Report of the Select Committee on the Employment of Military in the Case of Disturbances, P.P. 236 (1908)

Report of the American Commission on the Causes and Prevention of Violence (1969)

References to Quotations

References are to the works listed in the Bibliography except where stated otherwise –

Chapter 1

1 Franciscius, Andreas, *Itinerarium Britanniae, A Journey to London in 1497* (C. V. Mafatti, Barcelona, 1953), p. 36
2 Chamberlayne, Edward *Angliae Notitia*, quoted by Beloff, p. 9
3 Ariès, Philippe, *Centuries of Childhood* (1965), pp. 317–18
4 Rudé, *Crowd in History*, p. 230
5 Dickens, C., *Barnaby Rudge*, Chapter 15
6 Rudé, *Crowd in History*, pp. 241 and 221
7 *The Correspondence of Robert Southey with Caroline Bowles* (Ed. E. Dowden, 1881), p. 52
8 Webb, Vol. 4, pp. 412–13
9 Halévy, *A History of the English People in 1815* (1924), p. 512
10 Hamburger, pp. 17 and 115
11 Cole and Postgate, p. 473

Chapter 2

1 Bryant, *Makers of the Realm*, p. 154
2 Trevelyan, *History of England*, p. 81
3 *Ibid.*, p. 172
4 Keen, p. 168
5 Kendall, p. 30
6 Trevelyan, *History of England*, p. 256
7 Anon., *A Picture of English Life under Queen Mary* (Trans. C. V. Mafatti, Barcelona, 1953)
8 Jerrold, Douglas, *England, Past, Present and Future* (1950), p. 73
9 Discourse: William Stafford, *Examination of Certayne Ordinary Complaints A.D. 1581* (Ed. F. J. Furnivall, 1876), pp. 73–4
10 Osborne, p. 45
11 *Ibid.*, p. 62

Chapter 3

1 Clark, G. N., *The Later Stuarts* (1934), p. 114
2 Beloff, p. 11
3 Quoted in *ibid.*, p. 3
4 Radzinowicz, Vol. 4, p. 121
5 *Ibid.*, p. 142
6 *Ibid.*, p. 128
7 Clode, Vol. 2, p. 130
8 Thompson, p. 195

Chapter 4

1 Thompson, p. 203
2 Trevelyan, *English Social History*, p. 476
3 Darvall, p. 72
4 Thompson, pp. 628–9
5 *Ibid.*, p. 579
6 Darvall, p. 249
7 *Ibid.*, p. 314
8 *Ibid.*, p. 335
9 *Ibid.*, p. 299
10 Bamford, S., *The Life of a Radical* (1893), Vol. II, p. 142
11 *Ibid.*, pp. 155–7
12 Radzinowicz, Vol. 4, p. 156
13 Halévy, *A History of the English People, 1815–1830* (1926), Introduction, p. v
14 Radzinowicz, Vol. 4, p. 210
15 Disraeli, Preface to *Alton Locke*
16 Reith, p. 93
17 Hamburger, pp. 148–9
18 Mather, p. 12
19 Radzinowicz, Vol. 4, p. 246
20 *Ibid*, pp. 247–9
21 *Ibid.*, p. 251
22 Moylan, p. 64
23 Clode, Vol. 1, p. 320
24 Mather, p. 161
25 Radzinowicz, Vol. 4, p. 236
26 Halévy, *The Age of Peel and Cobden*, p. 204
27 *Ibid.*, pp. 211–12
28 H.O./O.S.2410
29 Halévy, p. 205

Chapter 5

1 Cole and Postgate, p. 450
2 Quoted by Laver, p. 230
3 Cole and Postgate, pp. 425–31
4 Webb, Beatrice, *My Apprenticeship* (Pelican edn. 1938), pp. 191–5

5 Trevelyan, *History of England,* pp. 707
6 Cole and Postgate, pp. 472–3
7 Fulford, p. 225

Chapter 6
1 Reynolds and Judge, p. 163
2 Taylor, p. 244
3 Cooper, Duff, *Old Men Forget* (1953), p. 154
4 Symons, p. 112
5 Williams, p. 191
6 Newsam, p. 32

Chapter 7
1 Siegfried, Chapter 4
2 Bryant, *Protestant Island,* p. 314
3 Cooper, Duff p. 155
4 Brownlie, pp. 190–1

Index

Index

Index

Justices of the peace, 33, 37, 46, 47, 51, 58, 59, 61, 62, 63, 66, 88, 106, 120; Cromwell and, 58; decline of (18th century), 67; failure to assist, an offence, 43; importance of Elizabethan, 51–2; open to bribery, intimidation, 46; penalties on, for negligence, 43, 62, 123–4
Justices of the Peace Act (1361), 37–8, 72–3, 205

Kendall, P. M. (*The Yorkist Age*), 45
Kennedy family, 4
Kennett, Barkley, 76, 81, 86
Kennington Common, 139, 146, 148
Kensal Green, 142
Kett's Rising, 48, 207
King, Dr. Martin Luther, 4
King's messengers, 61, 93
Kingsley, Charles, 173
Kipling, Rudyard, 165

Lancashire, 100, 102, 103, 104, 105, 114, 135
Lansbury, George, 175
Law(s), 7, 23, 25, 37, 41, 51, 58, 91, 106, 198, 202, 203; against public violence, 3, 72–6, 167; barbarity of 18th-century, 70, 71, 87, 113; common law, 27, 43, 73, 74, 83, 88, 115, 119, 204–5; divine right of kings and, 57; food riots and, 13, 14; game, 40; martial, 89; outlaws and, 36; power ruled by, 34; Press freedom, *see* Press; public assembly, *see* s.v.; regulates use of soldiers, 55, 60, 63, 71, 75, 76, 83–4, 89, 167, 170–1, 203; respect for, 47; seditious libel, 96; soldiers subject to civil, 76, 83–4, 89; tithes, 16; tythings *see* s.v.; wisely interpreted by courts, 71
Lawrence, Mrs. Pethick, 173
Leicestershire, 100
Liberal Party, 161, 165–6
Liberty/liberties, 8, 202, 208; demanded in Peasants' Revolt, 41; English liberty vs. French servility, 46; Fielding on, 69; folk-memory and, 18; groups defending, 4–5, 97–8; growth, 141; Edward III's reign and, 38–9; individual, 87, 97, 205; order vs., xi–xii, 8, 49, 53–4, 57, 69, 88, 145, 159, 194, 196, 197, 198, 208, 211, 212; political, 161; public good vs. individual, 205–6; public opinion and, 211; Saxon vs. Norman, 18; 'Wilkes and liberty,' 77, 80, 207
Linnell, Alfred, 157–8

Littledale, Judge, 23, 123
Liverpool, 169, 177, 180–2, 183
Liverpool, Lord (Prime Minister), 117–18
Lloyd George, 175, 179, 180, 185
Lollards, 43
London(ers), 1, 31, 44, 76, 109, 110, 111, 120, 121, 123, 137, 146, 155, 162, 196, 207; Chartism and, *see* Chartism; foreigner-baiting in, 10–11; Gordon Riots and, *see* s.v.; Great Fire of, 60; Hyde Park meetings and, *see* Hyde Park; mob behaviour, 11, 18, 19, 20, 24, 47, 56, 60, 61, 62, 64, 69, 78, 82–5, 119, 125–6, 139, 151, 152, 153, 155–6, 158, 159–60, 175, 181; night watch in, 59, 86; in Peasants' Revolt, *see* s.v.; police, *see* Police, Metropolitan; reaction to 'Peelers', 119; strikes in, *see* Strikes; trained bands retained in, 60, 62; vice in, 58; Wilkes riots and, *see* Wilkes riots
London Corresponding Society, 92
London School of Economics, xii
Lord Chancellor, 41, 75
Lord Chief Justice, 46, 82, 84
Lord lieutenant, 52, 58, 59, 60, 61, 62, 101, 104, 130, 134, 135
Loughborough, Lord, 87
Louis Philippe (Fr. king), 138
Luddism/Luddites, 6, 12, 16–17, 36, 98–109, 113, 114, 120, 122, 128, 129, 131, 132, 133, 135, 136, 137, 142, 144, 161, 175, 189, 190, 192, 199, 201, 206, 207, 209
Ludlam, Ned, 99
Lytton, Lord, 207

Macarthy, Mary, 212
Macaulay, 61, 121
Macdonald, Ramsay, 163, 165, 195
Maclean, Pte. Donald, 76, 79, 80
Macready, General Sir Charles, 168, 171, 179–80
Macready, William, 168
Magna Carta, 18, 34, 39, 56–7, 109
Maitland, General, 104, 105, 137, 192
Major-Generals, Cromwell's, 58
Manchester, 74, 110, 111, 113, 114, 115, 116, 128, 135, 136, 137, 138, 170, 172, 194
Mandeville, Geoffrey de, 31
Manhattan Island, 5
Mann, Tom, 164, 165, 171–2, 178, 181, 182, 184, 194, 206
Manors, 32–3, 37, 38, 39, 40, 43, 50, 53, 65